SHU CHING

People's Republic of China

1 Anhwei
2 Chekiang
3 Chinghai
4 Fukien
5 Heilungkiang
6 Honan
7 Hopeh
8 Hunan
9 Hupeh
10 Inner Mongolia
11 Kansu
12 Kiangsi
13 Kiangsu
14 Kirin
15 Kwangsi
16 Kwangtung
17 Kweichow
18 Liaoning
19 Ningsia
20 Shansi
21 Shantung
22 Shensi
23 Sinkiang
24 Szechuan
25 Tibet
26 Yunnan

China during Chou dynasty

China during Shang dynasty

Early governmental China

RUSSIA

MONGOLIA

JAMMU AND KASHMIR

NEPAL

BURMA

LAOS

NORTH VIETNAM

NORTH KOREA

YELLOW SEA

I Yellow River, also called Huang Ho, or Hwang Ho
   Present course
   Ancient course

II Yangtze River, also called Yangtze-Kiang.

SHU CHING

Book of History

A modernized edition of the translations of James Legge

CLAE WALTHAM

A GATEWAY EDITION
Henry Regnery Company • Chicago

First, and of greatest importance, there is the Book of Historical Documents, called the Shu *and, since the Han dynasty, the* Shu ching. *Its documents commence with the reign of Yao in the twenty-fourth century* B.C., *and come down to that of King Hsiang of the Chou dynasty.*

The earliest sections were not contemporaneous with the events they describe, but the others begin to be so in the twenty-second century B.C.

The reader will find a translation of the whole of this work without abridgment.

—James Legge

CONTENTS

James Legge and the *Shu ching, Book of History*　　ix

Part I: The Document of T'ang　　1
1. The Canon of Yao　　3

Part II: The Documents of Yü　　9
1. The Canon of Shun　　11
2. The Counsels of the Great Yü　　19
3. The Counsels of Kao Yao　　26
4. The Yi and Ch'i　　30

Part III: The Documents of Hsia　　37
1. Tribute to Yü　　39
2. The Speech at Kan　　55
3. Songs of the Five Sons　　57
4. The Punitive Expedition of Yin　　60

Part IV: The Documents of Shang　　65
1. The Speech by T'ang　　67
2. The Announcement by Chung Hui　　69
3. The Announcement by T'ang　　72
4. The Instructions of I　　74
5. The T'ai Chia　　77
6. The Common Possession of Pure Virtue　　82
7. The P'an Keng　　85
8. The Charge to Yüeh　　94
9. The Day of the Supplementary Sacrifice to Kao Tsung　　100
10. The Chief of the West's Conquest of Li　　102
11. The Count of Wei　　106

Part V: The Documents of Chou　　109
The House of Chou　　111
1. The Great Declaration　　113
2. The Speech at Mu　　119
3. The Successful Completion of the War　　121

4. The Great Plan   125
5. The Hounds of Lü   133
6. The Metal-Bound Coffer   135
7. The Great Announcement   139
8. The Charge to the Count of Wei   144
9. The Announcement to the Prince of K'ang   146
10. The Announcement About Drunkenness   153
11. The Timber of the Tzu Tree   158
12. The Announcement of the Duke of Shao   161
13. The Announcement Concerning Lo   167
14. The Numerous Officers   175
15. Against Luxurious Ease   179
16. The Prince of Shih   183
17. The Charge to Chung of Ts'ai   188
18. The Numerous Regions   190
19. The Establishment of Government   196
20. The Officers of Chou   201
21. The Chün Ch'en   205
22. The Testementary Charge   208
23. The Announcement of King K'ang   216
24. The Charge to the Duke of Pi   219
25. The Chün Ya   224
26. The Charge to Ch'iung   226
27. The Marquis of Lü on Punishment   228
28. The Charge to the Marquis Wen   237
29. The Speech at Pi   240
30. The Speech by the Marquis of Ch'in   242

Appendix: From the Prolegomena of James Legge   247
Introduction to the Chinese Classics Generally   249
Chronologic Table   259

Selected Bibliography   263
Index   265

James Legge
and the
Shu ching, Book of History

James Legge,[1] whose activity as a Sinologist spanned much of the nineteenth century, first conceived of translating the Chinese classics into English in 1841. It was 1856 before he mentioned the undertaking publicly; and the first volume was printed at Hong Kong in 1861. He was a pioneer in this field and was to devote more than half a century to his self-appointed task. In *The Legacy of China,* Raymond Dawson ranks him with Matteo Ricci and Marco Polo.

But only now, with the publication of this separate title from Legge's complete translations of the Chinese classics, is it possible for the general reader to have a copy of the *Shu ching, Book of History* in a modern edition with the early transliterations re-romanized according to current usage. Up to this time, the *Shu* was to be found either as part of the original bilingual

1. Born at Huntley, Aberdeenshire, Scotland, in 1815, James Legge graduated from King's College, Aberdeen, in 1835. In 1839 he went to Malacca for the London Missionary Society. He became principal of the Anglo-Chinese College there and moved with the college in 1843 to the newly acquired British colony of Hong Kong.

In 1861, Legge began publication of the first of his many translations from the Chinese, supervising the bilingual printing at Hong Kong. The expenses of publication were largely underwritten by three merchant-princes of China: Joseph Jardine, his brother, Sir Robert Jardine, and John Dent.

In 1873, Legge returned to England and in 1875 received the Julien Prize of the French Institute. The Chair of Chinese Language and Literature was constituted for him at Oxford University in 1876, a post he held until his death on November 29, 1897.

edition, overwhelming to all but scholars and Sinologists, or in the multivolume *Sacred Books of the East,* edited by F. Max Müller (Legge's second translation).

This edition fuses the two Legge translations into one modern version, and it includes relevant selections from his voluminous notes. The Legge translation of the documents is complete and unabridged. All Chinese names and terms have been re-romanized into the Wade-Giles system or into a modern spelling that has become standard usage. The index incorporates a glossary designed to be useful for general reference.

In the past, problems of romanization have been as numerous as the people translating and further complicated by differences of national spellings. Hopefully, these difficulties will begin to vanish when the language reform now going on among the Chinese themselves has been completed. The pronunciation of Chinese has already been standardized in accordance with the Peking, or Mandarin, dialect.

The general reader frequently encounters the *Shu ching, Book of History* referred to as the *Shang shu, Shoo King,* or *Historical Documents,* and some incidents from the *Shu* are encountered as excerpts which have been simplified and retold. But the *Shu* is a great book, and it should be allowed to speak for itself.

The *Shu ching, Book of History* is considered the oldest complete Chinese classic, although parts of both the *I ching, Book of Changes* and the *Shih ching, Book of Odes* have older sections. The *Shu* is basic to the subsequent literature of China. China's continuous history and the natural bent of her citizens for historical writings combine to endow the Chinese people with a collective consciousness. Thus, Chinese writers again and again refer to the personages and events that move across the pages of the *Shu.*

Recently the *Shu* has acquired another function: as twentieth century excavations brought to light the Shang bronzes and Chou jades, which have found their places in museums and in the pages of books on art, the *Shu* became their literary companion.

Through these documents, we can experience a sense of reality about the ancient people who made or used these artifacts.

It is hard for us today to realize that when Legge began his translations China had yet to be taken seriously as a nation. A great many of her claims to early civilization were simply set aside as fabrications. Legge did his work in the vitiating atmosphere of white supremacy, Victorian hypocrisy, and nineteenth century bigotry. The Manchus (Ch'ing dynasty) were still in power—fifty years away from Sun Yat-sen and the founding of the Chinese republic in 1912. The language barrier was considered so formidable that Legge was advised to seek the assistance of a native Chinese scholar "perfectly versed in Manchu." Legge rejected this idea because the Manchus themselves used Chinese interpreters. Furthermore, he did not want the "official" interpretation of the classics.

The general terseness of the Chinese language necessitates what Legge described, in his introduction to the *I ching, Book of Changes,* as the "leap from mind to mind." The oldest written Chinese characters are proportionately more cryptic than the modern characters and, in addition, Chinese characters vary quite a bit. When Legge made the acquaintance of a Chinese scholar qualified to enrich his translation of the *Shu,* he not only accepted his assistance, but in his preface paid Wang T'ao this tribute:

> This scholar, far excelling in classical lore any of his countrymen whom the author had previously known, came to Hong Kong in the end of 1863 and placed at his disposal all the treasures of a large and well-selected library. At the same time, entering with spirit into his labors, now explaining, now arguing, as the case might be, he has not only helped, but enlivened many a day of toil.

It is to the credit of both these scholars, and not merely fortuitous, that Legge's hundred-year-old translation of the *Shu ching, Book of History* is out of date only in the matter of romanization, the system of transliterating Chinese characters into our alphabet. Legge's style, which has been criticized as wooden, derives only from his determination to translate literally, transmitting the content as closely to the style of the original as possible.

Euro-American ideas of history are strictly defined. Western historians are suspicious of encapsulations of oral tradition, particularly those concerned with periods of time that are—in the Western sense—prehistoric. A verbal heritage without definite links to archaeological proof rarely finds acceptance. The no-man's-land between what is hypothesis and what is proven is rigidly patrolled.

But to the Chinese mind, for which a useful analogue is that of a revolving sphere, history exists in its original concept: inquiry into the past. Within this spherical mode of thinking—which not only revolves around the object of its inquiry but also is revolving upon the axis of its own psyche—history is total. It is far more than chronology and event. It is the cumulative evidence of all that has been. Within this spherical mode of thinking, nothing has existence of itself, isolatedly, but it exists as part of and at the same time in relation to everything else. To the Chinese, however much we may debate the historicity of these documents, the *Shu* simply *is* history.

Another characteristic of the Chinese mind is its subtlety, which gave rise to the false label of inscrutability. What seems to be inscrutable is actually an added dimension of consciousness: it is the expanded awareness that results in thought that turns upon concepts incorporating changes so rhythmic that they achieve constancy. This can also be called a system of correspondences, and this is the reason why nothing can exist in isolation.

The *Shu,* spanning more than seventeen centuries of China's early documents, offers unique insight into the development of this highly sophisticated—but basically simple—turn of mind. A primitive instance of the idea of correspondences is the fact that natural phenomena inspired the punitive expedition against Yin (Part III, Document 4). Much later, in "The Marquis of Lü on Punishments" (Part V, Document 27), this same idea of correspondences reappears skillfully articulated. Specifically, we read that punishments should be light in one age and heavy in another. To secure uniformity of seeming irregularity, officers are charged to consider certain relations of things, to observe the essential principle. This, then, becomes a system of infinite correspondences. And because the Chinese mind is rooted in what is practical, it carries its subtle functions into realms which in other cultures might easily vanish instead of developing into concepts.

The doctrine of the Mean, later to become a bulwark of Chinese philosophy, also has its beginnings articulated in the *Shu*. This is to be expected as, in spherical thought, history cannot be merely isolated events of the past but must also possess the ability to come full circle to face us from the future as well as buttress the present with philosophical wisdom.

The Chinese have never lost their sense of the past. It is a train that sweeps behind them through the centuries, a rich embroidery of philosophy, religion, geography, narrative, origins, and customs. And—in a way that we of the West are probably incapable of appreciating as yet—through ancestorism the Chinese remain close to their primordial images, or archetypes. The result of this is mental processes that are often more objective than ours, with fewer unconscious compulsions, and less at the mercy of instinct. While the Chinese heritage has not been presented to us as history, it has reached us through other disciplines: philosophy, as met in Hegel; sociology, as met in Max Weber; psychology, where East and West have been traced to a single rhizome in Jung; poetry, in Goethe's worldview; and religion, as in Taoism, Confucianism, and the practice of *ch'an,* later to become Zen Buddhism.

Legge seemed to sense all this. Also, he made a leap of faith, almost as if he knew that sleeping in the ground were Chinese Troys waiting for another Heinrich Schliemann to transform

legend into history. Legge died two years before the discovery
of the famous oracle bones of 1899, which were inscribed with
the early Chinese characters that amazed the world with historical proof of the Shang dynasty. Later, the 1,000-year chronology that Ssu-ma Ch'ien received from tradition was to be
verified with only minor corrections. Although Legge always
remained a scrupulous and indefatigable scholar, he recognized
that too much learned debate could vitiate a heritage. It seems
to the close reader of his entire works that he developed a
trivalence: he translated the text like a Chinese, annotated it
like an Oxford don, and, in his introductions and prolegomena,
argued like a Scot.

The basic use of history may still be to ask questions of the
past. If so, Legge helps us evaluate the answers we receive from
the *Shu*. He reminds us that there are gaps in the 1,700 years
spanned by the documents and that each of the five parts of the
Shu is to be interpreted differently. He summarizes these five
parts, each with its own style, flavor, and imponderables, in such
a way that we can see oral tradition turning into history.

Of Part I, which deals with the reign of Yao, Legge says:
"Legend and narrative are confusedly mixed together. . . ." Of
Part II, which deals with the reign of Shun, he says, "It may be
impossible to separate what is old from what is more recent—to
distinguish what the compilers added of their own. . . ." Of
Part III, which deals with the Hsia dynasty, a time not yet linked
to archaeological evidence, he says, ". . . professedly, the com-
pilations of a later time. . . ." Of Part IV, which deals with the
Shang dynasty, which made its incontrovertible link with archaeological finds only after Legge's death, he believes ". . . we
seem to be able to tread the field of history with a somewhat
confident step. . . ." Of Part V, which deals sequentially only
with the first five kings in the longest of all of China's dynasties,
he states, "The documents of Chou were contemporaneous with
the events they described and became public property not long
after their composition. Provision was made . . . by the statutes

of Chou for the preservation of the monuments of previous dynasties."

Legge recognized that China was not to be bound by our Western definitions of history. But he never forgot the uses of the scholarly discipline. He managed to keep conflicting theories on many related subjects ceaselessly promenading in his mind awaiting conclusive evidence. He became a psychopomp between East and West, never closing the windows of his mind. If we of the West set aside these documents as non-history, we cut ourselves off from relevant source material that not only sheds light on early China, the literature of China, the Chinese as a people and, indirectly, the whole Orient, but we also cut ourselves off from insight into human origins in general.

The authenticity of the documents of the *Shu ching, Book of History* that have come down to us has been the subject of controversy. Partly, this results from the famous burning of books of the Ch'in dynasty. But this dynasty was short-lived: 221–207 B.C. Under the next dynasty (Han), the great literary remains of ancient times were again reverenced. Scholars who had memorized the *Shu* rewrote the documents from memory or dictated them to recorders. Some unburned books were discovered in their hiding places. Fragments turned up in different regions of the empire. There was an atmosphere of restoring the learning of antiquity. But some scholars, in apparently misplaced zeal, reconstructed parts of the *Shu* from other books rather than from original relics; hence, the genuineness of these particular documents is a subject of dispute. However, these documents were unquestioned for more than a thousand years, and so influenced mores and literature.

Bernhard Karlgren's translation of the *Shu ching, Book of History* (The Museum of Far Eastern Antiquities, Bulletin 22, Stockholm, Sweden, 1950; *Book of Documents*) comprises what he considers "all the authentic chapters"—twenty fewer documents than Legge translates. Each of the disputed documents is identified for the reader within the text in this edition of the Legge translation.

In addition to the fact that the genuineness of certain documents has been challenged, there is the inherent difficulty of the text. As Karlgren states, the *Shu* ". . . through its lapidary style and archaic language, is often exceedingly obscure and frequently offers passages which, from the point of view of grammar, allow of several widely divergent interpretations. . . ."

Here and there in the text are Chinese characters that even the great native commentators have found inexplicable and have passed over—even though their lives' work had been writing commentaries on the classics. The Chinese have always been intensely practical but never literal. One must not press the material of the *Shu* too hard—its meaning can be received but not taken by force. Age has taken a toll of this great collection. Among the historiographers, human errors crept in. Classifications according to the divisions of canons, counsels, instructions, charges, speeches, and announcements—into which each of the documents is theoretically classed—do not always conform. Chronologic sequence is mixed here and there.

But it is not the purpose of this edition to enter into the erudite debates concerning controversial aspects of the *Shu*. The purpose of modernizing the text and abridging the notes is to make readily available to the general reader part of Legge's consummate knowledge of the history, customs, manners, culture, and literature that have shaped the Chinese people. This edition is not a criticism of Legge's original work but homage to it.

The serious student who wishes to join the scholarly colloquium in the footnotes and exegeses is urged to consult the original, bilingual translation. He will be readily able to orient himself by means of the five parts and the numbered, titled sections of this edition. To facilitate moving from this modernization to either the translation of 1865 or the translation of 1879, the chronologic details remain uncorrected, as the errors were minimal. Also, during the editing of this book, it became increasingly difficult to indicate where a phrase was taken verbatim from Legge's copious notes and where a paraphrase was used.

I wish to make grateful acknowledgment to Professor Karlgren and The Museum of Far Eastern Antiquities for permission to make liberal use of his translation of the *Shu: The Book of Documents.*

Methuen and Company, Ltd. of London and Quelle and Meyer of Heidelberg both gave permission to adapt from the excellent maps in *Ostasien: China–Japan–Korea* by Dr. Albert Kolb.

I wish to thank Wallace Carrithers for preparing the map showing the ancient areas of the *Shu* in relation to present-day China. In addition, I wish to thank him for his ingenuity in maintaining access to four different systems of romanization during the fusing of Legge's two translations.

Also, I am indebted to Jean Olson and Martha Moyer—to Mrs. Olson for the index and to Mrs. Moyer for the mechanical preparation of the manuscript. Both tasks required unusual skill and patience due to the inherent complexities of the subject matter.

While I wish to acknowledge my indebtedness, these individuals are not responsible for any errors that may remain.

Elizabethtown, Kentucky　　　　　　—CLAE WALTHAM
June, 1971

SHU CHING

*He whose vision cannot cover
History's three thousand years,
Must in outer darkness hover,
Live within the day's frontiers.*

—Goethe

The Document of T'ang

1. THE CANON OF YAO

Part I is called "The Document of T'ang" because Yao, before his elevation to the throne, had been marquis of the small state of T'ang. The place is not to be confused with the person of the same name, T'ang, founder of the Shang dynasty.

The character translated "canon" means a document of the most exalted nature, entitled to the greatest regard. This name is given expressly only to one other document: "The Canon of Shun" in Part II. The canons are the first of six classes of documents contained in the *Shu*.

We assume the time of Yao to be in the third millennium before the common era: between 2357 and 2255 B.C. Yao, the patriarch, is in his capital, concerned with preserving the offices and institutions of his government and disseminating knowledge of the solstices and equinoxes to establish agricultural practices that will insure adequate food. At this time, his domain is in the throes of a disastrous flood. The canon introduces us to persons, places, and things of this early time. Of particular note are:

The brothers Hsi and the brothers Ho, who are to regulate the calendar by the stars Huo and Hsü and the constellations Niao (Cor Hydra) and Mao (the Pleiades);

Kun, the father of Yü, founder of the Hsia dynasty, who is summoned to cope with the flood;

Shun, a poor man who will eventually succeed Yao, the present sovereign and the subject of this document;

Chief of the Four Mountains, an officer who is addressed by the title of his office. The four mountains are Tai in the east, in present-day Shantung; Hua in the west, in present-day Shansi; Mount Heng in the south, in present-day Hunan; and the northern Mount Heng, in present-day Hopeh. These peaks, Legge felt, were the probable limits of China at that time, and all within these points was under the care of the chief minister.

3

Document 1

Examining into antiquity, we find the sovereign Yao was styled Fang Hsün. He was reverent, intelligent, accomplished, and thoughtful—naturally and without effort. He was sincerely courteous and capable of all complaisance. The bright influence of these qualities extended through the four quarters of the land and reached to heaven above.

He distinguished the able and virtuous, and thence proceeded to the love of all in the nine classes of his kindred, who thus became harmonious. He also regulated and polished the people of his domain, who all became brightly intelligent. Finally, he united and harmonized the myriad states [those of the princes beyond the imperial domain]. And so the black-haired people were transformed. The result was universal concord.

He commanded the brothers Hsi and the brothers Ho, in reverent accord with their observation of the wide heavens, to calculate and delineate the movements and appearances of the sun, the moon, the stars, and the zodiacal spaces [houses], and so to deliver respectfully the seasons to be observed by the people.

He separately commanded the second brother Hsi to reside at Yü-i, in what was called the Bright Valley, there respectfully to receive as a guest the rising sun, and to adjust and arrange the labors of the spring. "The day," said he, "is of the medium length and the star is in Niao. You may thus exactly determine mid-spring. The people are dispersed in the fields and birds and beasts breed and copulate."

He further commanded the third brother Hsi to reside at Nan-chiao, in what was called the Brilliant Capital, to adjust and arrange the transformations of the summer, and respectfully to observe the exact limit of the shadow. "The day," said he, "is at its longest, and the star is in Huo. You may thus exactly determine mid-summer. The people are more dispersed; the birds and beasts have their feathers and hair thin and change their coats."

He separately commanded the second brother Ho to reside in the west, in what was called the Dark Valley, there respectfully to convoy the setting sun and to adjust and arrange the harvest labors of the autumn. "The night," said he, "is of medium length, and the star is in Hsü. You may thus exactly determine mid-autumn. The people feel at ease, and birds and beasts have their coats in good condition."

He further commanded the third brother Ho to reside in the northern region, in what was called the Somber Capital, and there to adjust and examine the changes of the winter. "The day," said he, "is at its shortest, and the star is in Mao. You may thus exactly determine mid-winter. The people keep in their houses, and the coats of birds and beasts are downy and thick."

The sovereign said, "Ah! you brothers Hsi and you brothers Ho, a round year consists of three hundred, sixty, and six days. By means of the intercalary month, you are to fix the four seasons and complete the determination of the period of a year. Thereafter, the various officers being regulated in accord with this, all the work of the seasons will be fully performed."

The sovereign said, "Who will search out for me a man according to the times, whom I can raise and employ?"

Fang Ch'i said, "Your heir-son Chu is highly intelligent."

The sovereign said, "Alas! he is insincere and quarrelsome. Could he do?"

The sovereign said, "Who will search out for me a man equal to the exigency of my affairs?"

Huan Tou said, "Oh! the merits of the minister of Works have just been displayed on a wide scale."

The sovereign said, "Alas! when all is quiet, he talks; but when employed, his actions turn out differently. He is respectful only in appearance. See! the floods assail the heavens!"

The sovereign said, "Oh! Chief of the Four Mountains, the waters of the inundation are destructive in their over-flow. In their vastness they embrace the hills and overtop great heights, threatening the heavens with their floods. The lower people groan and murmur! Is there a capable man to whom I can assign the correction of this calamity?"

All in the court said, "Ah! is there not Kun?"

The sovereign said, "Alas! how perverse is he! He is dis-obedient to orders and tries to injure his peers."

The Chief of the Four Mountains said, "Well, but try him—to see if he can accomplish the work."

Accordingly, Kun was employed.

The sovereign said to him, "Go; be reverent!"

For nine years Kun labored. But the work was not ac-complished.

The sovereign said, "Oh! Chief of the Four Mountains, I have been on the throne for seventy years. You can carry out my commands. I will resign my throne to you."

The Chief said, "I have not the virtue; I should disgrace the imperial seat."

The sovereign said, "Show me someone among the il-lustrious, or set forth one from among the poor and mean."

All then said to the sovereign, "There is an unmarried man among the lower people called Shun of Yü."

The sovereign said, "Yes, I have heard of him. What have you to say about him?"

The Chief said, "He is the son of a blind man. His father

was obstinately unprincipled; his stepmother was insincere; his half brother Hsiang was arrogant. Shun has been able, however, by his filial piety to live in harmony with them and to lead them gradually to self-government, so that they no longer proceed to great wickedness."

The sovereign said, "I will try him; I will wive him and thereby see his behavior with my two daughters."

Accordingly he prepared and sent down his two daughters to the north of the Kuei, to be wives in the family of Shun in Yü. The sovereign said to his daughters, "Be reverent!"

The Documents of Yü

1. THE CANON OF SHUN

Yü is the dynastic designation of Shun, as T'ang was that of Yao. According to tradition, Shun's ancestors had been lords of the principality of Yü until the time of Kun, father of Shun, who lost his patrimony and was reduced to the rank of a private man.

This canon opens at about 2283–85 B.C., when Yao summoned Shun to become a ruler of the land. In it, Shun's virtues are described, his gradual advancement, and the thirty years during which he shared the throne with Yao.

Upon the death of Yao, Shun chooses his own ministers and completes the organization of his government, calling upon his twenty-two appointed officers to be reverent. During Shun's reign, examinations are held every three years with appropriate rewards or demotions, and the people of San Miao are banished.

In this document we read of the five punishments and the five cardinal duties, the first two of many numerical categories that occur hereafter in the *Shu* and throughout later Chinese literature. The five punishments used are branding on the forehead, cutting off the nose, cutting off the feet, castration, and death inflicted in various ways. The five cardinal duties are virtues to be exercised in the relationships between husband and wife, father and son, sovereign and subject, older and younger brothers, and between friends.

The death of Shun, 2205 B.C., concludes this canon. This period of eighty years is dealt with in only a few pages, partly due to the abuse of time on the document, but certainly illustrative of the general terseness of the Chinese language.

Document 1

Examining into antiquity, we find the sovereign Shun was styled Ch'ung Hua. His character was entirely conformed to that of the former sovereign: he was profound,

11

wise, accomplished, and intelligent. He was mild and courteous and truly sincere. The report of his mysterious virtue was heard on high and he was appointed to occupy the imperial seat.

Shun carefully set forth the beauty of the five cardinal duties and they came to be universally observed. Being appointed General Regulator, the affairs of every department were arranged in their proper seasons. Being charged to receive the princes from the four quarters of the land, they were all docilely submissive. Being sent to the great plains at the foot of the mountains amid violent wind, thunder, and rain, he did not go astray.

The sovereign said, "Come, you Shun. For three years I have consulted you on all affairs, examined your words, and found that they can be carried into practice. Now you ascend the seat of the sovereign."

Shun wished to decline in favor of someone more virtuous, and not to be Yao's successor. On the first day of the first month, however, he received Yao's retirement from the imperial duties in the temple of the Accomplished Ancestor.

Shun examined the pearl-adorned turning sphere with its transverse tube of jade and reduced to a harmonious system the movements of the Seven Directors.[1]

Thereafter, Shun sacrificed especially, but with the ordinary forms, to God; sacrificed with reverent purity to the Six Honored Ones;[2] offered appropriate sacrifices to the

1. The examining instrument was probably a kind of armillary sphere representing the revolution of the heavens, with the transverse athwart the sphere for the purpose of celestial observation. Legge thought the Seven Directors designated the seven stars of the Big Dipper. According to the Karlgren translation, however, the Seven Directors meant the five planets plus the sun and moon.

2. The identities of the Six Honored Ones are not known.

hills and rivers; and extended his worship to the host of spirits.

He called in all the five jade symbols of rank. And when the month was over, he gave daily audience to the Chief of the Four Mountains and all the Pastors, finally returning their symbols to the various princes.[3]

In the second month of the year he made a tour of inspection eastward as far as lofty Mount Tai, where he presented a burnt offering to Heaven and sacrificed to the hills and rivers in order. Thereafter he gave audience to the princes of the east. He set in accord their seasons and months and regulated the days. He made uniform the standard tubes, the measures of length and of capacity, and the steelyards.[4] He regulated the five classes of ceremonies. As to the several articles of introduction: the five symbols of jade, the three kinds of silk, the two living animals and the one dead one: when all was over he returned the five symbols of jade.

In the fifth month he made a similar tour southward as far as the mountain of the south, where he observed the same ceremonies as at Mount Tai.

In the eighth month he made a tour westward as far as the mountain of the west, where he did as before.

In the eleventh month he made a tour northward as far as the mountain of the north, where he observed the same

3. When appointed, the princes received tokens that fit a form in the imperial treasury. An imposter might thus be detected. Shun, in returning the five jade symbols of rank, was confirming the appointments of the princes. They were called Pastors because, under the direction of the Chief of the Four Mountains, they were shepherds of men.

4. Standard tubes, made of bamboo, were twelve in number and approximated the chromatic scale. Their use was not only in music, but also to regulate measures of length. Steelyard refers to a weighing device of that generic name and does not imply that such a device was made of steel as we know that metal.

ceremonies as in the west. He then returned to the capital, went to the temple of the Accomplished Ancestor, and sacrificed a single bull.

In five years there was one tour of inspection, and there were four appearances of the princes at court. They gave a report of their government in words. This was clearly tested by their works. They received chariots and robes according to their merits.

Shun divided the land into twelve provinces, raising altars upon twelve hills in them. He also deepened the rivers.

He exhibited to the people the statutory punishments, enacting banishment as a mitigation of the five great inflictions; with the whip to be employed in the magistrates' courts, the stick to be employed in the schools for officers, and fines to be paid for redeemable offenses. Inadvertent offenses and those which might be ascribed to misfortune were to be pardoned. Those who transgressed presumptuously and repeatedly were to be punished with death. "Let me be reverent! Let me be reverent!" he said to himself. "Let compassion rule in punishment!"

Shun banished the minister of Works to Yu island; confined Huan Tou on Mount Ch'ung; drove the chief of San Miao and his people into San-wei and kept them there; and held Kun a prisoner until death on Mount Yü. These four criminals being thus dealt with, all under heaven acknowledged the justice of his administration.

After twenty-eight years the sovereign Yao deceased. The people mourned for him as for a parent for three years. Within the four seas all the eight kinds of instruments of music were stopped and hushed.

On the first day of the first month of the next year, Shun went to the temple of the Accomplished Ancestor.

He deliberated with the Chief of the Four Mountains how to throw open the doors of communication between himself and the four quarters of the land, and how he could see with the eyes and hear with the ears of all.

He consulted with the twelve Pastors and said to them, "The food: it depends on observing the seasons. Be kind to the distant and cultivate the ability of the near. Give honor to the virtuous and your confidence to the good, while you discountenance the artful. So shall the barbarous tribes lead on one another to make their submission."

Shun said, "Oh! Chief of the Four Mountains, is there any one who can with vigorous service attend to all the affairs of the sovereign? Whom I may appoint General Regulator to assist me in all affairs and manage each department according to its nature?"

All in the court replied, "There is Yü, the minister of Works."

The sovereign said, "Yes. Oh! Yü, you have regulated the water and the land. In this new office exert yourself."

Yü did obeisance with his head to the ground, and wished to decline in favor of Ch'i, minister of Agriculture, or Hsieh, or Kao Yao.

The sovereign said, "Yes, but let you go and undertake the duties."

The sovereign said, "Ch'i, the black-haired people are still suffering from famine. Let you, O prince, as minister of Agriculture, continue to sow for them the various kinds of grain."

The sovereign said, "Hsieh, the people are still wanting in affection for one another and do not docilely observe the five orders of relationship. It is yours, as minister of Instruction, reverently to set forth the lessons of duty belonging to those five orders. Do so with gentleness."

The sovereign said, "Kao Yao, the barbarous tribes trouble our great land. There are also robbers, murderers, insurgents, and traitors. It is yours, as minister of Crime, to use the five punishments to deal with their offenses. For the infliction of these there are the three appointed places. There are the five cases in which banishment in the appropriate places is to be resorted to, to which three localities are assigned. Perform your duties with intelligence and you will secure a sincere submission."

The sovereign said, "Who can superintend my works as they require?"

All in the court replied, "Is there not Ch'uei?"

The sovereign said, "Yes. Oh! Ch'uei, you must be minister of Works."

Ch'uei did obeisance with his head to the ground, and wished to decline in favor of Shu, Ch'iang, or Po Yü. The sovereign said, "Yes, but let you go and undertake the duties. Effect a harmony in all the departments."

The sovereign said, "Who is equal to the duty of superintending the grass and the trees, with the birds and beasts, on my mountains and in my marshes?"

All in the court replied, "Is there not Yi?"

The sovereign said, "Yes. Oh! Yi, let you be my Forester."

Yi did obeisance with his head to the ground and wished to decline in favor of Chu, Hu, Hsiung, or P'i.

The sovereign said, "Yes, but let you go and undertake the duties. You must manage them harmoniously."

The sovereign said, "Oh! Chief of the Four Mountains, is there any one able to direct my three religious ceremonies?" [5]

5. The three religious ceremonies were those observed in rites concerning the Spirits of Heaven, the Spirits of Earth, and the Spirits of Men.

All in the court answered, "Is there not Po-i?"

The sovereign said, "Yes. Oh! Po, you must be the Arranger in the Ancestral Temple. Morning and night be reverent. Be upright, be pure."

Po did obeisance with his head to the ground, and wished to decline in favor of K'uei or Lung. The sovereign said, "Yes, but let you go and undertake the duties. Be reverent!"

The sovereign said, "K'uei, I appoint you to be Director of Music and to teach our sons, so that the straightforward shall yet be mild; the gentle, dignified; the strong, not tyrannical; and the impetuous, not arrogant. Poetry is the expression of earnest thought; singing is the prolonged utterance of that expression; the notes accompany that utterance and are harmonized by the standard tubes. In this way the eight different kinds of musical instruments can be adjusted so that one shall not take from or interfere with another, and spirits and men are brought into harmony."

K'uei said, "I smite the musical stone, I gently strike it, and the various animals lead on one another to dance." [6]

The sovereign said, "Lung, I abominate slanderous speakers and destroyers of the right ways who agitate and alarm my people. I appoint you minister of Communication. Early and late give forth my orders and report to me, seeing that everything is true."

The sovereign said, "Oh! you twenty and two men, be reverent; so shall you be helpful to the business entrusted to me by Heaven."

Every three years there was an examination of merits, and after three examinations the undeserving were degraded and the deserving advanced. By this arrangement the duties

6. Musical stones were made of jade cut in an "L" shape and suspended from a hole at the apex of the right angle. When struck, they gave off a pleasing tone. The Chinese word "ch'ing" may also be translated as sonorous, or sounding, stones.

of all the departments were fully discharged. The people of San Miao were discriminated and separated.

In the thirtieth year of his age, Shun was called to employment. Thirty years he was on the throne with Yao. Fifty years afterwards he went on high and died.

2. THE COUNSELS OF THE GREAT YÜ

The counsels are the second of the six classes of documents in the *Shu*. Their style differs from that of the canons and occasionally falls into rhyme in the original. Counsels contain the wise remarks and suggestions of high officers on the subject of government, frequently in the style of maxims. The genuineness of this document has been challenged.

The Great Yü (also referred to elsewhere as "Ta Yü," "ta" meaning great or noble) is styled Wen Ming, "the Accomplished, the Commander." The time of this document is after Yü has controlled the flood and divided the land into nine provinces and five domains. The account of these labors appears out of chronological order and serves to introduce the documents of Hsia, China's first hereditary dynasty, founded by Yü.

In this document Yü, accompanied by Yi, is counseling the sovereign Shun. Yi appeared in the previous document when Shun appointed him to be his Forester. Yi assisted Yü in the work of burning and hewing the forests to make paths for men, controlling the flood waters, draining the marshes, forming lakes, and channeling the rivers to the sea. Yü and Yi had formed a celebrated friendship, such as David's friendship with Jonathan. The two friends are counseling Shun on principles and methods of government.

Shun wishes to turn over the throne to Yü, but Yü recommends Kao Yao, the minister of Crime who has sowed virtue throughout the land. However, like Shun before him, Yü is persuaded to assume the royal duties.

As acting sovereign, Yü calls together the princes who are to subdue the lords of Miao. With the brevity characteristic of the *Shu,* especially in the earlier sections, the document swiftly closes at a time thirty years later, when the submission of the lord of Miao is celebrated by dancing with shields and feathers in the courtyard of the sovereign.

Document 2

Examining into antiquity, we find that the Great Yü was styled Wen Ming. Having arranged and divided the land, all to the four seas, in reverent response to the sovereign, Yü said,

"If the sovereign can realize the difficulty of his sovereignty, and the minister the difficulty of his ministry, the government will be well ordered and the black-haired people will sedulously seek to be virtuous."

The sovereign said, "Yes. Let this really be the case and good words will nowhere lie hidden. No men of virtue and talents will be left neglected, away from court, and the myriad states will all enjoy repose. But to obtain the views of all, to give up one's opinion and follow that of others, to keep from oppressing the helpless and not neglect the straitened and poor—it was only the sovereign who could attain to this."

Yi said, "Oh! your virtue, O Sovereign, is vast and incessant. It is sagely, spirit-like, awe-inspiring, and adorned with all accomplishments. Great Heaven regarded you with its favoring decree and suddenly you obtained all within the four seas and became ruler of all under heaven."

Yü said, "Accordance with right leads to good fortune; following evil to bad: the shadow and the echo."

Yi said, "Alas! be cautious! Admonish yourself to caution when there seems to be no occasion for anxiety. Do not fail to observe the laws and ordinances. Do not find your enjoyment in idleness. Do not go to excess in pleasure. In your employment of men of worth, let none come between you and them. Put away evil without hesitation. Do not carry out plans about the wisdom of which you have doubts. Study that all your purposes may be with the light of reason. Do not go against what is right to get the praise of the people. Do not oppose the people to follow your own desires. Attend to these things without idleness or omission and from the four quarters the barbarous tribes will come and acknowledge your sovereignty."

Yü said, "Oh! think of these things, O Sovereign. The virtue of the ruler is seen in good government, and government is tested in nourishing of the people. There are water, fire, metal, wood, earth, and grain; these must be duly regulated. There are the rectification of the people's virtue, tools and other things that supply the conveniences of life, and securing abundant means of sustenance; these must be harmoniously attended to. When the nine services thus indicated have been orderly accomplished, let that accomplishment be celebrated by songs. Caution the people with gentle words, correct them with the majesty of law, stimulate them with the songs on those nine subjects in order that your success may not suffer diminution."

The sovereign said, "The earth has been reduced to order and the influences of heaven produce their complete effect. The six treasuries of nature and the three functions of government are all truly regulated and may be depended on for myriad generations. This is your merit."

The sovereign said, "Come, you Yü. I have occupied my throne for thirty and three years. I am between ninety and a hundred years old and the laborious duties weary me. Let you, eschewing all indolence, take the leadership of my people."

Yü replied, "My virtue is not equal to the position; the people will not repose in me. But there is Kao Yao with vigorous activity sowing abroad his virtue, which has descended on the black-haired people till they cherish him in their hearts. O Sovereign, think of him! When I think of him, my mind rests on him as the man fit for this office. When I would put him out of my thoughts my mind still rests on him. When I name and speak of him, my mind rests on him for this. The sincere outgoing of my thoughts about him is that he is the man. O Sovereign, think of his merits."

The sovereign said, "Kao Yao, owing to your being minister of Crime, hardly one of my ministers or people is found to offend against the government. You are intelligent in the use of the five punishments, thereby assisting the inculcation of the five cardinal duties. Your aim is the perfection of my government, that through punishment may come to be no punishments, and the people to be in accord with the path of the Mean. Continue to be zealous."

Kao Yao replied, "Your virtue, O Sovereign, is faultless. You condescend to your ministers with kindly ease; you preside over the multitudes with a generous forbearance. Punishments do not extend to the criminal's heirs; rewards reach to succeeding generations. You pardon inadvertent faults, however great, and punish purposed crimes, however small. In cases of doubtful crimes, you deal with them lightly; in cases of doubtful merit, you prefer the high estimate. Rather than put an innocent person to death, you will run the risk of irregularity and error. This life-loving virtue has penetrated the minds of the people and this is why they do not render themselves liable to punishment by your officers."

The sovereign said, "It is your excellence that I am able to follow and obtain what I desire in my government, the people responding everywhere as if moved by the wind."

The sovereign said, "Come, Yü. The inundating waters filled me with dread; you accomplished all that you had represented and completed your task, thus showing your superiority to other men. Full of toilsome earnestness in the service of the country, sparing in your expenditure on your family—and this without being full of yourself or elated —you again show your superiority to other men. You are without any prideful assumption, but no one under heaven can contest with you the palm of ability. You make no boasting, but no one under heaven can contest with you the palm of merit. I see how great is your virtue, how admirable your vast achievements. The determinate appointment of Heaven rests on your person; you must eventually ascend the throne of the great sovereign. The mind of man is restless, prone to err; its affinity for the right way is small. Be discriminating, be undivided in the pursuit of what is right that you may sincerely hold fast the Mean. Do not listen to unsubstantiated words; do not follow plans about which you have not sought counsel. Of all who are to be loved, is not the ruler the chief? Of all who are to be feared, are not the people the chief? If the multitude were without their sovereign, whom should they sustain aloft? If the sovereign had not the multitude, there would be none to guard the country for him. Be reverent! Carefully conduct yourself on the throne you will occupy, cultivating the virtues to be desired in you. If within the four seas there be distress and poverty, your Heaven-conferred revenues will come to a perpetual end. It is the mouth which sends forth what is good, and raises up war. My words I will not repeat."

Yü said, "Submit the meritorious ministers one by one to the trial of divination and let the favoring indication be followed."

The sovereign replied, "According to the rules for the regulation of divination, one should first make up his mind and afterward refer to the great tortoise shell. My mind in this matter was determined in the first place. I consulted and deliberated with all my ministers and people and they were of one accord with me. The spirits signified their assent and the tortoise shell and divining stalks concurred. Divination, when fortunate, should not be repeated."

Yü did obeisance with his head to the ground and firmly declined the throne.

The sovereign said, "You must not do so. It is you who can suitably take my place."

On the first morning of the first month, Yü received the appointment in the temple dedicated by Shun to the spirits of his ancestors, and took the leading of all the officers, as had been done by the sovereign at the commencement of his government.

The sovereign said, "Alas! O Yü, there is only the lord of Miao who refuses obedience; you must go and correct him."

Yü on this assembled all the princes and made a speech to the host, saying, "Ye multitudes here arrayed, listen all of you to my orders. Stupid is this lord of Miao, ignorant, erring, and disrespectful. Spiteful and insolent to others, he thinks that all ability and virtue are with himself. A rebel against right, he destroys all the obligations of virtue. Superior men are kept by him in obscurity and mean men fill all the offices. The people reject and will not protect him. Heaven is sending down calamities upon him. I therefore, along with you, my multitude of gallant men, bear the instructions of the sovereign to punish his crimes. Let you proceed with united heart and strength; so shall our enterprise be crowned with success."

At the end of three decades, the people of Miao continued rebellious against the sovereign's commands. Yi came to the help of Yü, saying,

"It is virtue that moves Heaven; there is no distance to which it does not reach. Pride brings loss, and humility receives increase; this is the way of Heaven. In the early time of the sovereign, when he was living by Mount Li,[1] he went into the fields and daily cried with tears to compassionate Heaven and to his parents, taking to himself all guilt and charging himself with their wickedness. At the same time, with respectful service he appeared before Ku Sou looking grave and awe-struck until Ku also became transformed by his example. Entire sincerity moves spiritual beings; how much more will it move this lord of Miao!"

Yü did homage to the excellent words and said, "Yes." Thereupon he led back his army, having drawn off the troops.

The sovereign set about diffusing on a grand scale the virtuous influences of peace. There was dancing with shields and feathers between the two staircases in the courtyard. In seventy days the lord of Miao came to make his submission.

1. Mount Li, in the present-day province of Shansi, was where Shun lived with Ku Sou, his father, and his stepmother. There are many legends of plots against Shun by his family. His filial piety despite this treatment was extolled to Yao by the Chief of the Four Mountains in "The Canon of Yao" (Part I).

3. THE COUNSELS OF KAO YAO

Kao Yao, minister of Crime to Shun, was celebrated for many centuries in China as a model for all administrators of justice. Here Kao Yao's counsels occur in a dialogue with Yü, in which he is the chief speaker. At the core of these counsels is a basic political concept of ancient China: that only if the sovereign is virtuous can his ministers and the people also be virtuous. The conversation takes place during the reign of Shun, probably about 2200 B.C.

Huan Tou, a minister to Yao, has been mentioned in several of the previous documents. He was one of four great criminals banished by Shun during the period he shared the imperial duties with Yao.

Of all the numerical categories employed throughout Chinese literature, that of five ("wu" in Chinese) predominates, possibly because of the five elements—metal, earth, wood, water, and fire, accompanied by their subtle essences. Here we encounter a new category of five: five ceremonies having to do with protocol. Of all numbers, five enjoys peculiar veneration. Of all colors, yellow enjoys peculiar veneration, probably because it was the color of the loess, the loamy soil on which sustenance depended.

Document 3

Examining into antiquity, we find that Kao Yao said, "If the sovereign sincerely pursues the course of his virtue, the counsels offered to him will be intelligent and the admonitions he receives will be harmonious."

Yü said, "Yes, but explain yourself."

Kao Yao said, "Oh! let him be careful about his personal cultivation, with thoughts that are far-reaching; thus he will effect a generous kindness and nice observance of distinc-

26

tions among the nine branches of his kindred. Also, all the intelligent will exert themselves in his service. In this way from what is near the sovereign will reach to what is distant."

Yü did reverence to the excellent words and said, "Yes."

Kao Yao continued, "Oh! it lies in knowing men and giving repose to the people."

Yü said, "Alas! to attain these things was a difficulty even to Yao. When a sovereign knows men, he is wise and can put every one into the office for which he is fit. When he gives repose to the people, his kindness is felt and the black-haired race cherish him in their hearts. When a sovereign can be thus wise and kind, what occasion will he have for anxiety about a Huan Tou or removing a lord of Miao? What has he to fear from insincere words, insinuating appearance, and great artfulness?"

Kao Yao said, "Oh! there are in all nine virtues to be discovered in conduct. When we say that a man possesses any virtue, it is as much as to say he does such and such a thing."

Yü asked, "What are the nine virtues?"

Kao Yao replied, "Affability combined with dignity, mildness with firmness, bluntness with respectfulness, aptness for government with reverence, docility with boldness, straightforwardness with gentleness, an easy negligence with discrimination, boldness with sincerity, and valor with righteousness. When these qualities are continuously displayed, have we not the good officer? When there is a daily display of three of these virtues, their possessor could early and late regulate and brighten the clan of which he was made chief. When there is a daily severe and reverent cultivation of six virtues, their possessor could brilliantly conduct the affairs of the state to which he was constituted ruler. When such men are all received and advanced, the possessors of those nine virtues will be employed in the public service. The men of a thousand and men of a hundred will be in their offices; the various ministers will emulate one another; all the officers will accomplish their duties at the proper times, observant of the seasons and the elements predominating in them; thus their various duties will be fully accomplished.

"Let not the Son of Heaven set the example of indolence or dissoluteness to the rulers of states. Let him be wary and fearful, remembering that in one day or two days there may occur ten thousand springs of things. Let not his various officers obstruct their places. The work is Heaven's; men must act for it!

"From Heaven are the social relationships with their several duties. To us it is given to enforce those five duties. Lo, then we have the five courses of generous conduct. From Heaven are the social distinctions with their several ceremonies; from us proceed the observances of those five ceremonies; and lo! they then appear in regular practice. When sovereign and ministers show a common reverence and united respect for these ceremonies do they not harmonize the moral nature of the people? Heaven graciously distinguishes the virtuous: are there not the five ceremonial robes with the five decorations? Heaven punishes the guilty; are there not the five punishments for that purpose? The business of government! Ought we not to be earnest in it? Ought we not to be earnest in it?

"Heaven hears and sees as our people hear and see; Heaven brightly approves and displays its terrors as our people brightly approve and would fear; such connection is there between the upper and lower worlds. How reverent ought the masters of the earth to be!

"My words are in accord with reason and may be put in practice."

Yü said, "Yes, your words may be put in practice and crowned with success."

Kao Yao said, "As to that I do not know; but I wish daily to be helpful. May the government be perfected!"

4. THE YI AND CH'I

This document takes its title from the names of two worthies. Yi, who was Shun's Forester, we already know as the friend and companion of Yü, who assisted him during the thirteen years he labored in controlling the great flood. Ch'i was minister of Agriculture. Neither Yi nor Ch'i appear as interlocutors in this section, and it is difficult for us to understand why the document bears their names; perhaps it is because only a fragment is extant.

This is the last section of *The Documents of Yü*. It opens with Yü narrating his work in controlling the flood, embodying in this account the legends attached to this achievement. This is followed by his counsels to Shun, from which the section derives its classification as a counsel.

And then abruptly K'uei, Shun's Director of Music, appears. Singing and playing music were established within Chinese culture from the earliest time. If the *Yo chi, Book of Music* had not been lost, we could understand a great deal more about this. We can assume that the principle of Chinese music, like the written characters, has endured with only slight changes over the centuries.

Today in the People's Republic of China, there is a new body of music celebrating Mao Tse-tung and the Chinese Cultural Revolution. In 1970 there were no less than thirty musical selections available, imported under U.S. Treasury License. These ranged from folk songs and dialogues set to music, to full-scale opera, all limited to the theme of celebration.

Part II is concluded after Shun and Kao Yao sing to each other on the mutual relation of the sovereign and his ministers. Then Shun sends Kao Yao away with the usual admonition toward reverence.

Document 4

The sovereign said, "Come, Yü, you also must have excellent words to bring before me."

Yü did obeisance and said, "Oh! what can I say after Kao Yao, O Sovereign? I can only think of maintaining a daily assiduity."

Kao Yao said, "Alas! will you describe it?"

Yü said, "The inundating waters seemed to assail the heavens and in their vast extent embraced the hills and overtopped the great mounds, so that the people were bewildered and overwhelmed. I mounted my four conveyances[1] and all along the hills hewed down the trees; at the same time, along with Yi, showing the multitudes how to get flesh to eat. I also opened passages for the streams throughout the nine provinces and conducted them to the seas. I deepened the channels and canals and conducted them to the streams; at the same time, along with Ch'i, sowing grain and showing the multitudes how to procure the food of toil in addition to the flesh meat. I urged them further to exchange what they had for what they had not, and to dispose of their accumulated stores. In this way all the people got grain to eat and the different states began to come under good rule."

1. Legge quotes from the *Shih chi, Historical Records* of Ssu-ma Ch'ien about these four conveyances. Yü says:

> "To travel along the dry land I used a
> carriage; to travel along the water, I
> used a boat; to travel through miry
> places, I used a sledge; to travel on
> the hills, I used spikes."

The sledge is thought to have been like a sieve, made to slide easily over marshes; spikes were thought to have been shoes fitted with awls underneath to prevent the feet from slipping.

Kao Yao said, "Yes, we ought to model ourselves after your excellent words."

Yü said, "Oh! carefully maintain, O Sovereign, the throne which you occupy."

The sovereign replied, "Yes."

Yü went on, "Find your repose in your proper resting-point. Attend to the springs of things, study stability, let your assistants be upright; then shall your movements be grandly responded to as if the people only waited for your will. Thus you will brightly receive the favor of God. Will not Heaven renew its appointment of you, and give you blessing?"

The sovereign said, "Alas! what are ministers? Are they not my associates? What are associates? Are they not my ministers?"

Yü replied, "Yes."

The sovereign went on, "My ministers constitute my legs and arms, my ears and eyes. I wish to help and support my people: you give effect to my wishes. I wish to spread the influence of my government through the four quarters: you act as my agents. I wish to see the emblematic figures of the ancients: the sun, moon, stars, mountain, dragons, and the flowery pheasant, which are depicted on the upper garment; the temple cups, pondweed, flames, grains of rice, hatchet, and the symbol of distinction, which are embroidered on the lower garment. I wish to see all these fully displayed with the five colors, so as to form the ceremonial robes; it is yours to see them clearly for me.

"I wish to hear the six pitch pipes, the five notes determined by them, and the eight kinds of musical instruments regulated again by these, examining thereby the virtues and defects of my government, according as the odes that go forth from the court set to music, and the ballads that come in from the people, are ordered by those five notes; it is yours to hear them for me.

"When I am doing wrong, it is yours to correct me; do not follow me to my face and, when you have retired, have other remarks to make. Be reverent, ye associates, who are before and behind and on each side of me! As to all the obstinately stupid and calumniating talkers who are found to be doing what is not right, there are the target to exhibit their true character, the scourge to make them recollect, and the book of remembrance.[2] Do we not wish them to live along with us? There are also the masters of music to receive the compositions and continually set them forth in song. If they become reformed they are to be received and employed; if they do not, let the terrors of punishment overtake them."

Yü said, "So far good! But let your light shine, O Sovereign, all under heaven, even to the grassy shores of the seas, and throughout the myriad states the most worthy of the people will all wish to be your ministers. Then, O Sovereign, you may advance them to office. They will set forth and you will receive their reports; you will make proof of them according to their merits; you will confer chariots and robes according to their services. Who would dare not to cultivate a humble virtue? Who would dare not to respond to you with reverence? If you, O Sovereign, do not act thus, all your ministers together will daily decline to a meritless character.

---

2. In ancient China, archery was used as a test of character. It was thought that unworthy men would not hit the mark frequently. The book of remembrance was probably a record on wood or cloth of the characters of the people kept by the heads of districts, according to the practice described in *The Official Book of Chou*. This reference implies the use of writing in this early period.

"Be not haughty like Chu of Tan,[3] who found his pleasure only in indolence and dissipation and pursued a proud oppressive course. Day and night without ceasing he was thus. He would make boats go where there was no water. He introduced licentious associates into his family. The consequence was that he brought the honors of his house to an end. I took warning from his course. When I married in T'u-shan, I remained with my wife only the four days *hsin, jen, kuei,* and *chia.* When my son Ch'i was wailing and weeping, I did not regard him but kept planning with all my might my labor on the land. Then I assisted in completing the five domains, extending over 5,000 li; in appointing in the provinces twelve officers. In the regions beyond, reaching to the four seas, I assisted in establishing the five chiefs. These all pursue the right path and are meritorious; but there are still the people of Miao, who refuse to acknowledge their duty. Think of this, O Sovereign."

The sovereign said, "That my virtue is followed is the result of your meritorious services so orderly displayed. And now Kao Yao is respectfully carrying out your arrangements, and employing the represented punishments with entire intelligence."

K'uei said, "When the musical stone is tapped or struck with force; when the lutes are strongly swept or gently touched to accompany the singing; then the progenitors of the sovereign come to the service, the guest of Yü[3] is in his place, and all the princes show their virtue in giving place to one another. In the court below there are the flutes and hand-drums, which join in at the sound of the rattle and

3. Chu was the son of Yao, probably lord of a principality called Tan. Later, when K'uei (Shun's Director of Music) speaks of the ancestral spirits that will descend when the musical stone is struck and makes reference to "the guest of Yü," it is to Chu of Tan that he refers.

cease at that of the stopper, when the organs and bells take their place. This makes birds and beasts fall to moving. When the nine parts of the service as arranged by the sovereign have all been performed, the male and female phoenix come with their measured gambolings into the court."

K'uei said, "Oh! when I smite the musical stone or gently strike it, the various animals lead on one another to dance and all the chiefs of the official departments become truly harmonious."

The sovereign on this made a song, saying, "We must deal cautiously with the favoring appointment of Heaven, at every moment and in the smallest particular." He then sang,

> "When the members work joyfully,
> The head rises grandly;
> And the duties of all the offices are
> fully discharged!"

Kao Yao did obeisance with his head to his hands and then to the ground, and with a loud and rapid voice said, "Think, O Sovereign. It is yours to lead on and originate things. Pay careful attention to your laws in doing so. Be reverent! Often examine what has been accomplished by your officers. Be reverent!" With this he continued the song,

> "When the head is intelligent,
> The members are good;
> And all affairs will be happily performed!"

Again he continued the song,

> "When the head is vexatious,
> The members are idle;
> And all affairs will go to ruin!"

The sovereign said, "Yes, go and be reverently attentive to your duties."

PART III

The Documents of Hsia

1. TRIBUTE TO YÜ

Before Yü, the throne had not passed to the heirs of rulers. Instead, the sovereign sought out a worthy successor and resigned the throne to him. According to tradition, this practice began with Fu Hsi, inventor of the eight trigrams on which the *I ching, Book of Changes* is based, and continued to Yü, who founded the first hereditary dynasty, Hsia.

This document, also called *Yü kung,* is the third and last of the three canons. As a tribute, it records those merits of Yü that earned him the throne; as a canon, it was a document of exalted nature, suitable to serve as a rule and pattern for the ages. It appears out of chronological order, apparently to introduce the documents of Hsia; the completion of the engineering labors it describes has already been referred to in Part II.

Since the archaeological finds in the provinces of Honan and Shansi in the twenties and thirties of this century confirmed the existence of the Shang dynasty, faith in the historicity of the Hsia dynasty has been strengthened. But since there has been no announcement of archaeological confirmation as yet, the Hsia remains classified as tradition not history, and its documents are read as literature.

Perhaps no other document in all the *Shu* illustrates so many aspects of ancient Chinese literature as this one. While its enumerations are tedious, its topics are interesting; it tells much in such an abbreviated style that reading it requires what Legge called "the leap from mind to mind"; it has undergone a dual process of accretion and compaction that renders its content monolithic.

The proliferation of names in the geographical descriptions of more than thirty-five rivers and their courses, forty-five hills and mountains, the detailed, yet sparse, information concerning the nine provinces and five domains, present the Western reader with what seems, at first reading, no more than a jumbled complexity. However, such enumerations may have been a means of survival to early travelers who used rivers for transportation, had reason to avoid barbarian tribes, and required some indication of the fauna and flora in strange regions. This document might have served the same purpose as the gazetteers of the North American continent that were used in the early nineteenth century.

Not all the place names can be identified. Many rivers have changed their courses, dried up, or merged with other rivers; the rocks of Chieh have disappeared into the sea; names of some of the mountains have been changed or are disputed. But there is much remaining that is of interest to us.

At the beginning, the nine provinces are dealt with one by one, beginning with Chi Chou where the capital was located. The articles of tribute tell us something about the manner, customs, and daily life of the inhabitants of those early times. We may have particular questions to which there are no answers, but there is general enlightenment.

The story of the provinces is followed by a description of the hills and mountains. Of particular interest to present-day readers are the Kunlun Mountains of the west, referred to frequently in other writings, and Mount Tai (also called Taishan and the Eastern Peak), the first of the four sacred mountains. Tai, with Mount Heng the Southern Peak, Mount Hua the Western Peak, and another Mount Heng the Northern Peak, constituted the Four Mountains ministry entrusted to an officer addressed as Chief of the Four Mountains by Yao (see Part I).

Next, the courses of nine rivers are traced. In all, more than thirty-five rivers are mentioned by name. Legge characterizes the Ho, Huai, Han, and Chiang as the four principal ones.

Of particular interest are the Ho and the Lo, both having legends connected with them. The Ho, later called the Huang (Hwang) Ho, is now generally referred to as the Yellow River. According to legend, out of the Ho rose a dragon-horse bearing on its back the marks that gave Fu Hsi the idea of the eight trigrams.

All of the tribute bearers made use of the Ho in reaching the capital. This river has changed its course many times, often with such disastrous results that it has been called "China's Sorrow." Earlier floods than the one we read of here may have driven inhabitants along its banks to live in trees, originating the folk-lore of the people called Nest-builders. Other people took to high ground and lived in caves.

A great tortoise with writing on its back was supposed to have risen from the waters of the Lo. The writing suggested to Yü, who was working nearby, the idea for "The Great Plan" (Part V, Document 4).

Yü regulated the waters by channeling and ditching and, in other places, by diking. Sometimes marshes were converted into lakes and sometimes they were drained.

After the rivers, we read of the five domains. The provinces were geographical areas, usually bounded by features such as mountains or rivers. The domains (or tenures), however, were political areas.

The time is during the vice-regency of Shun, when he shared the throne with Yao. According to tradition, Yü announced the completion of his work in 2276 B.C., the eightieth year of Yao's reign and the seventh year of Shun's association with him in the government. It is not exactly known how long Yü's labors took. Estimates vary. A legend tells of Yü three times passing his home and hearing the crying of his son whom he had not yet seen—but he did not pause in his work, so great was his zeal. The document is presented here as though Yü had worked single-handedly, but Legge gives this comment:

> We are too apt to think of him alone in connection with it. He had the merit of suggesting, directing, and superintending; but all the talent and strength of the empire was helping. Yi and Chi are mentioned . . . as his coadjutors. Passages from the *Shu* itself and the *Historical Records* indicate that he had all the resources of the empire at his disposal.

The document closes with the presentation of the dark-colored symbol of rank and the announcement of the completion of Yü's work. To many who regard Yao, Shun, and Yü as great and sage sovereigns, the golden age of ancient China also closes.

Document 1

Yü divided the land. Following the course of the hills, he cut down trees.[1] He determined the highest hills and largest rivers in the several regions.

With respect to Chi Chou, he did his work at Hu-k'ou hill. He took effective measures at the mountains Liang and Ch'i. Having repaired the works on T'ai-yüan,[2] he proceeded to the south of Mount Yo. He was successful with his labors at Tan-huai and went on to the cross-flowing stream of Chang.

The soil of this province was whitish and mellow. Its contribution of revenue was the first of the highest class, with some proportion of the second. Its fields were the average of the middle class.

The waters of the Heng and Wei were brought to their proper channels and the plain of Ta-lü was made capable of cultivation.

The wild people of the islands brought fur garments.

1. The location of mountains and rivers was basic to solving Yü's engineering problems. Cutting down trees provided pathways for men and was the first step in regulating the waters.

2. Chi Chou occupied the present-day province of Shansi with parts of Hopeh, Honan, and the western Liaotung Peninsula. Chi Chou's northern boundary was undefined, and the imperial seat was located there; for this reason it would be the first province to be worked on.

As to the repairs at T'ai-yüan, Legge infers from "repairs" that the work of Kun, Yü's father, had been partly effective. Some commentators state that Kun's error was in dealing with the flood waters where they encroached on the capital instead of at the sources of the rivers. Failure to control the flood caused Kun to be banished "until death a prisoner on Mount Yü" (Part II, Document 1).

Keeping close to the right they hugged the rocks of Chieh and entered the Ho.[3]

Between the Chi and the Ho was Yen Chou.[4]

The nine branches of the Ho were made to keep their proper channels. Lei-hsia was formed into a marsh in which the waters of the Yung and the Tsü united. The mulberry grounds were made fit for silkworms; then the people came down from the heights and occupied the land below.

The soil of this province was blackish and rich; the grass became luxuriant and the trees grew tall. Its fields were the lowest of the middle class. Its contribution of revenue was fixed at what would be deemed just the correct amount. But it was not required, as revenue from other provinces, until after it had been cultivated for thirteen years. Its articles of tribute were varnish and silk and, in baskets, woven ornamental fabrics.

They floated along the Chi and T'a and so reached the Ho.[5]

The sea and Mount Tai were the boundaries of Ch'ing Chou.[6]

3. The identity of the wild people of the islands is not known, but they probably came from the northern shore of Po Hai. The rocks of Chieh, to which the tribute bearers kept close, were well-known and often visited in ancient times. No trace of them remains.

4. Yen Chou was a small province, occupying parts of present-day Shantung and Hopeh. There were only a few hills in this province, and the people had been driven to them by the flood waters. The region was good for silkworms, but as these insects dislike excessive moisture, it was only after the flood waters were drained that their cultivation could be resumed.

5. We assume that "they" in "They floated along . . ." refers here, and in other descriptions of the provinces, to the tribute bearers. The Karlgren translation uses the singular "he."

6. Ch'ing Chou (not to be confused with Ching Chou) was in present-day Shantung. Some commentators think it was smaller than Yen Chou, but others hold that it crossed the sea and extended into the Liangtung Peninsula as far as modern Korea.

The territory of Yü-i was defined. The Wei and the Tsi were made to keep their old channels.

The soil of this province was whitish and rich. Near the sea were wide tracts of salt land. Its fields were the lowest of the first class and its contribution of revenue the highest of the second.

Its articles of tribute were salt, fine grass cloth,[7] various kinds of articles from the sea; with silk, hemp, lead, pine trees, and strange stones from the valleys of Tai. The wild people of Lai were taught tillage and pasturage, and brought in their baskets silk from the mountain mulberry tree.

They floated along the Wen and so reached the Chi.

The sea, Mount Tai, and the Huai were the boundaries of Hsü Chou.[8]

The Huai and the I rivers were regulated. The hills of Meng and Yü were brought under cultivation. The lake of Ta-ye was confined within its proper limits. The tract of Tung-yüan was successfully brought under management.

The soil of this province was red, clayey, and rich. The trees and grass became more and more bushy. Its fields were the second of the highest class; its contribution of revenue was the average of the second.

Its articles of tribute were earth of five different colors, variegated feathers of pheasants from the valleys of Mount Yü, the solitary dryandra from the south of Mount Yi, and the musical stones that seemed to float near the banks of the Ssu.[9] The wild tribes about the Huai brought oyster

7. The grass cloth was made from dolichos fiber and is sometimes known by that name. Dolichos fiber was also used for making shoes.

8. Hsü Chou occupied parts of present-day Kiangsu, Shantung, and Anhwei.

9. Legge quotes Ying-ta's comment on earth of the five different colors: " 'The emperors raised a mound of earth of the five colors as an altar to the spirits of the land. On the investiture of any prince a

pearls and fish, and their baskets full of deep azure silks and other silken fabrics, checkered and pure white.

They floated along the Huai and the Ssu and so reached the Ho.

The Huai and the sea formed the boundaries of Yang Chou.[10]

The lake of P'eng-li was confined to its proper limits and the wild geese had places to settle on. The Three Chiang were led to enter the sea and it became possible to still the marsh of Chen. The bamboos, small and large, then spread about. The grass grew long and thin and the trees rose high. The soil was miry.

The fields of this province were the lowest of the lowest class; its contribution of revenue was the highest of the lowest class, with a proportion of the class above.

Its articles of tribute were gold, silver, and copper; *yao* and *kun* stones; bamboos small and large; elephants' teeth, hides, feathers, hair, and timber. The wild people of the islands brought garments of grass, with silks woven in shell-patterns, in their baskets. Their bundles contained small

---

quantity of earth of the color characteristic of the region where his principality lay was cut away and given to him, which he took home to build an altar with. All the altars thus built, however, were covered with yellow earth. The earth was given to each prince in bundles covered with white rushes emblematic of purity.' "

Feathers were used extensively for ornament, and those from the pheasant would be particularly desirable.

The dryandra tree was prized for making lutes.

Musical stones were important in the music, rites, and ceremonies of early China. They were cut and polished by means of other, harder stones and bored through to make them capable of being suspended. When struck they gave off a pleasing tone (see the remarks of K'uei, Shun's Director of Music, at the close of Document 4 in Part II, "The Yi and Chi").

10. Yang Chou comprised the greater portions of present-day Anhwei and northern Hupeh and extended to an unknown extent south into Chekiang and Kiangsi.

oranges and pomelos—rendered when especially required.[11]

They followed the course of the Chiang and the sea, and so reached the Huai and the Ssu.

Mount Ching and the south of Mount Heng formed the boundaries of Ching Chou.[12]

The Chiang and the Han pursued their common course to the sea as if they were hastening to court. The Nine Chiang were brought to complete order. The T'o and Ch'ien streams were conducted by their proper channels. The land in the marsh of Yün became visible, and the marsh of Meng was brought under cultivation.

The soil of this province was miry. Its fields were the average of the lowest class; its contribution of revenue was the lowest of the highest class.

11. Legge quotes the *Shih chi, Historical Records* of Ssu-ma Ch'ien concerning gold, silver, and copper: "'Among the ancients there were three degrees of metal: the yellow metal, the highest in value; the white metal, the next; and the red metal, the lowest.'" The Karlgren translation reads "bronze of the three (colors) qualities."

In an article signed by William F. Collins in the *Encyclopedia Sinica,* edited by Couling, tin, or "hsi," is a character which in early periods indicated any white metal. "T'ieh" was iron; "kang" was a character translated as steel; and "lou" was translated as hard iron or steel.

The hides mentioned were probably rhinoceros hides, and the teeth of the elephants were, of course, the ivory tusks.

Legge left open the possibility that the climate of ancient China had undergone a great change since the time of this document; this is now generally acknowledged. Gernet states: "Yellow River China, which was covered by forests and marshlands, then had a hot and humid climate which seems to have lasted until the beginnings of the first millennium B.C." (Jacques Gernet, *Ancient China from the Beginnings to the Empire,* p. 31. Los Angeles: University of California Press, 1968.)

There is a growing body of ancient China aficionados who think that many animals such as the dragon and the phoenix, once considered fabulous, actually existed in the early, hot, humid climate but have since become extinct.

12. Ching Chou was the central province, embracing most of present-day Honan and also parts of Shantung and Hupeh.

Its articles of tribute were feathers, hair, ivory, and hides; gold, silver, and copper; the *ch'un* tree wood for bows, cedars and cypresses; grindstones, whetstones, flint stones to make arrowheads, and cinnabar. There were also the *ch'ün* and *lu* bamboos with the *hu* tree, all good for making arrows, of which the three regions were able to contribute the best specimens. The three-ribbed rush was put in cases, which again were wrapped up.[13] The baskets were filled with silken fabrics, azure and deep purple, and with strings of pearls that were not quite round. From the country of the Nine Chiang the great tortoise was presented when especially required and found.

They floated down the Chiang, the T'o, the Ch'ien, and the Han; crossed over the country to the Lo and proceeded to the southern part of the Ho.

The Ching mountain and the Ho were the boundaries of Yü Chou.[14]

The I, the Lo, the Ch'an, and the Chien were conducted to the Ho. The marsh of Yung-po was confined within its proper limits. The waters of the marsh of Ko were led to the marsh of Meng-chu.

The soil of this province was mellow; in the lower parts it was in some places rich, in others dark and thin. Its fields were the highest of the middle class. Its contribution of revenue was the average of the highest class with a proportion of the very highest.

Its articles of tribute were varnish, hemp, fine cloth of dolichos fiber, and the boehmerea. The baskets were filled

13. The tribute of three-ribbed rush was first put in cases and then wrapped up because it was used to strain the sacrificial wine at the imperial rites.
14. Yü Chou included parts of present-day Shantung and Hopeh, plus most of Honan.

with checkered silks, and of fine floss silk. Stones for polishing musical stones were rendered when required.[15]

They floated along the Lo and so reached the Ho.

The south of Mount Hua and the Black River were the boundaries of Liang Chou.[16]

The hills Min and Po were brought under cultivation. The T'o and Ch'ien streams were conducted by their proper channels. Sacrifices were offered to the hills Ts'ai and Meng upon the regulation of the country about them.

The country of the wild tribes about the Ho could now be successfully operated on.

The soil of this province was greenish and light. Its fields were the highest of the lowest class. Its contribution of revenue was the average of the lowest class, with proportions of the rates immediately above and below.

Its articles of tribute were: the best gold, iron, silver, steel, flint stones to make arrowheads, and musical stones; with the skins of bears, foxes, jackals, and nets woven of their hair.

From the hill of Hsi Ch'ing they came by the course of the Huan, floated along the Ch'ien, and then crossed the country to the Mien, then entered the Wei, and finally ferried across the Ho.

15. The boehmerea mentioned among the tributes was similar to the dolichos fibers from which grass cloth was made, but coarser. It resembled hempen cloth of either fine or coarse weave.

The stones that were brought in to polish the musical stones were selected because they were harder and thus could be used as tools.

16. Liang Chou included parts of present-day Shensi, Kansu, and Szechwan provinces.

Among the tributes, the Karlgren translation also mentions iron and steel. Legge footnotes the character for steel as meaning "hard iron." What exact degrees of hardness were achieved by smiths working at those early forges cannot be known.

The Black River and the Western Ho were the boundaries of Yung Chou.[17]

The Jo River was conducted westward. The Ching was led to mingle its waters with those of the Wei. The Ch'i and the Ch'ü were next led in a similar way to the Wei, and the waters of the Feng found the same river bed.

The mountains Ching and Ch'i were sacrificed to.[18] Those of Chung-nan and Ch'un-wu were also regulated all the way on to Niao-shu. Successful measures could now be taken with the plains and swamps, even to the marsh of Chu-ye. The country of San-wei was made habitable and the affairs of the people of San Miao were greatly arranged.

The soil of the province was yellow and mellow. Its fields were the highest of the highest class. Its contribution of revenue was the lowest of the second.

Its articles of tribute were the *ch'iu* jade and the *lin,* and the stones called *lang-kan.*[19]

Past Chi-shih mountain they floated on to Lung-men on the Western Ho. Then they met with other tribute bearers on the north of the Wei.

Hair-cloth and skins were brought from the mountains of Kunlun, Hsi-chih, and Ch'u-sou;[20] the wild tribes of the west all submitting to Yü's arrangements.

---

17. Yung Chou was the ninth and last province to be cultivated. It included nearly all of present-day Shensi and Kansu and extended indefinitely northwest.

18. Sacrifices, whenever noted, signify completion of phases of work.

19. There is much controversy over what kinds of stones were used for tributes. We assume some to be musical stones with other stones for polishing them. Some commentators also think lapis lazuli and coral were brought to the capital.

20. From the tributes of hair-cloth (felt) and skins (furs), we assume Yung Chou extended at least as far as the Kunlun Mountains.

The Mountains

Yü surveyed and described the hills,[21] beginning with Ch'ien and Ch'i and proceeding to Mount Ching then, crossing the Ho, the hills of Hu-k'ou and Lei Shou, going on to T'ai-yo mountain.

After these came Ti-chu and Hsi-ch'eng, from which he went on to Wang-wu. Then there were T'ai-hang and Mount Heng, from which he proceeded to the rocks of Chieh, where he reached the sea.

South of the Ho he surveyed Hsi-ch'ing, Chu-yü, and Niao-shu, going on to T'ai-hua followed by Hsiung-ehr, Wai-fang, and T'ung-po, from which he proceeded to Pei-wei.

He surveyed and described Po-ch'ung, going on to the other, southern, Mount Ching and Nei-fang, from which he went on to Ta-pie.

He did the same with the south of Mount Min and went on to Mount Heng. Then, crossing the Nine Chiang, he proceeded to the plain of Fu Ch'ien.

He traced the Jo River as far as the Ho-li Mountains, from which its superfluous waters went away among the Moving Sands.[22]

21. The document now deals with the mountain ranges. Legge reminds us that the surveying and describing is mental, concerned with taking a bird's-eye view. Within a few lines, more than twenty mountains are mentioned. Of these, Lei Shou (also called Mount Shou and Shou-yang) is noted as the place where the brothers Po-i and Shu Ch'i retired to starve to death rather than live under a corrupt government.

Here the reader is almost forced to speculate that at one time these concluding passages were to be read before the detailed descriptions of the nine provinces were given and the fixing of the revenue and tributes. The paragraphs dealing with the mountain ranges and river courses seem to describe the early planning of the work and, in point of chronology, might well be read between the first and second paragraphs.

22. Yü traces nine river courses and names many more. While these

He traced the Black River as far as San-wei, from which it went away to enter the southern sea.

He traced the Ho from Chi-shih as far as Lung-men and, thence southward, to the north of Mount Hua; eastward then to Ti-ch'u; eastward again to the ford of Meng;[23] eastward still, to the junction of the Lo; then on to Ta-pie. From this the Ho's course was northward, past the Chiang water, on to the plain of Ta-lü, north from which the river divided and became the Nine Ho when, uniting again, it formed the Meeting Ho and entered the sea.

From Po-ch'ung he traced the Yang which, flowing eastward, became the Han. Farther east it became the water of Ts'ang-lang and, after passing the three great dikes, went on to Ta-pie; southward from which it entered the Chiang. Eastward still, and whirling on, it formed the marsh of P'eng-li. From there its eastern flow was the northern Chiang, as which it entered the sea.

From Mount Min he traced the Chiang which, branching off to the east, formed the T'o. Eastward again, it reached the Li, passed the Nine Chiang, and went on to Tung-ling. Then, flowing east and winding to the north, it

---

names, some different designations of the same river, must have served a practical purpose at one time (possibly indicating sections of river), they cannot be ascertained today. Confucius has summarized "The Tribute to Yü" as follows: "Yü marked out the nine provinces; followed the course of the hills and deepened the rivers; defined the imposts on the land and the articles of tribute."

The Moving Sands refers to the famous loess, the yellow ground of North China. It is borne before the wind from the western plateaus and lies deep on the North China Plain. It gives the Yellow River its name and tinctures the Yellow Sea. It is rich in minerals and very fertile. Beneath its thick deposits may lie archaeological secrets of mining practices in ancient China.

23. There were several important fords of the Ho. Meng was the one most convenient to the capital.

joined the Han with its eddying movements. From there its eastern flow was the Middle Chiang, as which it entered the sea.

He traced the Yen water which, flowing eastward, became the Chi and entered the Ho. Thereafter it flowed out and became the Yung marsh. Eastward, it issued forth on the north of T'ao-ch'iu and flowed farther east to the marsh of Ko. Then it went northeast and united with the Wen. Thence it went north and finally entered the sea on the east.

He traced the Huai from the hill of T'ung-po. Flowing east, it united with the Ssu and the I and, still with an eastward course, entered the sea.

He traced the Wei from the hill Niao-shu. Flowing eastward, it united with the Feng and, eastward again, with the Ching. Farther east still, it passed the Ch'i and the Ch'ü and entered the Ho.

He traced the Lo from the hill Hsiung-ehr. Flowing to the northeast it united with the Chien and the Ch'an and, eastward still, with the I. Then on the northeast it entered the Ho.

Thus throughout the nine provinces order was effected: lands along the waters were everywhere made habitable; hills were cleared of their superfluous wood and sacrificed to; sources of rivers were cleared; marshes were well banked; access to the capital was secured for all within the four seas.[24]

24. This paragraph summarizes all the labors of Yü. Legge paraphrases Hu Wei's interpretation of four seas: ". . . all the habitable ground the ancient Chinese knew was conceived of as surrounded by water. . . ." The Chinese seem to have thought from the beginning in spherical concepts. To them the world stretched out on every side into limitless oceans without qualifying restrictions of the plane, such as an "end" of the earth where a traveler might fall off to his doom.

Legge quotes Wang Ts'ia: ". . . cutting down the wood was the first

The six treasuries of nature were fully attended to.[25] The different parts of the country were subjected to an exact comparison so contribution of revenue could be carefully adjusted according to the resources. The fields were all classified with reference to the three characters of the soil; and the revenues for the Middle Region were established.

He conferred lands and surnames.[26] He said, "Let me set the example of a reverent attention to my virtue, that none may act contrary to my conduct."

Five hundred li constituted the Imperial Domain.[27] From the first hundred li they brought as revenue the whole plant of the grain; from the second, the ears with a portion of the stalk; from the third, they brought only the straw but the people had to perform various services; from the fourth, the grain in the husk; from the fifth, the grain cleaned.

Five hundred li beyond constituted the Domain of the Nobles. The first hundred li was occupied by the cities and lands of the high ministers and great officers; the second, by the principalities of the barons; the other three hundred by various other princes.

Five hundred li farther beyond formed the Peace-secur-

---

step in the regulation of the waters; the sacrificing was the announcement of the completed work."

25. The six treasuries of nature (in the original translation "six magazines *of material wealth*") are generally considered to have been water, fire, metal, wood, earth, and grain.

26. Legge footnotes: "Yü assigned . . . different portions of territory to those whose birth, or services, or virtue, most entitled them to the distinction. . . . The surname . . . was given not only from the birthplace, but after the name of the fief conferred, from the office held . . . or one of his ancestors, from any remarkable incident in his life, and from a variety of other circumstances; the history of surnames among the Chinese is just like the same history in other nations. . . ."

27. The 500 li of the Imperial Domain is to be understood as 500 li extending east, west, south, and north in two directions from each of the four corners; thus the whole domain contained not 250,000 square li but 1,000,000.

ing Domain. In the first three hundred li they cultivated the lessons of learning and moral duties; in the other two hundred they showed the energies of war and defense.

Five hundred li more remote still formed the Domain of Restraint. The first three hundred were occupied by the tribes of the I; the other two hundred, by criminals undergoing the lesser banishment.

The most remote five hundred li constituted the Wild Domain. The first three hundred were occupied by the tribes of the Man; the other two hundred by criminals undergoing the greater banishment.

On the east reaching to the sea, on the west extending to the Moving Sands, to the utmost limits of north and south—his fame and influence filled up all within the four seas. Yü presented the dark-colored symbol of his rank and announced the completion of his work.[28]

28. Legge related the "dark-colored symbol" to one of the tokens usually presented by the sovereign to the nobles (see Part I, Document 1 where Shun calls in the tokens). It is a debatable point. In the Karlgren translation the sovereign makes a presentation to Yü. Legge concludes his lengthy footnote:

"Yü found somewhere such a dark-colored precious stone so remarkable that he thought it worthy to be presented to the sovereign. The sovereign was Yao, but the stone would be presented in the first place to Shun as his vice-regent."

All that is certain is that upon the completion of these great labors of controlling the flood waters, there was an exchange of an object that was probably symbolic. It is also probable that a ceremony was planned, accompanied by music and dancing with appropriate costuming. This is conjecture.

The next document, "The Speech at Kan," ushers in a less-conjectural era.

2. THE SPEECH AT KAN

The *Shu* tells us nothing of Yü's accession to the throne nor of the events of his reign. He died after a reign of only eight years.

Yü was succeeded by his son Ch'i, whose reign dates from 2197 B.C., and to whom this speech is attributed. The time assigned to it is the third year of his nine-year reign. The word "Kan" refers to a place, river, marsh, or wilderness, in the principality of Hu (in present-day Shensi).

The six leaders of the six hosts mentioned in the document were nobles. The chariots were the principal part of an ancient Chinese army; it is a long time before we read of a cavalry. A war chariot generally carried three people: a charioteer in the center, an archer on the left, and a spearman on the right. They all wore mail.

The crimes of the lord of Hu are not clearly stated. It was understood, however, that every dynasty chose a new month for the beginning of the year. If the lord of Hu failed to begin the year with the month Yü had fixed, he was refusing to submit to the new dynasty and thus rebellious.

The *Shu* does not mention the issue of the battle. We may suppose that Ch'i was successful at Kan. We know nothing of the later events of his reign. He died in 2189 B.C. and was succeeded by his son T'ai K'ang.

This document may be regarded as recorded contemporaneously with the events described. It is the first of the speeches, forming one classification of the documents of the *Shu*.

Document 2

There was a great battle at Kan. Previous to it, the king called together the six leaders of his six hosts and said:

"Ah! all ye who are engaged in my six armies, I have a solemn announcement to make to you.

"The lord of Hu wildly wastes and despises the five elements that regulate the seasons and has idly abandoned the three acknowledged commencements of the year. On this account Heaven is about to destroy him and bring to an end his appointment to Hu. I am now reverently executing the punishment appointed by Heaven.

"If you, the archers on the left, do not do your work on the left it will be a disregard of my orders. If you, the spearmen on the right, do not do your work on the right it will be a disregard of my orders. If you, charioteers, do not observe the rules for the management of your horses it will be a disregard of my orders.

"You who obey my orders shall be rewarded before the spirits of my ancestors; you who disobey my orders shall be put to death before the altar of the spirits of the land, and I will also put to death your children."

3. SONGS OF THE FIVE SONS

The genuineness of this document has been challenged. However, those *Shu* documents that were forged were accepted in good faith for a thousand years. They not only exerted a general influence on the people, but references to them appear in other literature. Forgery or not, this document speaks authoritatively out of the uniquely Chinese sense of clan or sib responsibility.

T'ai K'ang ascended the throne in 2188 B.C. and reigned for twenty-nine years. I, prince of Ch'iung, challenged his supremacy. We know nothing of this sovereign beyond what is stated here.

Following a short introduction, the sovereign's brothers' poems appear. The first brother deplores how he had lost the affections of the people; the second speaks of his dissolute extravagance; the third mourns his loss of the throne; the fourth deplores departure from the principles of Yü; the fifth laments the miserable condition of all of them.

Document 3

T'ai K'ang occupied the throne like a personator of the dead.[1] By idleness and dissipation he extinguished his virtue until the black-haired people all wavered in their allegiance. He, however, pursued his pleasure and wanderings without any self-restraint. He went out to hunt beyond the Lo and a hundred days elapsed without his returning. On this I, prince of Ch'iung, taking advantage of the discontent of the people, resisted the sovereign's return on the south of the Ho.

---

1. Included in the rites of sacrificial services to the dead was a personator of the deceased. The Chinese characters signify that T'ai K'ang was merely a sham sovereign.

The sovereign's five brothers had attended their mother in following him and were waiting for him on the north of the Lo. When they heard of I's movement, all full of dissatisfaction, they related the cautions of the great Yü in the form of songs.

The first said,

> "It was the lesson of our great ancestor:
> The people should be cherished;
> They should not be downtrodden;
> The people are the root of a country;
> The root firm, the country is tranquil.
> When I look at all under heaven,
> Of the simple men and simple women,
> Any one may surpass me.
> If the One Man[2] err repeatedly,
> Should dissatisfaction be waited for until it appears?
> Before it is seen it should be guarded against.
> In my dealing with the millions of the people
> I should feel as much anxiety as if I were driving
>   six horses with rotten reins.
> The ruler of men—
> How should he be but reverent of his duties?"

The second said,

> "It is in the lessons:
> When the palace is a wild of lust
> And the country is a wild for hunting;
> When wine is sweet and music the delight,
> When there are lofty roofs and carved walls . . .
> The existence of any one of these things
> Has never been but the prelude to ruin."

2. One Man was a designation for the sovereign.

The third said,

> "There was the lord of T'ao and T'ang,
> Who possessed this region of Chi.[3]
> Now we have fallen from his ways
> And thrown into confusion his rules and laws;
> The consequence is extinction and ruin."

The fourth said,

> "Brightly intelligent was our ancestor,
> Sovereign of the myriad regions.
> He had canons, he had patterns,
> Which he transmitted to his posterity.
> The standard stone and the equalizing quarter
> Were in the royal treasury.[4]
> Wildly have we dropped the clue he gave us,
> Overturning our temple, and extinguishing our sacrifices."

The fifth said,

> "Oh! whither shall we turn?
> The thoughts in my breast make me sad.
> All the people are hostile to us;
> On whom can we rely?
> Anxieties stand thick in our hearts;
> Thick as are our faces, they are covered with blushes.
> We have not been careful of our virtue;
> And though we repent, we cannot overtake the past."

3. The "lord of T'ao and T'ang who possessed this region of Chi" refers to Yao, who was lord of the principalities of T'ao and T'ang; Chi is the Chi Chou of "The Tribute to Yü."

4. Regulations of measures by the sovereign was a means of justice, ensuring the tranquillity of the people. The standard stone and the equalizing quarter insured uniformity.

4. THE PUNITIVE EXPEDITION OF YIN

The genuineness of this document, like the preceding one, is challenged.

Hsi and Ho, ministers of the Board of Astronomy, are descendants of the brothers mentioned in "The Canon of Yao." They had grossly neglected their duties and given themselves over to licentious indulgence. In particular, they had been unobservant of an eclipse of the sun in autumn, a capital offense. The sovereign commissions the marquis of Yin to execute the death sentence upon them.

This document is classified as a speech. The period is during the reign of Chung K'ang, 2159–47 B.C.

Document 4

When Chung K'ang commenced his reign over all within the four seas, the marquis of Yin was commissioned to take charge of the six hosts. At this time the Hsi and Ho had neglected the duties of their office and were abandoned to drink in their private cities. The marquis of Yin received the king's charge to go and punish them.

The marquis made an announcement to his hosts, saying, "Ah! ye, all my men, there are the well-counseled instructions of the sage-founder of our dynasty, clearly verified in their power to give stability and security: 'the former kings were carefully attentive to the warnings of Heaven[1] and their ministers observed the regular laws of their offices. All the officers watchfully did their duty to assist the government and their sovereign became entirely intelligent.' Every year, in the first month of spring, the herald with his wooden-tongued bell goes along the roads proclaiming, 'Ye

1. Eclipses and other celestial phenomena were considered warnings from heaven.

officers able to instruct, be prepared with your admonitions. Ye workmen engaged in mechanical affairs, remonstrate on the subjects of your employments. If any of you do not attend with respect to this requirement, the country has regular punishments for you.'

"Now here are the Hsi and Ho. They have allowed their virtue to be subverted and are besotted by drink. They have violated the duties of their office and left their posts. They have been the first to let the regulating of the heavenly bodies get into disorder, putting far from them their proper business. On the first day of the last month of autumn, the sun and moon did not meet harmoniously in Fang.[2] The blind musicians beat their drums; the junior officers galloped, and the common people employed about the public offices ran about. The Hsi and the Ho, however, as if they were mere personators of the dead in their offices, heard nothing and knew nothing. Stupidly they went astray from their duties in the matter of the heavenly appearances and rendered themselves liable to the death appointed by the former kings. The statutes of government say, 'When they anticipate the time, let them be put to death without mercy; when their reckoning is behind the time, let them be put to death without mercy.'

"Now I, with you, am entrusted with the execution of the punishment appointed by Heaven. Unite your strength, all of you warriors, for the royal House. Give me your help, I pray you, reverently to carry out the dread charge of the Son of Heaven.

"When the fire blazes over the ridge of Kun,[3] gems and stones are burned together; but if a minister of Heaven

2. *Fang:* the constellation Scorpio.
3. The "ridge of Kun" may refer to Kunlun Mountain in the northwest.

exceed in doing his duty the consequences will be fiercer than blazing fire. While I destroy, therefore, the chief criminals, I will not punish those who have been forced to follow them. And those who have long been stained by their filthy manners will be allowed to renovate themselves.

"Oh! when sternness overcomes compassion, things are surely conducted to a successful issue. When compassion overcomes strictness, no merit can be achieved. All ye, my warriors, exert yourselves, take warning, and obey my orders!"

This concludes the last existing document of the dynasty of Hsia. The reigns of seventeen men are assigned to it. Chung K'ang's was the fourth; his reign lasted thirteen years and ended in 2146 B.C.

Chung K'ang was succeeded by his son Hsiang. In the first year of his reign he had to withdraw across the Ho into present-day Honan, driven, Legge believes, by I, who was by now exercising supreme authority in Chi Chou.

Here and there within the large body of detailed footnotes amassed and sequenced by Legge, occasionally there appears a splendid word picture of the people and events of ancient China. One of these word pictures is contained in the conclusion of Part III under the general heading "Conclusion and connecting note." It concerns Chieh, the last sovereign of the line of Hsia. This tyrant is notorious throughout later literature and held up as an archetype of evil. Legge was always the aroused scholar and all too often the sleeping poet. But of the last Hsia sovereign he writes with poetic abandon:

> The first three and thirty years of his long reign are a blank. Possessing extraordinary strength, able to twist bars of iron about like ropes, he gloried in his vigor and wearied out the people with expeditions of war. In 1786 B.C. he proceeded to attack the chief of Shi, in the neighborhood of Mount Mung in the present Shantung. The chief propitiated his anger by presenting him with

his daughter Mei Hsi, of surpassing beauty but more depraved, if possible, than the ruler himself. All thoughts of prudence were lost amid the enjoyment of her charms. He gratified all her caprices. He made her a chamber of carnelian, with side apartments of ivory, a splendid tower, and a bed glittering with gems. Around this he heaped up, in their wild dissoluteness, mounds of flesh, hung dried meats on all the trees, filled a pond with wine until they could row a boat on it, while 3,000 people would make their appearance at the beat of drum and drink up the liquor like so many oxen. All government was neglected.

In the meantime the avenger was growing up. T'ang succeeded to his father's principality in 1784 B.C., and soon drew the regard of all thoughtful men to himself. The great officers who felt ashamed of Chieh's vices and mourned the condition of the realm, betook themselves to Shang. The people who groaned beneath the oppression of their lords, too many of whom followed Chieh's example, sighed for the gentle rule of T'ang.

Chieh was roused to fits of jealousy and at one time got T'ang in his power and imprisoned him. He let him go, however, and at last, 1766 B.C., after many misgivings, T'ang took the field against his sovereign.

There could be no doubt as to the result. Heaven and earth combined with men to show their detestation of the tyrant. Two suns fought in the sky. The earth shook. Mountains were moved from their strong foundations. Rivers were dried up. Chieh was routed and fled south to Ch'ao. There he was kept a prisoner until his death three years after. His son and some of his adherents made their way to the wilds of the north and mingled among the barbarian tribes.

Thus miserably ended the dynasty of Hsia having extended, including the usurpations of I and Tsu, over 439 years.

Here comes to a close that portion of the *Shu ching, Book of History* of which, so far, there has been no authentication through dated archaeological discovery. It is affirmed, not confirmed. As Legge put it: "Beyond the time of T'ang we cannot be so sure of our way. Our information is comparatively scanty. It has in itself less of verisimilitude. Legend and narrative are confusedly mixed together."

PART IV

The Documents of Shang

1. THE SPEECH BY T'ANG

The ruling house of Shang traced its origin to remote antiquity through Hsieh, who was appointed by Shun to be minister of Instruction. For his services, Hsieh was invested with the principality of Shang, in present-day Shensi.

T'ang had summoned his hosts to take the field with him against Chieh, tyrant and last ruler of Hsia. But he finds his people are reluctant. He calls them together to set forth his reasons for the attack, seeks to persuade them to his cause, and threatens death to them and their children if they do not obey his orders. The place is Po, far from the ancestral fief, at a site that corresponds to present-day Honan. The year is estimated 1766 B.C. This document is classified as a speech, signifying a military address.

Document 1

The king said, "Come, ye multitudes of the people, listen all to my words. It is not I, the Little Child,[1] who dare to undertake a rebellious enterprise; Heaven has given the charge to destroy the sovereign of Hsia for his many crimes.

"Now, ye multitudes, you are saying, 'Our prince does not compassionate us but is calling us away from our husbandry to attack and punish Hsia.' I have indeed heard these words of you all. But the sovereign of Hsia is guilty and, as I fear God,[2] I dare not but punish him.

1. "Little Child" is a designation of the ruler used by him in humility (see note 4, below). It emphasizes the humble position of a child in relation to its father.
2. The term "God" is also used by Karlgren. Whether or not the character so translated is synonymous with the Western concept of God has been endlessly debated. Legge disagreed with the prevailing opinion of his day and declared that the Chinese and English had similar concepts of God.

"Now you are saying, 'What are the crimes of Hsia to us?' The king of Hsia in every way exhausts the strength of his people and exercises oppression in the cities of Hsia. His people have all become idle and will not assist him. They are saying, 'When wilt thou, O sun, expire? [3] We will all perish with thee.'

"Such is the course of the sovereign of Hsia. And now I must go punish him.

"I pray you, assist me, the One Man, [4] to carry out the punishment appointed by Heaven. I will greatly reward you. On no account disbelieve me; I will not eat my words. If you do not obey the words I have spoken to you I will put your children to death with you. You will find no forgiveness."

3. It is said that Chieh, when warned that his cruelties would cost him the throne, replied that his place on the throne was as firm as the position of the sun in the sky.

4. One Man as a designation of the ruler implies the position of sovereign as ordained by Heaven—the Son of Heaven.

2. THE ANNOUNCEMENT
BY CHUNG HUI

This announcement is one of several announcements that form a large classification of documents in the *Shu* and are addressed to the general population, as contrasted with speeches, which are directed to the armed hosts.

Previously, during a time of need, T'ang had sent provisions to aid the farmers in the nearby principality of Ko. But the earl of that region stole the provisions and victimized the bearers. Chung Hui reminds the people that T'ang's motive is punitive justice and his first object, the earl of Ko. Now the evil ways of Chieh are to be set right.

The document lauds T'ang's virtues and concludes with a description of the sage behavior of kings. The announcement was made to the people by T'ang's chief minister, Chung Hui, to secure their support. It is the early period of the Shang-Yin dynasty, which endured for six centuries in several capitals. The genuineness of this document has been challenged.

Document 2

When T'ang the Successful was keeping Chieh in banishment in Nan Ch'ao,[1] he had a feeling of shame on account of his conduct and said, "I am afraid that in future ages men will fill their mouths with me as an apology for their rebellious proceedings."

On this Chung Hui made the following announcement: "Oh! Heaven gives birth to the people with such desires that, without a ruler, they must fall into disorders; Heaven again gives birth to the man of intelligence to regulate them. The sovereign of Hsia had his virtue entirely obscured; the people were as if they had fallen amid mire and burning charcoal.

1. Nan Ch'ao was in present-day Anhwei.

Heaven hereupon endowed our king with valor and prudence to serve as a sign and director to the myriad regions, and to continue the old ways of Yü. You are now following the proper course, honoring and obeying the appointment of Heaven. The king of Hsia was an offender, falsely and calumniously alleging the sanction of supreme Heaven to spread abroad his commands among the people. On this account God viewed him with disapprobation, caused our Shang to receive the appointment, and employed you to enlighten the multitudes of the people.

"Scorners of the worthy and parasites of the powerful, many such followers T'ang had indeed; but from the first our country was to the sovereign of Hsia like weeds among the springing corn and blasted grains among the good.[2] Our people great and small were in constant apprehension, fearful though not guilty of crime. How much more was this the case when our prince's virtues became a theme eagerly listened to! Our king did not indulge in dissolute music and women; he did not seek to accumulate property and wealth. To great virtue he gave great offices and to great merit great rewards. He employed others as if their excellences were his own. He was not slow to correct his errors. Rightly indulgent and rightly benevolent, such virtue earned him the confidence of millions of the people.

"When the earl of Ko showed his enmity to the provision-bearers, the work of punishment began with Ko. When it went on in the east, the wild tribes of the west murmured; when it went on in the south, those of the north murmured; they said: 'Why does he make us alone the last?' To whatever people he went, they congratulated one another in their

2. This sentence is obscure and has been the subject of controversy. Likening the people of Shang to weeds and blasted grains is the point at issue; it is to be understood that it was only Chieh who defined the worthy people of Shang in this way.

families, saying, 'We have waited for our prince; our prince is come and we revive.' The people's honoring our Shang is a thing of long existence.

"Show favor to the able and right-principled among the princes and aid the virtuous; distinguish the loyal and let the good have free course. Absorb the weak and punish the willfully blind; take their states from the disorderly and deal summarily with those going to ruin. When you thus accelerate the end of what is of itself ready to perish, and strengthen what is itself strong to live, how the states all flourish! When a sovereign's virtue is daily being renewed he is cherished throughout the myriad regions; when his mind is full only of himself he is abandoned by the nine branches of his kindred.[3]

"Exert yourself, O king, to make your virtue still more illustrious; set up the standard of the Mean before the people. Order your affairs by righteousness; order your heart by propriety; so shall you transmit a grand example to posterity. I have heard the saying, 'He who finds instructors for himself comes to the supreme dominion; he who says that others are not equal to himself comes to ruin. He who likes to put questions becomes enlarged; he who uses only his own views becomes smaller than he was.' Oh! he who would take care for the end must be attentive to the beginning. There is establishment for the observers of propriety and overthrow for the blinded and wantonly indifferent. To revere and honor the path prescribed by Heaven is the way ever to preserve the favoring appointment of Heaven."

3. The different degrees, grades, and branches of relations within the family or clan as recognized at that time cannot be accurately stated.

3. THE ANNOUNCEMENT BY T'ANG

When T'ang returned to Po, he made this announcement to tell the people that he had taken the throne from Chieh in reverent submission to the will of heaven. He calls upon them and their princes to cooperate with him. In support of his action he speaks of having sought the counsel of "the great sage." This is I Yin, who became T'ang's chief minister and later adviser to his heir. I Yin appears often in Chinese literature, the pattern for faithful ministers. The genuineness of this document has been challenged.

The time is close to 1766 B.C. Chieh is in exile. The Shang dynasty is now founded, the earliest of the traditional dynasties to be confirmed by archaeological discoveries.

Document 3

When T'ang returned from vanquishing Hsia and came to Po, he made a grand announcement to the myriad regions.

The king said, "Ah! ye multitudes of the myriad regions, listen clearly to the announcement of me, the One Man. The great God has conferred even on the inferior people a moral sense, compliance with which would show their nature invariably right. To make them tranquilly pursue this course is the work of the sovereign.

"The king of Hsia extinguished his virtue and played the tyrant, extending his oppression over you, the people of the myriad regions. Suffering from his cruel injuries, unable to endure the wormwood and poison, you protested with one accord your innocence to the spirits of heaven and earth. The way of Heaven is to bless the good and make the bad miserable. It sent down calamities on the house of Hsia to make manifest its guilt. Therefore I, the Little Child, charged with the decree of Heaven and its bright terrors,

72

did not dare to forgive the criminal. I presumed to use a dark-colored victim-bull and, making clear announcement to the Spiritual Sovereign in the high heavens, requested leave to deal with the ruler of Hsia as a criminal. Then I sought for the great sage, with whom I might unite my strength, to request the favor of Heaven for you, my multitudes. High Heaven truly showed its favor to the inferior people; the criminal has been degraded and subjected. What Heaven appoints is without error. Brilliantly now, like the blossoming of plants and trees, the millions of the people show a true reviving.

"It is given to me, the One Man, to secure the harmony and tranquillity of your states and clans. But I know not whether I offend the Powers above and below. I am fearful and trembling, as if in danger of falling into a deep abyss. Throughout all the regions that enter on a new life under me, do not, ye princes, follow lawless ways; make no approach to insolence and dissoluteness; let everyone be careful to keep his statutes that we may receive the favor of Heaven. The good in you I will not dare to keep concealed; for the evil in me I will not dare to forgive myself. I will examine these things in harmony with the mind of God. When guilt is found in you who occupy the myriad regions, let it rest on me, the One Man.[1] When guilt is found in me, the One Man, it shall not attach to you who occupy the myriad regions.

"Oh! let us attain to be sincere in these things, and so we shall likewise have a happy consummation."

1. This sentence enunciates one of the basic structures of the Chinese concept of the responsibility of rulers: that the ruler is ultimately responsible to everyone and for everything.

4. THE INSTRUCTIONS OF I

I is the surname of I Yin, accounted for by his having been born on the river of that name; Yin was his designation. He may also have been known as Aheng or Chih or both.

T'ang died about 1753 B.C. and was succeeded by his grandson T'ai Chia, so far as the evidence of the *Shu* goes. I Yin, as his chief minister, undertook the guidance of the young heir-king. This document and the next two are classified as instructions and relate the counseling of I Yin to T'ai Chia. The genuineness of all three documents has been challenged.

Document 4

In the twelfth month of the first year, on the day *yi-ch'ou,* I Yin sacrificed to the former king and reverently presented the heir-king before the shrine of his grandfather. All the princes from the domain of the nobles and the royal domain were present. All the various officers also were in attendance with their several duties to receive the orders of the chief minister. I Yin then clearly described the complete virtue of the meritorious ancestor for the instruction of the new king.

He said, "Oh! of old the former kings of Hsia cultivated earnestly their virtue and there were no calamities from Heaven. The spirits of the hills and rivers likewise were all in tranquillity. The birds and beasts, the fishes and tortoises, all realized the happiness of their nature. But their descendant Chieh did not follow their example and great Heaven sent down calamities, employing the agency of our ruler who received its favoring appointment. The attack on Hsia may be traced to the orgies in Ming-t'iao,[1]

1. Ming-t'iao was a place not far from Chieh's capital, in present-day Shansi, where Chieh's notorious orgies that alienated the people were held.

74

but our attack on it began in Po. Our king of Shang brilliantly displayed his sagely prowess; for oppression he substituted his generous gentleness and the millions of the people gave him their hearts. Now your Majesty is entering on the inheritance of his virtue. All depends on how you commence your reign. To set up love, it is for you to love your relations; to set up respect, it is for you to respect your elders. The commencement is in the family and the state; the consummation is in all within the four seas.

"Oh! the former king began with careful attention to the bonds that hold men together. He listened to expostulation and did not seek to resist it; he conformed to the wisdom of the ancients; occupying the highest position, he displayed intelligence; occupying a lower position, he displayed his loyalty; he acknowledged the good qualities of the men whom he employed and did not seek that they should have every talent; in the government of himself, he seemed to think that he could never sufficiently attain. It was thus he arrived at the possession of the myriad regions. How painstaking was he in these things!

"He sought out wise men who should be helpful to you, his descendant and heir. He laid down the punishments for officers and warned those who were in authority, saying, 'If you dare to have constant dancing in your palaces and drunken singing in your chambers, that is called the fashion of sorcerers; if you dare to set your hearts on wealth and women and abandon yourselves to wandering about or to hunting, that is called the fashion of dissipation; if you dare to despise sage words, to resist the loyal and upright, to put far from you the aged and virtuous and to seek the company of procacious[2] youths, that is called the fashion

2. Apparently a misspelling of a euphemism for sodomitic (proctacious).

of disorder. Now if a high noble or officer be addicted to one of these three fashions with their ten evil ways, his family will surely come to ruin; if the prince of a country be so addicted, his state will surely come to ruin. The minister who does not try to correct such vices in the sovereign shall be punished with branding.' These rules were minutely inculcated also on the sons of officers and nobles in their lessons.

"Oh! let you who now succeed to the throne revere these warnings. Think of them! Sacred counsels of vast importance, admirable words forcibly set forth! The ways of God are not invariable: on the good doer he sends down all blessings, and on the evil doer he sends down all miseries. Let you be virtuous in things small and large and the myriad regions will have cause for rejoicing. If you be not virtuous in large and small things it will bring the ruin of your ancestral temple."

5. THE T'AI CHIA

In this document T'ai Chia, the new sovereign, does not obey the instructions set forth by I Yin in the previous document. Therefore, I Yin, as chief minister, keeps T'ai Chia in partial confinement near the gravesite of his grandfather during the three-year period of mourning. Here T'ai Chia learns penitence and virtue.

After this, I Yin brings the king with honors to Po to undertake the duties of government. I Yin congratulates T'ai Chia on his reformation and, in response, T'ai Chia asks I Yin to continue his counsels.

The document is classified as an instruction and concludes with general statements by I Yin on proper conduct of a sovereign. Of particular note is the statement that I Yin "made a writing," the first direct mention of a written communication. The genuineness of this document has been challenged.

Document 5

The king, on succeeding to the throne, did not follow the advice of I Yin. I Yin then made the following writing: "The former king kept his eye continually on the bright requirements of Heaven and so maintained the worship of the spirits of heaven and earth, of those presiding over the land and the grain, and of those of the ancestral temple; all with a sincere reverence. Heaven took notice of his virtue and caused its great appointment to light on him, that he should soothe and tranquilize the myriad regions. I, Yin, then gave my assistance to my sovereign in the settlement of the people; thus it is that you, O heir-king, have received the great inheritance. I have seen it myself in Hsia with its western capital:[1] that when rulers went through a prosperous

1. An-yi, west of Po, is the Hsia capital I Yin refers to.

course to the end, their ministers also did the same and afterwards, when their successors could not attain to such a consummation, neither did their ministers. Take warning, O heir-king. Reverently use your sovereignty. If you do not play the sovereign as the name requires, you will disgrace your grandfather."

The king would not think of these words, nor listen to them.

On this I Yin said, "The former king, before it was light, sought to have large and clear views and then sat waiting for the morning. He also sought on every side for men of ability and virtue to instruct and guide his posterity. Do not frustrate his charge to me and bring on yourself your own overthrow. Be careful to strive after the virtue of self-restraint; cherish far-reaching plans. Be like the forester who, when he has adjusted the spring, goes to examine the end of the arrow, whether it be placed according to rule, and then lets go; reverently determine your aim and follow the ways of your grandfather. Thus I shall be delighted and be able to show to all ages that I have discharged my trust."

The king was not yet able to change his course.

I Yin said to himself, "This is real unrighteousness and is becoming by practice second nature. I cannot bear to be near so disobedient a person. I will build a place in the palace at T'ung[2] where he can be in silence near the grave of the former king. This will be a lesson which will keep him from going astray all his life."

The king went accordingly to the palace at T'ung to dwell during the period of mourning. In the end he became sincerely virtuous.

2. The site of T'ung was probably in present-day Shansi.

On the first day of the twelfth month of his third year, I Yin took the royal cap and robes and escorted the young king back to Po. At the same time he made the following writing:

"Without the sovereign, the people cannot have that guidance necessary to the comfort of their lives; without the people, the sovereign would have no sway over the four quarters of the kingdom. Great Heaven has graciously favored the house of Shang and granted to you, O young king, at last to become virtuous. This is indeed a blessing that will extend without limit to ten thousand generations."

The king did obeisance with his face to his hands and his head to the ground, saying, "I, the Little Child, was without understanding of what was virtuous and was making myself one of the unworthy. By my desires I was setting at nought all rules of conduct, violating by self-indulgence all rules of propriety, and the result must have been speedy ruin to my person. Calamities sent by Heaven may be avoided, but from calamities brought on by one's self there is no escape. Heretofore I turned my back on the instructions of you, my tutor and guardian; my beginning has been marked by incompetency. Let me still rely on your correcting and preserving virtue, keeping this in view that my end may be good!"

I Yin did obeisance with his face to his hands and his head on the ground and said, "To cultivate his person and, by being sincerely virtuous, bring all below to harmonious concord with him: this is the work of the intelligent sovereign. The former king was kind to the distressed and suffering, as if they were his children, and the people submitted to his commands with sincere delight. Even in the states of the neighboring princes the people said, 'We are waiting for our sovereign. When our sovereign comes, we shall not suffer the punishments that we now do.'

"O king, zealously cultivate your virtue. Regard the example of your meritorious grandfather. At no time permit yourself pleasure and idleness. In honoring your ancestors, think how you can prove your filial piety; in receiving your ministers, think how you can show yourself respectful; in looking to what is distant, try to get clear views; have your ears ever open to lessons of virtue—then shall I acknowledge and respond to the excellence of your majesty with an untiring devotion to your service."

I Yin again made an announcement to the king, saying, "Oh! Heaven has no partiality; only to those who are reverent does it show affection. The people are not constant to those whom they cherish; they cherish only him who is benevolent. The spirits do not always accept the sacrifices that are offered to them; they accept only the sacrifices of the sincere. A place of difficulty is the Heaven-conferred seat. When there are those virtues, good government is realized; when there are not, disorder comes. To maintain the same principles as those who secured good government will surely lead to prosperity; to pursue the courses of disorder will surely lead to ruin. He who at last, as at first, is careful whom and what he follows is a truly intelligent sovereign. The former king was always zealous in the reverent cultivation of his virtue so that he was the fellow of God. Now, O king, you have entered on the inheritance of his excellent line; fix your inspection on him.

"Your course must be as in ascending high: you begin from where it is low; and when in traveling far: you begin where it is near. Do not slight the occupations of the people; think of their difficulties. Do not yield to a feeling of repose on your throne; think of its perils. Be careful for the end at the beginning. When you hear words against which your mind sets itself, you must enquire whether they be not right; when you hear words that accord with your own views, you must enquire whether they be not contrary to what is right. Oh! what attainment can be made without anxious thought? What achievement can be made without earnest effort? Let the One Man be greatly good, and the myriad regions will be rectified by him.

"When the sovereign does not, with disputatious words, throw the old rules of government into confusion and the minister does not, for favor and gain, continue in an office whose work is done: then the country will lastingly and surely enjoy happiness."

6. THE COMMON POSSESSION
OF PURE VIRTUE

It is now much later, chronologically, than the two previous documents. I Yin is about to enter his retirement. As T'ang's chief minister and the regent for his grandson, he has had a long and arduous career in the early years of the new dynasty of Shang.

In the Chinese historical tradition, I Yin is revered as a great chief minister. According to the Chinese historian Ssu-ma Ch'ien, he lived until 1713 B.C., the eighth year of the reign of the next king. The genuineness of this document has been challenged.

The time is the last half of the eighteenth century B.C. The document is classified as an instruction and contains the last of I Yin's aphorisms and advice to his young sovereign.

Document 6

I Yin, having returned the government to the hands of his sovereign and being about to announce his retirement, set forth admonitions on the subject of virtue.

He said, "Oh! it is difficult to rely on Heaven; its appointments are not constant. But if the sovereign sees to it that his virtue be constant, he will preserve his throne; if his virtue be not constant the nine provinces will be lost by him. The king of Hsia could not maintain the virtue of his ancestors unchanged, but scorned the spirits and oppressed the people. Great Heaven no longer extended its protection to him. It looked out among the myriad regions to give its guidance to one who should receive its favoring appointment, fondly seeking a possessor of pure virtue whom it might make lord of all the spirits. Then there were

82

I, Yin, and T'ang, both possessed of pure virtue and able to satisfy the mind of Heaven. He received in consequence the bright favor of Heaven. He became master of the multitudes of the nine provinces and proceeded to change Hsia's commencement of the year.[1] It was not that Heaven had any private partiality for the lord of Shang; it simply gave its favor to pure virtue. It was not that Shang sought the allegiance of the lower people; the people simply turned to pure virtue. Where the sovereign's virtue is pure, his movements are all fortunate; where his virtue is wavering and uncertain, his movements are all unfortunate. Good and evil do not wrongly befall men; Heaven sends down misery or happiness according to their conduct.

"Now, O young king, you are newly entering on your great appointment. You should be making new your virtue. At last, as at first, have this as your one object, so shall you make a daily renovation. Let the officers whom you employ be men of virtue and ability, let the ministers about you be the right men. The minister, in relation to his sovereign above him, has to promote his virtue and, in relation to the people beneath him, has to seek their good. How hard must it be to find the proper man! What careful attention must be required! Thereafter there must be harmony cultivated with him and a oneness of confidence placed in him.

"There is no invariable model of virtue; a supreme regard to what is good gives the model of it. There is no invariable characteristic of what is good to be supremely regarded; it is found where there is a conformity to the uniform consciousness in regard to what is good. Such virtue will make the people with their myriad surnames all say, 'How

1. The sovereign of each dynasty chose a month for the beginning of each year. This was called the commencement of the year. (See Part III, "The Speech at Kan," fourth paragraph of introductory remarks.)

great are the words of the king!' and 'How single and pure is the king's heart!' It will avail to maintain in tranquillity the great possession of the former king and to secure forever the happy life of the multitudes of the people.

"Oh! to retain a place in the seven-shrined temple[2] of ancestors is a sufficient witness of virtue. To be acknowledged as chief by the myriad heads of families is a sufficient evidence of one's government.

"The sovereign without the people has none whom he can employ; the people without the sovereign have none whom they can serve. Do not think yourself so large as to deem others small. If ordinary men and women do not find the opportunity to develop their ability, the people's lord will be without the proper aids to complete his merit."

Between this document and the next, "The P'an Keng," the reigns of fourteen kings intervene. So far as the chronology of the *Shu* is concerned, there is a gap of over 300 years.

The chronologic table shows a King Wu Ting who succeeded T'ai Chia. This king, about whom no document is extant, is not to be confused with the second King Wu Ting who reigned more than 396 years later.

2. The ancestral temples, or halls, were of prime importance to Chinese families from the beginning. Tablets, representative of the deceased, were installed in a special space and kept for seven generations; the tablets of illustrious ancestors sometimes were maintained for longer periods.

7. THE P'AN KENG

P'an Keng was the seventeenth ruler of the dynasty that now begins to be called Yin as well as Shang.

The king wishes to move the people to Yin, the sixth site of the capital. Because the people and nobles are reluctant to go, P'an Keng makes three speeches to induce them. Certain passages of this document are difficult to understand. According to Chang Chi-yun, this is because they were written in the slang idiom of the time.

In the king's first speech, it seems to be implied that the removal of the people is due to some kind of an emergency, and that in order to cope with it the tortoise shell has been divined. In the second speech, the removal of the capital is in progress. Some of the people remain in the old capital; P'an Keng makes an earnest appeal to them.

In the third speech all are exhorted to forget past differences and join in the great destiny that awaits them in their new capital at Yin (near present-day Anyang in Honan where archaeological excavations have disclosed the great Shang bronzes, polished jade, chariots, and other remains).

P'an Keng reigned from 1401 to 1374 B.C. and was one of the most revered of China's ancient rulers. The document falls into the classification of announcements, being composed of speeches to the general population.

Document 7

The First Speech

P'an Keng wished to remove the capital to Yin but the people would not go to dwell there. He therefore appealed to all the discontented, and made the following protestations:

"Our king Tsu Yi came and fixed on Keng for his capital.

85

He did so from a deep concern for our people, because he would not have them all die where they cannot help one another to preserve their lives. I have consulted the tortoise shell and obtained the reply: 'This is no place for us.' When the former kings had any important business they gave reverent heed to the commands of Heaven. In a case like this especially they did not indulge the wish for constant repose; they did not abide ever in the same city. Up to this time the capital has been in five regions. If we do not follow the example of these old times, we shall be refusing to acknowledge that Heaven is making an end of our dynasty here. How little can it be said of us that we are following the meritorious course of the former kings! As from the stump of a felled tree there are sprouts and shoots, Heaven will perpetuate its decree in our favor in this new city. The great inheritance of the former kings will be continued and renewed. Tranquillity will be secured to the four quarters of the kingdom."

P'an Keng, in making the people aware of his views, began with those who were in high places. He took the constantly recurring circumstances of former times to lay down the right law and measure for the present emergency, saying, "Let none of you dare to suppress the remonstrances of the poor people."

The king commanded all to come to him in the courtyard of his palace.

The king spoke to this effect: "Come, all of you; I will announce to you my instructions. Take counsel how to put away your selfish thoughts. Do not with haughty disregard of me follow after your own ease. Of old, our former kings had it as a principal object in their plans to employ the men of old families to share in the government. When they wished to proclaim and announce what was to be attended to, these men did not conceal the royal views; on this account the kings greatly respected them. They did not exceed the truth in their communications with the people; on this account the people became greatly changed in their views. Now, however, you keep clamoring, and get the confidence of the people by alarming and shallow speeches. I do not know what you keep wrangling about. In this removal I am not myself abandoning my proper virtue;[1] but you conceal the goodness of my intentions and do not stand in awe of me, the One Man. I see you as clearly as one sees a fire; but I by my undecided plans have produced your error.[2]

"When the net has its line, there is order and not confusion; when the husbandman labors upon his fields and reaps with all his might, there is the abundant harvest. If you can put away your selfish thoughts you will bestow real good upon the people, reaching also to your own relatives and friends, you may boldly venture to make your words great and say that you have accumulated merit. But you do not fear the great evils which through our not removing are extending far and near. You are like idle husbandmen who yield themselves to ease and are not strong to toil and labor on their acres and who in such a case cannot have either rice or millet. You do not speak in a spirit of harmony and goodness to the people and are giving birth to bitter evils for yourselves. You play the part of destroyers and authors of calamity, of villains and traitors; the punishment shall come on your own persons. You set the example of evil and must feel its smart; what will it avail you then to repent?

1. The proper virtue of the sovereign was to love the people.
2. This is the first of several instances of sovereign responsibility in this document: when the people are in error, the king is to blame. The necessary corollary is that harmony in the ruled results from harmony in the ruler.

Look at the poor people: they can still look to one another and give expression to their remonstrances, but when they begin to speak you are ready with your extravagant talk. How much more ought you to have me before your eyes, with whom it lies to make your lives long or short! Why do you not report their words to me but instead go about to excite one another by empty speeches, frightening and involving the multitudes in misery? When a fire is blazing in the plains so that it cannot be approached, can it still be beaten out? So it will not be I who will be to blame. You cause unrest in this way, and must suffer the consequences.

"Ch'ih Jen[3] has said, 'In men we seek those of old families; in vessels we do not seek old ones, but new.' Of old, the kings my predecessors, and your forefathers and fathers, shared together the ease and toil of the government; how should I dare to lay undeserved afflictions on you? For generations the labors of your fathers have been approved and I will not conceal your goodness. Now when I offer the great sacrifices to my predecessors, your forefathers are present to share in them. They observe the happiness I confer and the sufferings I inflict. I cannot dare to reward virtue that does not exist.

"I have announced to you the difficulties of the intended removal, being bent on it like an archer whose only thought is to hit. Do not despise the old and experienced and do not make little of the helpless and young. Seek long continuance in this new city which is to be your abode; exert yourselves to listen to the plans of me, the One Man. I will make no distinction between men as being more distantly or more nearly related to me. The criminal in this matter shall die the death, and the good man shall have his virtue distinguished. The prosperity of the country ought to come from

3. Ch'ih Jen is assumed to have been an ancient historiographer.

all of you. If it fail of prosperity, that must arise from me, the One Man, erring in the application of punishment. Be sure, all of you, to make known this announcement. From this time forward, attend respectfully to your business; have the duties of your offices regularly adjusted; bring your tongues under the rule of law lest punishment come upon you when repentance will be of no avail."

The Second Speech

P'an Keng arose and was about to cross the Ho with the people, moving to the new capital. Accordingly, he addressed himself to those of them who were still dissatisfied, made a full announcement to their multitudes, to induce a sincere acquiescence. They all attended and, being charged to take no liberties in the royal courtyard, he called them near and said, "Listen clearly to my words and do not disregard my commands.

"Oh! Of old time my royal predecessors cherished, every one and above every other thing, a respectful care of the people, who again upheld their sovereign with a mutual sympathy. Seldom was it that they were not superior to any calamitous time sent by Heaven. When great calamities came down on Yin the former kings did not fondly remain in their place. What they did was with a view to the people's advantage, and therefore they moved their capitals. Why do you not reflect that I, according to what I have heard of the ancient sovereigns, in my care of you and actings toward you, am only wishing to rejoice with you in a common repose? It is not that any guilt attaches to you, so that this movement should be like a punishment. If I call upon you to cherish this new city, it is simply on your account, and as an act of great accordance with your wishes. My present undertaking to remove with you is to give repose and stability to the country. You, however, have no sympathy with the anxieties of my mind; but you all keep a great reserve in declaring your minds, when you might respectfully think by your sincerity to move me, the One Man. You only exhaust and distress yourselves. The case is like that of sailing in a boat; if you do not cross the stream at the proper time, you will destroy all the cargo. Your sincerity does not respond to mine and we are in danger of going together to destruction. You, notwithstanding, will not examine the matter; though you anger yourselves, what cure will that bring?

"You do not consult for a distant day, nor think of the calamity that must befall you if you do not move. You greatly encourage one another in what must prove to your sorrow. Now you have the present, but you will not have the future; what prolongation of life can you look for from above? My measures are forecast to prolong your lease of life from Heaven. Do I force you by the terrors of my power? My object is to support and nourish you all. I think of my ancestors, the spiritual sovereigns: when they made your forefathers toil on similar occasions it was only for their good; I wish in the same way greatly to nourish you and cherish you.

"Were I to err in my government and remain long here, my high sovereign, the founder of our dynasty, would send down on me great punishment for my crime and say, 'Why do you oppress my people?' If you, the myriads of the people, do not attend to the perpetuation of your lives and cherish one mind with me, the One Man, in my plans, the former kings will send down on you great punishment for your crime, and say, 'Why do you not agree with our young grandson, but go on to forfeit your virtue?' When they punish you from above, you have no way of escape. Of old, my royal predecessors made your ancestors and fathers toil only for their good. You are equally the people whom I wish to cherish. But your conduct is injurious; it is cherished in your hearts. Whereas my royal predecessors made your ancestors and fathers happy, they, your ancestors and fathers, will now cut you off and abandon you and not save you from death. Here are those ministers of my government, who share with me in the offices of the kingdom; yet they only think of hoarding up cowries[4] and gems. Their ancestors and fathers earnestly represent their course to my high sovereign, saying, 'Execute great punishments on our descendants.' So do they advise my high sovereign to send down great calamities on those men.

"Oh! I have now told you my unchangeable purpose; let you perpetually respect my great anxiety; let us not get alienated and removed from one another; share in my plans and thoughts and think only of following me; let every one of you set up the true rule of conduct in his heart. If there be bad and unprincipled men, precipitately or carelessly disrespectful to my orders, taking advantage of this brief season to play the part of villains or traitors, I will cut off their noses,[5] or utterly exterminate them. I will leave none of their children. I will not let them perpetuate their seed in this new city.

"Go! Preserve and continue your lives. I will now transfer you to the new capital and there establish your families forever."

The Third Speech

P'an Keng, having completed the removal and settled the places of residence, proceeded to adjust the several positions

---

4. Cowrie shells were used as currency until 338 B.C.
5. Cutting off the nose was one of the five punishments.

of all classes at an assembly; and then he soothed and comforted the multitudes, saying to them, "Do not play nor be idle, but exert yourselves to build here a great destiny for us.

"Now I have disclosed my heart and belly, my reins and bowels, and fully declared to you, my people, all my mind. I will not treat any of you as offenders; and do not you any more help one another to be angry and form parties to defame me, the One Man.

"Of old, my royal predecessor T'ang, that his merit might exceed those who were before him, proceeded to the hill site. Thereby he removed our evils and accomplished admirable good for our country. Now you, my people, were by your position dissipated and separated, so that you had no abiding place. And yet you asked why I was troubling your myriads and requiring you to remove. But God being about to restore the virtuous service of my high ancestor and secure the good order of our kingdom, I, sincere and respectful of my ministers, felt a reverent care for the lives of the people and have made a lasting settlement in this new city.

"I, a youth, did not neglect your counsels; I only used the best of them. Nor did any of you presumptuously oppose the decision of the tortoise shell. So we are here to enlarge our great inheritance.

"Oh! ye chiefs of regions, ye heads of departments, all ye, the hundreds of officers, would that ye had a sympathy with my people! I will exert myself in the choice and guiding of you; ye shall think reverently of my multitudes. I will not employ those who are fond of enriching themselves; but will use and revere those who are vigorously, yet reverently, laboring for the lives and increase of the people, nourishing them and planning for their enduring settlement.

"I have now brought forward and announced to you my

mind, whom I approve and whom I disallow; let none of you but reverence my will. Do not seek to accumulate wealth and precious things, but in fostering the life of the people seek to find your merit. Reverently display your virtue in behalf of the people. For ever maintain this one purpose in your hearts."

8. THE CHARGE TO YÜEH

Yüeh had been a recluse living in obscurity in Fu Yen or "among the Crags of Fu." He was later called Fu Yüeh, as if surnamed Fu. In this document he is summoned by the second King Wu Ting to become his chief minister.

Two reigns, not mentioned in the remaining documents of the *Shu,* intervene between P'an Keng and Wu Ting. It is Wu Ting who delivers the charge that gives this document its title. Charges are the addresses delivered by a king or high officer upon investiture of a fief, duty, or other occasion. Here, the charge is delivered to Yüeh upon his appointment as chief minister.

Wu Ting, under his dynastic title name of Kao Tsung, is referred to in Hexagram 63 of the *I ching, Book of Changes*: he "attacked the demon-land and subdued it in three years."

This demon-land seems to have been the country of the wild tribes in the north, who never ceased to press upon the more civilized Chinese until they made themselves masters of the empire about 2,500 years after Wu Ting's time.

Wu Ting subdued rebellion and made peace within all his borders. He arrested the decline of the Shang dynasty that had begun with the reigns of P'an Keng's successors, Hsiao Hsin and Hsiao Yi. During the reign of the latter, Tan Fu removed to Ch'i and called his settlement Chou, the name which his descendants would give to the dynasty that was to overthrow the Shang. During Wu Ting's reign, Ch'ang, the father of the founder of the Chou dynasty, was born. He was later known as King Wen.

This document bears some resemblance to "The T'ai Chia" (Part IV, Document 5): I Yin had removed T'ai Chia to the grave of his grandfather to spend the period of mourning. However, here we are told that Wu Ting spent his mourning period in a mourning shed. Legge quotes Chu Hsi: " 'The lessons of I Yin to T'ai Chia are different from those of Yüeh to Wu Ting. The words of I Yin are repeated again and again, as the small

94

natural comprehension of T'ai Chia required. This was not necessary with Wu Ting. His natural ability was good, and he was not chargeable with many faults.' "

Wu Ting is about to inaugurate his reign, 1324–1264 B.C. Although the classification of charge is given to this document, there is much of the nature of a counsel about the dialogue. Its genuineness has been challenged.

Document 8

The king passed the season of sorrow in the mourning shed for three years.[1] When the period of mourning was over, he still did not speak to give commands.

All the ministers remonstrated with him, saying, "Oh! he who is the first to apprehend we pronounce intelligent, and the intelligent man is the model for others. The Son of Heaven rules over the myriad regions; all the officers look up to and reverence him. The king's words form the commands for them. If he do not speak, the ministers have no way to receive their orders."

On this the king made a writing, for their information, to the following effect: "As it is mine to secure what is right in the four quarters of the kingdom, I have been afraid that my virtue is not equal to that of my predecessors and therefore have not spoken. But while I was reverently and silently thinking of the right way, I dreamed that God gave me a good assistant who should speak for me." He then minutely described the appearance of the person, and caused search to be made for him everywhere by means of a picture.

---

1. A young king, mourning for his father, had to "afflict" himself in various ways for twenty-five months, nominally for three years. Among other privations, he had to exchange the comforts of a palace for a rough shed in one of the courtyards. During the time of mourning, the direction of affairs was left to the chief minister.

Yüeh, a builder in the wild country of Fu Yen, was found like to it.

On this the king raised and made Yüeh his prime minister, keeping him also at his side.

He charged him, saying, "Morning and evening present your instructions to aid my virtue. Suppose me a weapon of steel; I will use you for a whetstone. Suppose me crossing a great stream; I will use you for a boat with its oars. Suppose me in a year of great drought; I will use you as a copious rain. Open your mind, and enrich my mind. Be you like medicine which must distress the patient in order to cure his sickness. Think of me as one walking barefoot whose feet are sure to be wounded if he do not see the ground.

"Let you and your companions all cherish the same mind to assist your sovereign, that I may follow my royal predecessors and tread in the steps of my high ancestor to give repose to the millions of the people. Oh! respect this charge of mine; so shall you bring your work to a good end."

Yüeh replied to the king, saying, "Wood by the use of the line is made straight, and the sovereign who follows reproof becomes sage. When the sovereign can thus make himself sage, his ministers anticipate his orders without being especially charged. Who would dare not to act in respectful compliance with this excellent charge of your Majesty?"

Yüeh having received his charge, and taken the presidency of all the officers, presented himself before the king, and said, "Oh! intelligent kings act in reverent accord with the ways of Heaven. The founding of states and setting up of capitals; the appointing of sovereign kings, of dukes and other nobles with their great officers and heads of departments: these were not designed to minister to the idleness and pleasures of one but for the good government of the people. It is Heaven which is all-intelligent and observing; let the sage king take it as his pattern. Then his ministers will reverently accord with him and the people consequently will be well governed.

"It is the mouth that gives occasion for shame; the coat of mail and helmet give occasion to war. The upper robes and lower garments[2] for reward should not be lightly taken from their chests; before spear and shield are used, one should examine himself. If your Majesty will be cautious in these things and, believing this about them, attain to the intelligent use of them, your government will in everything be excellent. Good government and bad depend on the various officers. Offices should not be given to men because they are favorites but only to men of ability. Honors should not be conferred on men of evil practices, but only on men of worth.

"Anxious thought about what will be best should precede your movements, which also should be taken at the time proper for them. Indulging the consciousness of being good is the way to lose goodness; boasting of ability is the way to lose the merit it might produce.

"For all affairs let there be adequate preparation; with preparation there will be no calamitous issue. Do not open the door for favorites, from whom you will receive contempt. Do not be ashamed of mistakes and go on to make them crimes. Let your mind rest in its proper objects, and the affairs of your government will be pure. Officiousness in sacrificing is called irreverence; ceremonies when burdensome lead to disorder. To serve the spirits acceptably in this way is difficult."

2. The robes in the imperial stores were intended to reward the good and meritorious but, if distributed carelessly, were productive of evil effects.

The king said, "Excellent! Your words, O Yüeh, should indeed be put in practice by me. If you were not so good in counsel, I should not have heard these rules for my conduct."

Yüeh did obeisance with his head to the ground, and said, "It is not the knowing that is difficult, but the doing. But since your Majesty truly knows this, there will not be the difficulty and you will become really equal in complete virtue to our first king. When I, Yüeh, refrain from speaking what I ought to speak, the blame will rest with me."

The king said, "Come, O Yüeh. I, the Little One, first learned with Kan P'an.[3] Afterwards I lived concealed among the rude countrymen, then I went to the country inside the Ho and lived there. From the Ho I went to Po; and the result has been that I am unenlightened. Teach me what should be my aims. Be to me as the yeast and the malt in making sweet spirits, as the salt and the prunes in making agreeable soup. Use various methods to cultivate me; do not cast me away; so shall I attain to practice your instructions."

Yüeh said, "O king, a ruler should seek to learn much from his ministers with a view to establishing his affairs. But to learn the lessons of the ancients is the way to attain this. That the affairs of one not making the ancients his masters can be perpetuated for generations—this I have not heard.

"In learning, there should be a humble mind and the maintenance of a constant earnestness. In such a case the

3. It is supposed that Kan P'an had been minister to Wu Ting's father, Hsiao I, and died during the king's period of mourning. The reasons for Wu Ting's having been disadvantaged and therefore unenlightened are not given. Legge hazarded the opinion that it was probably due to troubles in the kingdom.

learner's improvement will surely come. He who sincerely cherishes these things will find all truth accumulating in his person. Teaching is one half of learning. When a man's thoughts from first to last are constantly fixed on learning, his virtuous cultivation comes unperceived.

"Survey the perfect pattern of our first king; so shall you forever be preserved from error. Then shall I be able reverently to meet your views, and on every side to look for men of eminence to place in the various offices."

The king said, "Oh! Yüeh, that all within the four seas look up to my virtue is owing to you. As his legs and arms form the man, so does a good minister form the sage king. Formerly, there was I Yin,[4] who raised up and formed its royal founder. He said, 'If I cannot make my sovereign like Yao or Shun I shall feel ashamed in my heart, as if I were beaten in the market-place.' If any common man did not get all he should desire, he said, 'It is my fault.' Thus he assisted my meritorious ancestor, so that he became equal to great Heaven. Let you give your intelligent and preserving aid to me; let not I Yin engross all the good service to the house of Shang.

"The sovereign should share his government with none but worthy officers. The worthy officer should accept his support only from the proper sovereign. May you now succeed in making your sovereign a true successor of the founder of his line and in securing the lasting happiness of the people!"

Yüeh did obeisance with his head to the ground, and said, "I will venture to respond to, and display abroad, your Majesty's excellent charge."

4. I Yin is referred to here in both the first and second translations as Pao Heng, meaning the protector and steelyard (or equalizer). In the second mention of I Yin he is styled Aheng. I Yin is used throughout this modernization for clarity.

9. THE DAY OF THE SUPPLEMENTARY SACRIFICE TO KAO TSUNG

After his death, Wu Ting was apotheosized with the title Kao Tsung in a ceremony at the ancestral temple. At the close of this ceremonial sacrifice, the personators of the dead in the sacrifice of the regular and more solemn service of the preceding day were feasted.

The crowing pheasant appearing on the day of the sacrifice of Kao Tsung is considered ominous. Ssu-ma Ch'ien says that the pheasant sat on the ear (one of the handles) of a tripod. This incident provides Tsu Chi with an opportunity to censure Wu Ting's son, Tsu Keng.

The document is classified as an instruction. The year is 1265 B.C.

Document 9

On the day of the supplementary sacrifice of Kao Tsung, there appeared a crowing pheasant. Tsu Chi said, "To rectify this affair, the king must first be corrected."

Accordingly he delivered a lesson to the king, saying, "In its inspection of men below, Heaven's first consideration is of their righteousness; it bestows on them accordingly length of years or the contrary. It is not Heaven that cuts short men's lives; they bring them to an end themselves. Some men who have not complied with virtue will not acknowledge their offenses. When Heaven has by evident tokens charged them to correct their conduct, they still say, 'What are these things to us?'

"Oh! your Majesty's business is to care reverently for the people. And all your ancestors were the heirs of the kingdom by the gift of Heaven; in attending to the sacrifices to them, be not excessive in those to your father."

10. THE CHIEF OF THE WEST'S CONQUEST OF LI

Between this document and the last, the reigns of seven more kings have passed. We are in the last period of the Shang dynasty, and the house of Chou is on the rise. The account of the fall of the Shang dynasty bears striking similarities to the account of the fall of Hsia. It is possible, as many have suggested, that much in the account of one downfall owes its origin to the other. In his *The Birth of China,* Creel points out that there are discrepancies in the documents of this period and raises the possibility that the Chou, as they came to power, replaced the Shang version of history with their own.

But to deal with a forgery is not necessarily purposeless. We are still dealing with a traditional view and one that prevailed for centuries. This view shaped millions of Chinese as Shakespeare's view of history shaped the ideas of millions of Anglo-Saxons. History, no less than tradition, should be evaluated, but often the effect of tradition outweighs that of history.

Legge summarizes the last days of the Shang dynasty in a lengthy footnote which tells us something about the manners and customs and people of that time, whether Shang or Chou:

Chou Hsin (Shou) succeeded to the kingdom 1154 B.C. He had two brothers older than himself: Ch'i, known as the count of Wei, and Chung-yen. But when they were born, their mother had only a secondary place in the harem. Before the birth of Chou Hsin (Shou), however, she was raised to the dignity of queen and she and King Ti Yi were persuaded, against their better judgment, to name him on that account successor to the throne in preference to Ch'i.

Chou Hsin (Shou) appears in history with all the attributes of a tyrant. His natural abilities were more than ordinary; his sight and hearing were astonishingly acute; his strength made him a match for the strongest animals; he could make the worse appear to be the better reason when his ministers attempted to remonstrate with him; he was intemperate, extravagant, and would sacrifice everything to the gratification of his passions. He was the first, we are told, to use ivory chopsticks, which made the count of Ch'i sorrowfully remonstrate with him. "Ivory chopsticks," said he, "will be followed by cups of gem; and then you will be wanting to eat bears' paws and leopards' wombs, and proceed to other extravagancies. Your indulgence of your desires may cost you the empire." Such admonitions were of no use.

In 1147 B.C. in an expedition against the prince of Su, he received from him a lady of extraordinary beauty called Ta Chi, of whom he became the thrall. It is the story of Chieh and Mei Hsi over again. Ta Chi was shamelessly lustful and cruel. The most licentious songs were composed for her amusement, and the vilest dances exhibited. A palace was erected for her, with a famous terrace or tower, two li wide, and the park around stocked with the rarest animals. This expenditure necessitated heavy exactions, which moved the resentment of the people. At Sha-ch'u there was still greater extravagance and dissipation. There was a pond of wine; the trees were hung with flesh; men and women chased each other about quite naked. In the palace there were nine market-stances where they drank all night. The princes began to rebel when Ta Chi said that the majesty of the throne was not sufficiently maintained, that punishments were too light and executions too rare. She therefore devised two new instruments of torture. One of them was called the heater and consisted of a piece of metal, made hot in a fire, which people were obliged to take up in their hands. The other was a copper pillar, greased all over, and laid above a pit of live charcoal. The culprit had to walk across the pillar and when his feet slipped and he fell down into the fire, Ta Chi was greatly delighted. This was called the punishment of roasting. These enormities made the whole empire groan and fume with indignation.

Chou Hsin (Shou) appointed the Chief of the West, the prince of Ch'u, and the prince of Go his three principal ministers. The two last met a sad fate. The prince of Ch'u added his own daughter to the harem and, when she would not enter into its debaucheries, Chou Hsin (Shou) put her to death, and made minced meat of her father. The prince of Go ventured to remonstrate and was sliced to pieces for his pains. Ch'ang fell at the same time under suspicion and was put in prison, in a place called Yu Li.

These events are referred to 1144 B.C. Ch'ang, it is said, occupied himself, in prison, with the study of Fu Hsi's diagrams, and composed a considerable portion of the present *I ching*. In 1142, his sons and subjects propitiated the tyrant with immense gifts; the exigencies of the kingdom were likewise very pressing in consequence of risings and incursions of the wild tribes; Ch'ang was released, and invested with greater authority than before. If he had raised the flag of rebellion, he could easily have dethroned the king, but he preserved his allegiance, obtained the abolition of the punishment of roasting, and drew the hearts and thoughts of princes and people more and more to himself and his house. History tells us of his exploits, virtually regent of the kingdom, till his death in 1135 B.C., when he was succeeded by his son Fa, who inherited his authority and his virtues. Ten years pass on, of the events of which nothing important is related, and we come to 1124 B.C., to which the conquest of Li is referred.

The identity of the Chief of the West may have been King Wen (also called Ch'ang) or his son King Wu (also called Fa).

King Wen's father had been appointed Chief of the West, an area which embraced Yü's provinces of Yung, Liang, and Ching. This jurisdiction descended to his son and grandson. Now the conquest of the state of Li, which was within the royal domain, threatens the throne and the king himself. Tsu I, hearing of the conquest, hurries to inform Shou of the danger and warns him that the dynasty is falling because of his evil conduct.

The time is in the last period of Chou Hsin's (Shou's) reign: 1154–1123 B.C. The document is classified among the announcements, though the reason is not clear.

Document 10

The Chief of the West having subdued Li, Tsu I was afraid and hastened to report it to the king.

He said, "Son of Heaven, Heaven is bringing to an end the

dynasty of Yin. The wisest men and the shell of the great tortoise do not presume to know anything fortunate for it. It is not that the former kings do not aid us, men of this later time, but your dissoluteness and sport are bringing on the end yourself. On this account Heaven has cast us off; there are no good harvests to supply us with food. Men have no regard for their heavenly nature and do not obey the statutes of the kingdom. Yea, our people now all wish the dynasty to perish, saying, 'Why does not Heaven send down its indignation? Why does not someone with its great appointment make his appearance? What has the present king to do with us?' "

The king said, "Oh! was not my birth in accord with the appointment of Heaven in favor of my house?"

On this Tsu I returned to his own city and said, "Your crimes, which are many, are registered above and can you still appeal to the appointment of Heaven in your favor? Yin will perish very shortly. As to all your deeds, can they but bring ruin on your country?"

11. THE COUNT OF WEI

Ch'i, count of Wei, was probably an elder brother of Shou by the same concubine (later elevated to queen, before the birth of Shou).

Saddened with the thought of the impending ruin of the dynasty, the count seeks the counsel of two other nobles to see if the dynasty can be saved.

The year is 1123 B.C., the last of the Shang (Yin) dynasty. This conference of the three high nobles forms the substance of this document, which is classified among the announcements of the *Shu*.

Document 11

The count of Wei spoke to the following effect: "Grand Master and Junior Master, we may conclude that the house of Yin can no longer exercise rule over the four quarters of the kingdom. The great deeds of our founder were displayed in former ages, but by our maddened indulgence in spirits we have destroyed the effects of his virtue in these later times. The people of Yin, small and great, are given to highway robberies, villainies, and treachery. The nobles and officers imitate one another in violating the laws and there is no certainty that criminals will be apprehended. The smaller people consequently rise up and commit violent outrages on one another. Yin is now sinking in ruin. Its condition is like one crossing a large stream who finds neither ford nor bank. That Yin should be hurrying to ruin at the present pace!"

He added, "Grand Master and Junior Master, we are manifesting insanity. The most venerable members of our families are withdrawn to the wilds. You indicate no course to be taken, but only tell me of the impending ruin. What is to be done?"

The Grand Master made the following reply: "O son of our former king, Heaven in anger is sending down calamities and wasting the country of Yin. Hence has arisen that mad indulgence in spirits. The king has no reverence for things which he ought to reverence, but insults the venerable aged, the men who have long been in office.

"The people of Yin will now steal even the pure and perfect sacrificial victims devoted to the spirits of heaven and earth; their conduct is ignored and, though they proceed to eat the sacrifice victims, they suffer no punishment.

"On the other hand, when I look down and survey the people of Yin, the methods by which they are governed are hateful exactions, which call forth outrages and hatred; and this without ceasing. Such crimes equally belong to all in authority. Multitudes are starving with none to whom to appeal. Now is the time of Shang's calamity; I will arise and share in its ruin. When ruin overtakes Shang, I will not be the servant of another house. But I tell you, O king's son, to go away is the course for you. Formerly I injured you by what I said;[1] if you do not now go away, our sacrifices will entirely perish. Let us rest quietly in our several parts, and each present himself to the former kings as having done so. I do not think of making my escape."

Legge's concluding footnote to his first translation of *The Documents of Shang*:

The dynasty closes, in the chronology, in 1122 B.C., the same year to which the conference between the count of Wei and his

1. According to tradition, the Grand Master had recommended Ch'i, count of Wei, as successor to the throne instead of Shou—which made the latter intensely jealous of Ch'i.

friends is referred. It was in the year after, however, that Chou Hsin died. For the contest between him and King Wu we must look to the commencing documents of the next Part (V).

The house of Chou after many delays at last took the field against the tyrant. The two armies met in the plain of Mu, in present-day Honan. Chou Hsin's troops failed him in the hour of need. He was totally defeated and fled to the palace which had been the scene of so many debaucheries with Ta Chi.

Arrayed in his most gorgeous robes, and covered with gems, he set fire to the "Stag Tower" which he had built for her and perished in the flames. Yet not so but that his body was found. King Wu cut off the head and had it exhibited on a pole.

Ta Chi appareled herself splendidly and went out to meet the conqueror, thinking he might be conquered by her charms. She was made prisoner, however, by a detachment of his troops and put to death by his order without having the opportunity to present herself before him.

PART V

The Documents of Chou

THE HOUSE OF CHOU

The Chou were people of the West. Their surname was Ch'i. They claimed as their ancestor Ch'i, minister of Agriculture to Shun. Shun had given Ch'i a small fief on the Wei, near Hsian in present-day Shensi.

King Wen (or Wen Wang) was imprisoned by Chou Hsin (Shou) at Yu Li where, it is said, he occupied himself with studying the diagrams of the *I ching, Book of Changes*. The *t'uan,* or short summary under each of the sixty-four hexagrams of the *I ching,* are ascribed to him. After his death when his son King Wu (Fa, also Wu Wang) came to the throne, King Wen was apotheosized as founder of the Chou dynasty.

Tan, duke of Chou, the fourth son of King Wen, was among the great figures of early China. He secured the dynasty after the death of King Wu, acting as regent for the young King Ch'eng. He is credited with writing the *yao* of the *I ching,* the line by line interpretations of the hexagrams. The *t'uan* and the *yao* by this father and son became lessons to generations of Chinese.

The *Shih ching, Book of Odes* says of King Wen:

> Full of earnest activity was King Wen—
> And his fame is without end.
> The gifts of God to Chou
> Extend to the descendants of King Wen—
> To the descendants of King Wen
> In the direct line and the collateral branches
>   for a hundred generations.
> All the officers of Chou
> Shall also be illustrious from age to age.

The Chou are inextricably linked with the three ancient great books of China: the *Shu ching, Book of History,* the *I ching, Book of Changes,* and the *Shih ching, Book of Odes.* The dynasty lasted for more than 900 years, although from the eighth century B.C. to the founding of the empire under Ch'in Shih Huang Ti, it gradually declined.

The Chou dynasty is often thought of in periods. It is called Western Chou from its founding to about 771 B.C. It is called Eastern Chou after it moved east to its new capital of Lo. The period from about 450 to 221 B.C., marking the close of the Chou dynasty, is designated as the Warring States period.

The documents of Chou in the *Shu* come to an end in the seventh century B.C.

1. THE GREAT DECLARATION

The genuineness of this document is questioned. It does not appear in the Karlgren translation, nor is it stated what classification the document falls into.

The "thirteenth year" in the opening phrase refers to the thirteenth year after King Wu had succeeded his father King Wen as Chief of the West.

The ford of Meng (also known as Meng-tsin) is the ford mentioned in "The Tribute to Yü." Here on the Ho River the princes who acknowledged King Wu had assembled, having already entered the western confederation of King Wen. It is a time of preparation for battle against Chou Hsin (Shou).

Document 1

In the spring of the thirteenth year there was a great assembly at the ford of Meng.

The king said, "Ah! ye hereditary rulers of my friendly states, and all ye my officers, managers of my affairs—listen clearly to my declaration.

"Heaven and earth is the parent of all creatures; and of all creatures man is the most highly endowed. The sincerely intelligent among men becomes the great sovereign; and the great sovereign is the parent of the people. But now Shou, the king of Shang, does not reverence Heaven above and inflicts calamities on the people below. Abandoned to drunkenness and reckless in lust, he has dared to exercise cruel oppression. He has extended the punishment of offenders to all their relatives. He has put men into office on the hereditary principle. He has made it his pursuit to have palaces, towers, pavilions, embankments, ponds, and all other extravagances—to the most painful injury of you,

113

the myriads of the people. He has burned and roasted the loyal and good. He has ripped up pregnant women. Great Heaven was moved with indignation and charged my deceased father Wen to display its terrors; but he died before the work was completed.

"On this account I, Fa, the Little Child, have by means of you, the hereditary rulers of my friendly states, contemplated the government of Shang; but Shou has no repentant heart. He sits squatting on his heels, not serving God nor the spirits of heaven and earth, neglecting also the temple of his ancestors and not sacrificing in it. The sacrificial victims and the vessels of millet all become the prey of wicked robbers. Still he says, 'The people are mine; the heavenly appointment is mine,' never trying to correct his contemptuous mind.

"Heaven, for the help of the inferior people, made for them rulers, and made for them instructors, that they might be able to aid God and secure the tranquillity of the four quarters of the kingdom. In regard to who are criminals and who are not, how dare I give any allowance to my own wishes? 'Where the strength is the same, measure the virtue of the parties; where the virtue is the same, measure their righteousness.'

"Shou has hundreds of thousands and myriads of officers, but they have hundreds of thousands and myriads of minds; I have only three thousand officers, but they have one mind. The iniquity of Shang is full. Heaven gives command to destroy it. If I did not obey Heaven, my iniquity would be as great.

"I, the Little Child, early and late am filled with apprehensions. I have received the command of my deceased father Wen; I have offered special sacrifice to God; I have performed the due services to the great earth; and I lead the multitude of you to execute the punishment appointed by Heaven. Heaven compassionates the people. What the people desire, Heaven will effect. You must aid me, the One Man, to cleanse for ever all within the four seas. Now is the time! It should not be lost."

On the day *wu-wu,* the king halted on the north of the Ho. When all the princes with their hosts were assembled the king reviewed the hosts and made the following declaration: "Oh! ye multitudes of the West, listen all to my words.

"I have heard that the good man, doing good, finds the day insufficient; and that the evil man, doing evil, also finds the day insufficient. Now Shou, king of Shang, with strength pursues his lawless way. He has cast away the time-worn sires and cultivates intimacies with wicked men. Dissolute, intemperate, reckless, oppressive, his ministers have become like to him; they form combinations and contract animosities and depend on their power to exterminate one another. The innocent cry to Heaven. The odor of such a state is plainly felt on high.

"Heaven loves the people, and the sovereign should reverently carry out this mind of Heaven. Chieh, sovereign of Hsia, would not follow the example of Heaven but sent forth his poisonous injuries through the states of the kingdom. Heaven therefore gave its aid to T'ang the Successful, and charged him to make an end of the appointment of Hsia.

"But the crimes of Shou exceed those of Chieh. He has degraded from office the greatly good man the count of Wei; he has behaved with cruel tyranny to his reprover and helper Pi Kan. He says that with him is the appointment of Heaven; he says that a reverent care of his conduct is not worth observing; he says that sacrifice is of no use; he says that tyranny is no harm. The case for him to look to was not far off: it was that king of Hsia. It would seem that Heaven is going by means of me to rule the people. My dreams coincide with my divinations; the auspicious omen is double. My attack on Shang must succeed.

"Shou has hundreds of thousands and millions of ordinary men, divided in heart and divided in practice; I have of ministers able to govern ten men,[1] one in heart and one in practice. Though he has his nearest relatives with him, they are not like my virtuous men. Heaven sees as my people see; Heaven hears as my people hear.

"The people are blaming me, the One Man, for my delay; I must now go forward. My military prowess is displayed; I enter his territories to take the wicked tyrant. My punishment of evil will be great, more glorious than that executed by T'ang. Rouse ye, my heroes! Do not think that he is not to be feared; better think that he cannot be withstood. His people stand in trembling awe of him, as if the horns were falling from their heads.[2] Oh! unite your energies, unite your hearts; so shall you forthwith surely accomplish the work to last for all ages!"

The time was on the morrow, when the king went round his six hosts in state, and made a clear declaration to all his officers. He said,

"Oh! my valiant men of the West, Heaven has enjoined the illustrious courses of duty, of which the several require-

1. Confucius said of these ten ministers that one was a woman: ". . . there was a woman among them. The able ministers were no more than nine men" (Analects, VIII.20). It is a subject of controversy whether this woman was King Wu's wife or mother.
2. The reference to horns implies that the people had existed only as cattle.

ments are quite plain. And now Shou, king of Shang, treats with contemptuous slight the five regular virtues and abandons himself to wild idleness and irreverence. He has cut himself off from Heaven and brought enmity between himself and the people.

"He cut through the leg-bones of those who were wading in the morning;[3] he cut out the heart of the worthy man, Pi Kan. By the use of his power, killing and murdering, he has poisoned and sickened all within the four seas. His honors and confidence are given to the villainous and bad. He has driven from him his instructors and guardians. He has thrown to the winds the statutes and penal laws. He has imprisoned and enslaved the upright officer the count of Ch'i. He neglects the sacrifices to heaven and earth. He has discontinued the offerings in the ancestral temple. He makes contrivances of wonderful device and extraordinary cunning to please his woman Ta Chi.

"God will no longer indulge him, but with a curse is sending down on him this ruin. With untiring zeal support me, the One Man, reverently to execute the punishment appointed by Heaven. The ancients have said, 'He who soothes us is our sovereign; he who oppresses us is our enemy.' This solitary fellow Shou, having exercised great tyranny, is your perpetual enemy. It is said again, 'In planting a man's virtue, strive to make it great; in putting away a man's wickedness, strive to do it from the root.' Here I, the Little Child, by the powerful help of you, all my officers, will utterly exterminate your enemy. Let you, all my officers, march forward with determined boldness to sustain your prince. Where there is much merit, there shall be large

3. A legend says that Shou (Chou Hsin), upon seeing some people wading in winter, ordered their legs cut through that he might inspect their bone marrow.

reward; where you do not so advance, there shall be conspicuous disgrace.

"Oh! the virtue of my deceased father Wen was like the shining of the sun and moon. His brightness extended over the four quarters of the land, and shone signally in the western region. Hence it is that our Chou has received the allegiance of many states. If I subdue Shou, it will not be from my prowess but from the faultless virtue of my deceased father Wen. If Shou subdue me, it will not be from any fault of my deceased father Wen, but because I, the Little Child, am not good."

2. THE SPEECH AT MU

Mu is a tract of open country not far from the Shang capital. It is the morning of the day of battle for which King Wu (Fa) prepared his host by the speeches in "The Great Declaration." Once more he rouses his men by a martial speech.

The king singles out by name eight confederate princes of the tribes of Yung, Shu, Ch'iang, Mao, Wei, Lu, P'ang, and P'o—from western sites in present-day areas of Szechwan, Yunnan, and Hupeh.

Document 2

The time was the gray dawn of the day *chia-tzu*. On that morning the king came to the open country of Mu in the borders of Shang and addressed his army. In his left hand he carried a battle-axe, yellow with gold, and in his right he held a white ensign which he waved, saying, "Far are ye come, ye men of the western regions!"

He added, "Ah! ye hereditary rulers of my friendly states; ye managers of affairs; ministers of Instruction, of War, and of Works; the great officers subordinate to these, and the many other officers; the master of my body guards; the captains of thousands and captains of hundreds; and ye, O men of Yung, Shu, Ch'iang, Mao, Wei, Lu, P'ang, and P'o, lift up your lances, join your shields, raise your spears: I have a speech to make."

The king then said, "The ancients have said, 'The hen should not announce the morning. The crowing of a hen in the morning indicates the subversion of the family.' Now Shou, the king of Shang, follows only the words of his wife. In his blindness he has neglected the sacrifices which he ought to offer and makes no response for the favors that

119

he has received; he has blindly thrown away his paternal and maternal relations, not treating them properly. There are only the vagabonds from all quarters, loaded with crimes, whom he honors and exalts, whom he employs and trusts, making them great officers and high nobles so that they can tyrannize the people and exercise their villainies in the cities of Shang.

"Now, I, Fa, am simply executing respectfully the punishment appointed by Heaven. In today's business do not advance more than six or seven steps and then stop and adjust your ranks; my brave men, be energetic! Do not exceed four blows, five blows, six blows, or seven blows, and then stop and adjust your ranks; my brave men, be energetic! Display a martial bearing. Be like tigers and panthers, like bears and grizzly bears, here in the borders of Shang. Do not rush on those who fly to us in submission, but receive them to serve our western land; my brave men, be energetic! If you are not thus energetic in all these matters, you will bring destruction on yourselves."

3. THE SUCCESSFUL COMPLETION OF THE WAR

With this document we accept the inauguration of the Chou dynasty. However, the document itself offers difficulties. Probably, parts of it are lost and what remains is out of the original order. It does not appear in the Karlgren translation, and its classification is doubtful. Its genuineness is questioned.

We assume that after he had defeated Chou Hsin (Shou), King Wu returned to Feng to sacrifice in the ancestral temple and perform those duties and rites necessary to tranquilize the people and administer the new dynasty.

Near the conclusion of the document, a description of the battle at Mu appears.

Document 3

In the first month, the day *jen-ch'en* immediately followed the end of the moon's waning. The next day was *kuei-chi,* when the king, in the morning, marched from Chou to attack and punish Shang. In the fourth month, at the first appearance of the moon, the king came from Shang to Feng where he hushed all the movements of war and proceeded to cultivate the arts of peace. He sent back his horses to the south of Mount Hua and let loose his oxen in the open country of T'ao-lin, showing to all under heaven that he would not use them again.

On the day *ting-wei,* he sacrificed in the ancestral temple of Chou, when the princes of the royal domain, and of the Tien, Hou, and Wei domains, all hurried about carrying the dishes. The third day after was *keng-hsü;* he presented a burnt offering to Heaven and worshiped toward the hills and rivers, solemnly announcing the successful completion of the war.

After the moon began to wane, the hereditary princes of the various states, and all the officers, received their appointments from Chou.

The king spoke to the following effect: "Oh! ye host of princes, the first of our kings[1] founded his state, and commenced the enlargement of its territory. Kung Liu was able to consolidate the services of his predecessor. But it was King T'ai who laid the foundations of the royal inheritance. The king Ch'i was diligent for the royal house; and my deceased father, King Wen, completed his merit and grandly received the appointment of Heaven to soothe the regions of our great land. The great states feared his strength; the small states thought fondly of his virtue. In nine years, however, the whole kingdom was not united under his rule and it fell to me, the Little Child, to carry out his will.

"Detesting the crimes of Shang, I announced to great Heaven and the sovereign Earth, to the famous hill and the great river[2] by which I passed, saying, 'I, Fa, the principled, king of Chou by a long descent, am about to administer a great correction to Shang. Shou, the present king of Shang, is without principle, cruel and destructive to the creatures of Heaven, injurious and tyrannical to the multitudes of the people, lord of all the vagabonds under heaven, who collect about him as fish in the deep and beasts in the prairie. I, the Little Child, having obtained the help of virtuous men, presume reverently to comply with the will of God and make an end of his disorderly ways. Our flowery and great land, and the tribes of the south and north, equally follow

1. The "king" to which King Wu refers is Ch'i, Shun's minister of Agriculture. His state is T'ai, a small fief on the Wei presented to him by Shun. Of Kung (duke) Liu little is known. King T'ai (also known as Tan Fu) acquired Ch'i about 1327 B.C. and called his principality Chou. King Wu is capsulating a family history that extends through nine centuries. This is further justification for his assumption of power.
2. The famous hill was probably Mount Hua, and the river the Ho.

and consent with me. Reverently obeying the determinate counsel of Heaven, I pursue my punitive work to the east to give tranquillity to its men and women. They meet me with their baskets full of dark-colored and yellow silks, thereby showing the virtues of us, the kings of Chou. Heaven's favors stir them up so that they come with their allegiance to our great state of Chou. And now, ye spirits, grant me your aid that I may relieve the millions of the people, and nothing turn out to your shame.'"

On the day *wu-wu,* the army crossed the ford of Meng, and on *kuei-hai* it was drawn up in array in the borders of Shang, waiting for the gracious decision of Heaven. On *chia-tzu,* at early dawn, Shou led forward his troops, looking like a forest, and assembled them in the wild of Mu. But they offered no opposition to our army. Those in the front inverted their spears and attacked those behind till they fled; the blood flowed till it floated the pestles of the mortars. Thus did King Wu once don his armor, and the kingdom was grandly settled. He overturned the existing rule of Shang and made government resume its old course. He delivered the count of Ch'i from prison, and raised a mound over the grave of Pi Kan. He bowed forward to the cross bar of his carriage at the gate of Shang Yung's village.[3] He dispersed the treasures of the Stag Tower, and distributed the grain of Chu-ch'iao,[4] thus conferring great gifts on all within the four seas, so that the people joyfully submitted to him.

He arranged the nobles in five orders,[5] assigning the ter-

3. Probably the home of a worthy that Shou had disgraced.
4. Stag Tower was the name of the famous tower built by Chou Hsin (Shou) for Ta Chi; Chu-ch'iao was where grain was hoarded.
5. The five orders of nobles were duke, marquis, earl, count, and baron.

ritories to them according to a threefold scale. He gave office only to the worthy and employment only to the able. He attached great importance to the people's being taught the duties of the five relations of society, and to measures for ensuring a sufficient supply of food, attention to the rites of mourning, and to sacrifices. He showed the reality of his truthfulness and proved clearly his righteousness. He honored virtue and rewarded merit. Then he had only to let his robes fall down, fold his hands, and the kingdom was orderly ruled.

4. THE GREAT PLAN

This document sets forth a model government by which the people may be rendered happy and tranquil, in harmony with their condition through the perfect character of the king and his perfect administration.

It is included in the documents of Chou because the count of Ch'i (also referred to as Ch'i, count of Wei) presents it as a counsel to King Wu. The count of Ch'i was Grand Master at the court of Shang. In Part IV, Document 11, "The Count of Wei," Ch'i stated: "When ruin overtakes Shang, I will not be the servant of another dynasty." He refused allegiance to King Wu and fled.

King Wu admired and respected the count's fidelity to the fallen dynasty and invested him with the territory into which he had fled. It was to acknowledge this, so it is said, that the count of Ch'i presented himself at King Wu's court to set forth this plan, supposedly handed down from the time of Yü the Great, founder of the Hsia dynasty. The *Shu* makes no mention of the legend that Yü, while working near the river Lo, saw a large tortoise rise from the Lo bearing on its back well-defined marks that were the inspiration for the writing of "The Great Plan." Nor does the *Shu* make any explanation of how the plan came into the possession of the count of Ch'i.

This document, a counsel like "The Great Declaration," dates from the thirteenth year of King Wu's accession to the principality of Chou as Chief of the West, the same year he attacked Shang.

Document 4

In the thirteenth year, the king went to enquire of the count of Ch'i, and said to him, "Oh! count of Ch'i, Heaven, working unseen, secures the tranquillity of the lower people, aiding them to be in harmony with their condition. I

125

do not know how the unvarying principles of its method in doing so should be set forth in due order."

The count of Ch'i thereupon replied, "I have heard that in old time Kun dammed up the inundating waters and thereby threw into disorder the arrangement of the five elements. God was consequently roused to anger and did not give him the Great Plan with its nine divisions; thus the unvarying principles of Heaven's method were allowed to go to ruin. Kun was therefore kept a prisoner till his death and his son Yü rose up and entered on the same undertaking. To him Heaven gave the Great Plan with its nine divisions and the unvarying principles of its method were set forth in their due order.

"Of those divisions the first is called the five elements; the second, reverent attention to the five personal matters; the third, earnest devotion to the eight objects of government; the fourth, the harmonious use of the five dividers of time; the fifth, the establishment and use of royal perfection; the sixth, the discriminating use of the three virtues; the seventh, the intelligent use of the means for the examination of doubts; the eighth, the thoughtful use of the various verifications; the ninth, the encouraging use of the five sources of happiness, and the awesome use of the six occasions of suffering.

"First, the five elements: the first is water; the second, fire; the third, wood; the fourth, metal; and the fifth, earth. The nature of water is to soak and descend; of fire to blaze and ascend; of wood to be crooked and straight; of metal to yield and change; while that of earth is seen in seed-sowing and in-gathering. That which soaks and descends becomes salt; that which blazes and ascends becomes bitter; that which is crooked and straight becomes sour; that which yields and changes becomes acrid; and from seed-sowing and in-gathering comes sweetness.

"Second, the five personal matters: the first is bodily demeanor; the second, speech; the third, seeing; the fourth, hearing; the fifth, thinking. The virtue of bodily appearance is respectfulness; of speech, accord with reason; of seeing, clearness; of hearing, distinctness; of thinking, perception. Respectfulness becomes manifest in gravity; accord with reason, in orderliness; clearness, in wisdom; distinctness, in deliberation; and perception, in sageness.

"Third, the eight objects of government: the first is food; the second, wealth and articles of convenience; the third, sacrifices; the fourth, the business of the minister of Works; the fifth, that of the minister of Instruction; the sixth, that of the minister of Crime; the seventh, the courtesy to be paid to guests; the eighth, the army.

"Fourth, the five dividers of time: the first is the year or the planet Jupiter; the second, the moon; the third, the sun; the fourth, the stars, planets, and the zodiacal spaces; and the fifth, the calendaric calculations.

"Fifth, of royal perfection: the sovereign, having established in himself the highest degree and pattern of excellence, concentrates in his own person the five sources of happiness and proceeds to diffuse them, and give them to the multitudes of the people. Then they, on their part, embodying your perfection will give it back to you and secure the preservation of it. Among all the multitudes of the people there will be no unlawful confederacies, and among men in office there will be no bad and selfish combinations; let the sovereign establish in himself the highest degree and pattern of excellence.

"Among all the multitudes of the people there will be

those who have ability to plan and to act, and who keep themselves from evil: let you keep such in mind. There will be those who, not coming up to the highest point of excellence, yet do not involve themselves in evil: let the sovereign receive such. And when a placid satisfaction appears in their countenances and they say, 'Our love is fixed on virtue,' let you then confer favors on them; those men will in this way advance to the perfection of the sovereign. Let him not oppress the friendless and childless, nor let him fear the high and distinguished. When men in office have ability and administrative power, let them be made still more to cultivate their conduct; and the prosperity of the country will be promoted. All such right men, having a competency, will go on in goodness.

"If you cannot cause them to have what they love in their families, they will forthwith proceed to be guilty of crime. As to those who lack the love of virtue, although you confer favors and emoluments on them, they will only involve you in the guilt of employing the evil.

> "Without deflection, without unevenness,
> Pursue the royal righteousness.
> Without selfish likings,
> Pursue the royal way.
> Without selfish dislikings,
> Pursue the royal path.
> Without deflection, without partiality,
> The royal path is level and easy;
> Without perversity, without one-sidedness,
> The royal path is right and straight.
> Seeing this perfect excellence,
> Turn to this perfect excellence."

He went on to say, "This amplification of the royal perfection contains the unchanging rule, and is the great lesson; yea, it is the lesson of God. All the multitudes of the people, instructed in this amplification of the perfect excellence and carrying it into practice, will thereby approximate to the glory of the Son of Heaven, and say, 'The Son of Heaven is the parent of the people, and so becomes the sovereign of all under the sky.'

"Sixth, the three virtues: the first is correctness and straightforwardness; the second, strong rule; the third, mild rule. In peace and tranquillity, correctness and straightforwardness must prevail; in violence and disorder, strong rule; in harmony and order, mild rule. For the reserved and retiring there should be the stimulus of the strong rule; for the high-minded and distinguished, the restraint of the mild rule.

"It belongs only to the sovereign to confer honors and rewards, to display the terrors of majesty, and to receive the revenues of the kingdom. There should be no such thing as a minister's conferring honors or rewards, displaying the terrors of majesty, or receiving the revenues. Such a thing is injurious to the clans and fatal to the states of the kingdom; smaller affairs are thereby managed in a one-sided and perverse manner and the people fall into assumptions and excesses.

"Seventh, the means for the examination of doubts:[1] of-

---

1. The examination of doubts was done by divination, which underwent changes in method. Early references to divining are objective and tangential, leaving modern readers uncertain of the details of practice. Legge quotes Chu Hsi on the subject: " 'The tortoise after great length of years becomes intelligent; and the *ch'i* plant (yarrow) will yield, when a hundred years old, a hundred stalks from one root and is also a spiritual and intelligent thing. The two divinations were in reality a questioning of spiritual beings, the plant and the shell being employed, because of their mysterious intelligence, to indicate their intimations. The way of divination by the shell was by the application of fire to scorch it until the indications appeared on it; and that by the stalks of

ficers having been chosen and appointed for divining by the tortoise shell and the stalks of the yarrow, they are to be charged on occasion to execute their duties. In doing this, they will find the appearances of rain, of clearing up, of cloudiness, of want of connection, and of crossing; and the inner and outer trigrams. In all the indications are seven: five given by the shell and two by the stalks; and by means of these any errors in the mind may be traced out. These officers having been appointed, when the divination is proceeded with, three men are to interpret the indications and the consenting words of two of them are to be followed.

"When you have doubts about any great matter, consult with your own mind; consult with your high ministers and officers; consult the tortoise shell and divining stalks. If you, the shell, the stalks, the ministers and officers, and the common people all agree about a course, this is what is called a great concord; the result will be the welfare of your person and good fortune to your descendants. If you, the shell, and the stalks agree, while the ministers, officers, and the common people oppose, the result will be fortunate. If the ministers and officers agree with the shell and stalks, while you and the common people oppose, the result will be fortunate. If the common people, the shell, and the stalks agree, while you, the ministers, and officers oppose, the result will be fortunate. If you and the shell agree while the stalks, the ministers, officers, and the common people op-

---

the plant was to manipulate in a prescribed way forty-nine of them, eighteen different times, until the diagrams appeared.' "

Since divination was used from the earliest times, it is assumed that the process underwent many changes and that it was sometimes employed to focus the mind and sometimes merely used by charlatans to dupe the unwary. Also, one can infer a connection between the examination of doubts and the rites connected with ancestorism and translate these into modern psychological terms of individuation and the collective unconscious. (See "divination" in index-glossary.)

pose, internal operations will be fortunate, and external undertakings unlucky. When the shell and stalks are both opposed to the views of men, there will be good fortune in being still; active operations will be unlucky.

"Eighth, the various verifications.[2] They are rain, sunshine, heat, cold, wind, and seasonableness. When the five come all complete, and each in its proper order, even the various plants will be richly luxuriant. Should any one of them be either excessively abundant or excessively deficient, there will be evil.

"There are the favorable verifications: namely, ceremony, which is emblemed by seasonable rain; orderliness, emblemed by seasonable sunshine; wisdom, emblemed by seasonable cold; sageness, emblemed by seasonable wind. There are also the unfavorable verifications: namely, recklessness, emblemed by constant rain; assumption, emblemed by constant sunshine; indolence, emblemed by constant heat; hastiness, emblemed by constant cold; stupidity, emblemed by constant wind."

2. "Various verifications" hardly satisfied Legge as adequate to the character he sought to translate. He quoted Ts'ai Ch'en, a disciple of Chu Hsi and commentator on the *Shu:* " 'To say that on occasion of such and such a personal matter being realized there will be the favorable verification corresponding to it, or that on the occasion of the failure of such realization there will be the corresponding unfavorable verification, would betray a pertinacious obtuseness and show that the speaker was not a man to be talked with on the mysterious operations of nature. It is not easy to describe the reciprocal meeting of Heaven and men. The hidden springs touched by failure and success and the minute influences that respond to them—who can know these but the man who has apprehended all truth?' "

The phrase "various verification" is linked to correspondences of things and is an integral although extremely subtle aspect of the spherical nature of Chinese concepts. The Karlgren translation also employs the phrase "various verifications." What is emblemed is the material; the correspondences are subtle. The nature of Heaven and the nature of man are emblemed both in things seen and things unseen; thus, the correspondences are between the natural and the spiritual, corporeal and incorporeal, the formless *t'ai chi* and the formed thing.

He went on to say, "The king should examine the character of the whole year; the high ministers and officers that of the month; and the inferior officers that of the day. If, throughout the year, the month, the day, there be an unchanging seasonableness, all the grains will be matured; the measures of government will be wise; heroic men will stand forth distinguished; in the families of the people there will be peace and prosperity. If, throughout the year, the month, the day, the seasonableness be interrupted, the various kinds of grain will not be matured; the measures of government will be dark and unwise; heroic men will be kept in obscurity; in the families of the people there will be an absence of repose.

"By the common people the stars should be examined. Some stars love wind and some love rain. The courses of the sun and moon give winter and summer. The way in which the moon follows the stars gives wind and rain.

"Ninth, the five sources of happiness: the first is long life; the second, riches; the third, soundness of body and serenity of mind; the fourth, love of virtue; the fifth is an end crowning the life. Of the six extreme evils, the first is misfortune shortening the life; the second, sickness; the third, distress of mind; the fourth, poverty; the fifth, wickedness; the sixth, weakness."

5. THE HOUNDS OF LÜ

Lü was the name of a tribe to the west of the provinces of Chou. At all times, while the civilized arts of ancient China were being developed, the Chinese were surrounded by tribes. Some tribes were in docile submission and brought their tributes, others were in revolt, while still others were nomadic.

The Grand Guardian, who here gives King Wu this instruction, is Shih, duke of Shao, an appanage within the imperial domain. Document 12, "The Announcement of the Duke of Shao," is also concerned with Shih, whose surname was Ch'i and who was consequently a member of the house of Chou and thought to have been a son of King Wen by a concubine and thus half brother to Wu.

The genuineness of this document has been challenged.

Document 5

After the conquest of Shang, the way being open to the nine wild and the eight savage tribes, the western tribe of Lü sent as tribute some of its hounds, on which the Grand Guardian made "The Hounds of Lü" by way of instruction to the king.

He said, "Oh! the intelligent kings paid careful attention to their virtue, and the wild tribes on every side acknowledged subjection to them. The nearer and the more remote all presented the productions of their countries, in robes, food, and vessels for use. The kings then displayed the things thus drawn forth by their virtue, distributing them to the princes of the states of different surnames from their own to encourage them not to neglect their duties. The more precious things and pieces of jade they distributed among their uncles in charge of states, thereby increasing

133

their attachment to the throne. The recipients did not despise the things, but saw in them the power of virtue.

"Complete virtue allows no contemptuous familiarity. When a ruler treats superior men with such familiarity, he cannot get them to give him all their hearts; when he so treats inferior men, he cannot get them to put forth for him all their strength. Let him keep from being in bondage to his ears and eyes, and strive to be correct in all his measures. By trifling intercourse with men, he ruins his virtue; by finding his amusement in things of mere pleasure, he ruins his aims. His aims should repose in what is right; he should listen to words also in their relation to what is right.

"When he does not do what is unprofitable to the injury of what is profitable, his merit can be completed. When he does not value strange things and scorn things that are useful, his people will be able to supply all that he needs. Even dogs and horses that are not native to his country he will not keep. Fine birds and strange animals he will not nourish in his state. When he does not look on foreign things as precious, foreigners will come to him; when it is real worth that is precious to him, his own people near at hand will be in a state of repose.

"Oh! early and late never be but earnest. If you do not attend jealously to your small actions, the result will be to affect your virtue in great matters. In raising a mound of nine fathoms, the work may be unfinished for want of one basket of earth. If you really pursue this course which I indicate, the people will preserve their possessions and the throne will descend from generation to generation."

6. THE METAL-BOUND COFFER

This is the first appearance in the *Shu* of Tan, duke of Chou, a name famous in Chinese history. A man of both counsel and action, he was the legislator and consolidator of the Chou dynasty. Many consider him second only to Confucius.

The duke of Chou was the fourth of King Wen's ten sons. At least one son conspired against the new dynasty with the survivors of the Shang dynasty. Hsien, lord of Kuan, and two of the younger brothers spread false rumors about the duke of Chou's personal ambition.

This narrative is among the most famous in the *Shu* and has been retold countless times, the vindication of the duke of Chou unfolding along classic lines.

Within the document is a rare picture of one of the early rites of ancestorism. The *pi* was a flat disc with a hole representative of heaven in its center; the *kuei* was the ceremonial jade symbol of a duke. The ancestors that the duke of Chou petitions are King Wen, his father; King Chi, the father of Wen; and King T'ai, the father of Chi.

King Wu did not die until 1116 B.C., five years after the illness that caused the duke of Chou to conceive of dying in his stead. He was succeeded by his son Sung, to be known as King Ch'eng, then thirteen years old. The duke of Chou was to act as regent for seven years.

Document 6

Two years after the conquest of Shang, the king fell ill and was quite disconsolate. The two other great dukes[1] said, "Let us reverently consult the tortoise shell about the king."

But the duke of Chou said, "You must not so distress our former kings."

1. The two dukes not named were Shih, duke of Shao (to whom "The Hounds of Lü" was ascribed) and T'ai, lord of Ch'i.

He then took the business on himself and reared three altars of earth on the same cleared space. Having made another altar on the south of these, and facing the north, he took there his own position. Having put a round symbol of jade, *pi,* on each of the three altars and holding in his hands the long symbol of his own rank, *kuei,* he addressed the kings T'ai, Chi, and Wen.

The Grand Historiographer had written on tablets his prayer, which was to this effect: "Your great descendant is suffering from a severe and violent disease. If you three kings in heaven have the charge of watching over him, Heaven's great son, let me, Tan, be a substitute for his person. I was lovingly obedient to my father; I am possessed of many abilities and arts which fit me to serve spiritual beings. Your great descendant, on the other hand, has not so many abilities and arts as I, and is not so capable of serving spiritual beings. And moreover he was appointed in the hall of God to extend his aid all over the kingdom, so that he might establish your descendants in this lower earth. The people of the four quarters all stand in reverent awe of him. Oh! do not let that precious Heaven-conferred appointment fall to the ground, and all the long line of our former kings will also have one in whom they can ever rest at our sacrifices. I will now seek your decision from the great tortoise shell. If you grant me my request, I will take these symbols and this mace, and return and wait for your orders. If you do not grant it, I will put them by."

The duke then divined with the three tortoise shells and all were favorable. He opened with a key the place where the oracular responses were kept, looked at them, and they also were favorable. He said, "According to the form of the prognostic the king will take no injury. I, the Little Child, have got the renewal of his appointment from the three kings, by whom a long futurity has been consulted for. I have now to wait for the issue. They can provide for our One Man."

When the duke returned, he placed the tablets of the prayer in a metal-bound coffer and next day the king got better.

Afterward, upon the death of King Wu, the duke's elder brother, he of Kuan, and his younger brothers, spread a baseless report through the kingdom to the effect that the duke would do no good to the king's young son. On this the duke said to the two other great dukes, "If I do not take the law to these men, I shall not be able to make my report to the former kings."

He resided accordingly in the east for two years, when the criminals were taken and brought to justice. Afterward, he made a poem to present to the king and called it "The Owl." The king on his part did not dare to blame the duke.

In the autumn, when the grain was abundant and ripe but before it was reaped, Heaven sent a great storm of thunder and lightning, along with wind, by which the grain was broken down and great trees torn up. The people were greatly terrified. The king and great officers, all in their caps of state, proceeded to open the metal-bound coffer and examine the writings in it, where they found the words of the duke when he took on himself the business of being a substitute for King Wu. The two great dukes and the king asked the historiographer and all the other officers acquainted with the transaction about the thing, and they replied, "It was really thus. But ah! the duke charged us that we should not presume to speak about it."

The king held the writing in his hand and wept, saying, "We need not now go on reverently to divine. Formerly the duke was thus earnest for the royal house, but I, being a child, did not know it. Now Heaven has moved its terrors to display his virtue. That I, the Little Child, now go with my new views and feelings to meet him, is what the rules of propriety of our kingdom require."

The king then went out to the borders to meet the duke, when Heaven sent down rain and, by virtue of a contrary wind, the grain all rose up. The two great dukes gave orders to the people to take up the trees that had fallen and replace them. The year then turned out very fruitful.

7. THE GREAT ANNOUNCEMENT

This announcement is from the duke of Chou, who speaks now for the young King Ch'eng. The new dynasty has been troubled by a revolt among the wild tribes along the Huai, and this revolt has emboldened the survivors of Chou Hsin (Shou), conspiring with the disloyal sons of King Wen, to rise against the present king. The tranquilizing king is King Wu. The identities of the "ten men of worth," or if both references are to the same ten men, cannot be ascertained.

These disorders have occurred in the east, causing troubles in the west, which is the seat of government; therefore, a punitive expedition will be sent eastward.

Document 7

The king speaks to the following effect: "Ho! I make a great announcement to you, the princes of the many states, and to you, the managers of my affairs: we are unpitied, and Heaven sends down calamities on our house without the least intermission. It greatly occupies my thoughts that I, so very young, have inherited this illimitable patrimony with its destinies and domains. I cannot display wisdom and lead the people to prosperity; and how much less should I be able to reach the knowledge of the decree of Heaven! Yes, I who am but a little child am in the position of one who has to go through a deep water; I must go and seek where I can cross over. I must diffuse the elegant institutions of my predecessor and display the appointment which he received from Heaven; so shall I not be forgetful of his great work. Nor shall I dare to restrain the majesty of Heaven in sending down its inflictions on the criminals.

"The tranquilizing king left to me the great precious

139

tortoise shell, to bring into connection with me the intelligence of Heaven. I divined by it and it told me that there would be great trouble in the region of the west, and that the western people would not be still. Accordingly we have these senseless movements. Small and reduced as Yin now is, its prince greatly dares to take in hand its broken line. Though Heaven sent down its terrors on his house, yet knowing of the evils in our kingdom and that the people are not tranquil, he says, 'I will recover my patrimony.' And so he wishes to make our Chou a border territory again.

"One day there was a senseless movement and the day after ten men of worth appeared among the people, to help me to go forward to restore tranquillity and perpetuate the plans of my father. The great business I am engaging in will thus have a successful issue. I have divined also by the tortoise shell and always got a favorable response. Therefore I tell you, the princes of my friendly states, and you, the directors of departments, my officers, and the managers of my affairs, I have obtained a favorable reply to my divinations. I will go forward with you from all the states and punish those vagabond and transported ministers of Yin.

"But you the princes of the various states, and you the various officers and managers of my affairs, all retort, saying, 'The hardships will be great, that the people are not quiet has its source really in the king's palace and in the mansions of the princes in that rebellious state.[1] We little ones, and the old and reverend men as well, think the expedition ill-advised. Why does your Majesty not go con-

---

1. This is a reference to those brothers of the Duke of Chou who were traitorous and added to the troubles of the new government.

trary to the divinations?' I, in my youth, also think continually of these hardships, and say, Alas! these senseless movements will deplorably afflict the wifeless men and widows! But I am the servant of Heaven, which has assigned me this great task, and laid the hard duty on my person. I therefore, the young one, do not pity myself; and it would be right in you, the many officers, the directors of departments, and the managers of my affairs, to comfort me, saying, 'Do not be distressed with sorrow. We shall surely complete the plans of your tranquilizing father.'

"Yes, I, the little child, dare not disregard the charge of God. Heaven, favorable to the tranquilizing king, gave such prosperity to our small country of Chou. The tranquilizing king divined and acted accordingly, and so he calmly received his great appointment. Now when Heaven is evidently aiding the people, how much more should we follow the indications of the shell! Oh! the clearly intimated will of Heaven is to be feared: it is to help my great inheritance!"

The king says, "You, who are the old ministers, are fully able to remember the past; you know how great was the toil of the tranquilizing king. Where Heaven now shuts up our path and distresses us is the place where I must accomplish my work; I dare not but do my utmost to complete the plans of the tranquilizing king. It is on this account that I use such efforts to remove the doubts and carry forward the inclinations of the princes of my friendly states. And Heaven assists me with sincere expressions of sympathy, which I have ascertained among the people. How dare I but aim at the completion of the work formerly begun by the tranquilizer? Heaven, moreover, is thus toiling and distressing the people: it is as if they were suffering from disease; how dare I allow the appointment which my predecessor, the tranquilizer, received, to be without its happy fulfillment?"

The king says, "Formerly, at the initiation of this expedition, I spoke of its difficulties, and thought of them daily. But when a deceased father, wishing to build a house had laid out the plan, if his son be unwilling to raise up the hall, how much less will he be willing to complete the roof! Or if the father had broken up the ground and his son be unwilling to sow the seed, how much less will he be willing to reap the crop! In such a case could the father, who had himself been so reverently attentive to his objects, have been willing to say, 'I have a son who will not abandon his patrimony?' How dare I therefore but use all my powers to give a happy settlement to the great charge entrusted to the tranquilizing king? If among the friends of an elder brother or a deceased father there be those who attack his son, will the elders of the people encourage the attack, and not come to the rescue?"

The king says, "Oh! take heart, ye princes of the various states, and ye managers of my affairs. The enlightening of the country was from the wise, even from the ten men who obeyed and knew the charge of God, and the real assistance given by Heaven. At that time none of you presumed to change the rules prescribed by the tranquilizing king. And now when Heaven is sending down calamity on the country of Chou and the authors of these great distresses make it appear on a grand scale as if the inmates of a house were mutually to attack one another, you are without any knowledge that the decree of Heaven is not to be changed!

"I ever think and say, Heaven in destroying Yin was doing husbandman's work; how dare I but complete the work on my fields? Heaven will thereby show its favor to my predecessor, the tranquilizer. How should I be all for the oracle of divination, and presume not to follow your advice? I am following the tranquilizer, whose purpose embraced all within the limits of the land. How much more must I proceed, when the divinations are all favorable! It is on these accounts that I make this expedition in force to the east. There is no mistake about the decree of Heaven. The indications given by the tortoise shell are all to the same effect."

8. THE CHARGE TO THE COUNT OF WEI

The count of Wei, brother of Chou Hsin (Shou), last sovereign of the Shang dynasty, was the principal personage in Document 11 of Part IV, "The Count of Wei." And it is supposed that King Wu had allowed the count of Wei continuance in his appanage.

Under ancestorism, it was not the custom completely to extinguish a lineage and its ancestral sacrifices. Under the Chou, representatives from both Hsia and Shang were denominated guests of the king and came to his court to assist in the services in the ancestral temple. Wu Keng, son of Chou Hsin, had been entrusted with the duty of continuing the sacrifices to T'ang and other great sovereigns of the line of Shang.

However, in the revolt that called forth "The Great Announcement" (Document 7), Wu Keng had been active and was already put to death when the duke of Chou called the count of Wei to court and, in the name of the young King Ch'eng, invested him with the duchy of Sung. There he was to be the representative of the line of the departed kings of Shang. The genuineness of this document has been challenged.

Document 8

The king speaks to the following effect: "Ho! eldest son of the king of Yin, examining into antiquity, I find that the honoring of the virtuous belongs to their descendants who resemble them in worth, and I appoint you to continue the line of the kings your ancestors, observing their ceremonies and taking care of their various relics. Come also as a guest to our royal house and enjoy the prosperity of our kingdom, for ever and ever without end.

"Oh! your ancestor, T'ang the Successful, was reverent and sage, with a virtue vast and deep. The favor and help

144

of great Heaven lighted upon him and he grandly received its appointment, to soothe the people by his gentleness and remove the wicked oppressions from which they were suffering. His achievements affected his age and his virtue was transmitted to his posterity. And you are the one who pursues and cultivates his plans; this praise has belonged to you for long. Reverently and carefully have you discharged your filial duties; gravely and respectfully you behave to spirits and to men. I admire your virtue and pronounce it great and not to be forgotten. God will always enjoy your offerings; the people will be reverently harmonious under your sway. I raise you therefore to the rank of high duke, to rule this eastern part of our great land.

"Be reverent. Go and diffuse abroad your instructions. Be carefully observant of your robes and other accompaniments of your appointment; follow and observe the proper statutes; thus to prove a bulwark to the royal house. Enlarge the fame of your meritorious ancestor; be a law to your people; thus for ever to preserve your dignity. So also shall you be a help to me, the One Man; future ages will enjoy the benefit of your virtue; all the states will take you for a pattern; thus you will make our dynasty of Chou never weary of you.

"Oh! go and be prosperous. Do not disregard my charge."

9. THE ANNOUNCEMENT TO THE PRINCE OF K'ANG

Feng was the ninth son of King Wen, generally referred to as K'ang Shu, K'ang being the name of his appanage. This document is called an announcement but is nevertheless a charge to Feng upon his appointment to be marquis of Wei, where the capital of Chou Hsin (Shou), last sovereign of the Shang dynasty, was located. The marquisate of Wei is not to be confused with the count of Wei's principality, also named Wei.

The opening paragraph is out of place and appears again later (Part V, Document 13). This has occasioned some doubts about the genuineness of the document. Also, it is not clear whether the king referred to is King Wu or the duke of Chou speaking for the young King Ch'eng, who would be nephew to the prince of K'ang. Either assumption poses problems, but Legge felt that to assume the duke of Chou was speaking for the young king presented fewer problems. Though the duke speaks as a deputy of the king, he nevertheless addresses the prince of K'ang as his younger brother.

Document 9

In the third month, when the moon began to wane, the duke of Chou commenced the foundations, and proceeded to build the new great city of Lo, of the eastern states. The people from every quarter assembled in great harmony. From the Hou, Tien, Nan, Ts'ai, and Wei domains, the various officers stimulated this harmony of the people and introduced them to the business there was to be done for Chou. The duke encouraged all to diligence, and made a great announcement about the performance of the works.

The king speaks to this effect: "Head of the princes, and my younger brother, little one, Feng: it was your greatly distinguished father, King Wen, who was able to illustrate his virtue and be careful in the use of punishments. He did not dare to treat with contempt even wifeless men and widows. He employed the employable and revered the reverent; he was terrible to those who needed to be awed: so getting distinction among the people. It was thus he laid the foundation of the sway of our small portion of the kingdom,[1] and one or two neighboring regions were brought under his improving influence, until throughout our western land all placed in him their reliance. The fame of him ascended up to the high God, and God approved. Heaven accordingly gave a grand charge to King Wen to exterminate the great dynasty of Yin and grandly receive its appointment, so that the various countries belonging to it and their peoples were brought to an orderly condition. Then your unworthy elder brother[2] exerted himself; and thus it is that you Feng, the little one, are here in this eastern region."

The king says, "Oh! Feng, bear these things in mind. Now your success in the management of the people will depend on your reverently following your father Wen; carry out his virtuous words which you have heard, clothe yourself with them. Moreover, where you go, seek out among the traces of the former wise kings of Yin what you may use in protecting and regulating their people. Again, you must in the remote distance study the ways of the old accomplished men of Shang, that you may establish your heart and know how to instruct the people. Further still, you must search out besides what is to be learned of the wise

1. This refers to the original principality of Chou.
2. The Karlgren translation does not carry the adjective "unworthy." Possibly all the sons of King Wen referred to each other as "unworthy" as a token of filial respect.

kings of antiquity and employ it in tranquilizing and protecting the people. Finally, enlarge your thoughts to the comprehension of all heavenly principles and virtue will be richly displayed in your person, so that you will not render worthless the king's charge."

The king says, "Oh! Feng, the little one, be respectfully careful, as if you were suffering from a disease. Awful though Heaven be, it yet helps the sincere. The feelings of the people can for the most part be discerned; but it is difficult to preserve the attachment of the lower classes. Where you go, employ all your heart. Do not seek repose, nor be fond of ease and pleasure. I have read the saying, 'Dissatisfaction is caused not so much by great things, or by small things, as by a ruler's observance of principle or the reverse, and by his energy of conduct or the reverse.' Yes, it is yours, O little one—it is your business to enlarge the royal influence, and harmoniously to protect this people of Yin. Thus also shall you assist the king, consolidating the appointment of Heaven and renovating this people."

The king says, "Oh! Feng, deal reverently and intelligently in your infliction of punishments. When men commit crimes which are purposed and not by chance, intentionally doing what is contrary to the laws, they must be put to death even though their crimes be small. But in the case of great crimes which are not purposed but from mischance and misfortune, accidental, you must not put them to death if the transgressors confess their guilt without reserve."

The king says, "Oh! Feng, there must be orderly regulation of this matter. When you show a great discrimination, subduing men's hearts, the people will admonish one another and strive to be obedient. Deal firmly yet tenderly with evil, as if it were a disease in your own person, and the people will entirely put away their faults. Deal with them as if you were protecting your own infants, and the people will be tranquil and orderly: it is not you, O Feng, who can presume to inflict a severe punishment or death upon a man; do not, to please yourself, punish a man or put him to death." Moreover, he says, "It is not you, O Feng, who can presume to inflict a lighter punishment, cutting off a man's nose or ears; do not, to please yourself, cause a man's nose or ears to be cut off."

The king says, "In things beyond your immediate supervision, have laws set forth which the officers may observe; these should be the penal laws of Yin which were rightly ordered." He also says, "In examining the evidence in criminal cases, reflect upon it for five or six days, yea, for ten days or three months. You may then boldly come to a decision in such cases."

The king says, "In setting forth the business of the laws, the punishments will be determined by what were the regular laws of Yin. But you must see that those punishments, and especially the penalty of death, be righteous. And you must not let them be warped to agree with your own inclinations, O Feng. Then shall they be entirely accordant with right, and you may say, 'They are properly ordered'; yet you must say at the same time, 'Perhaps they are not yet entirely accordant with right.' Yes, though you are the little one, who has a heart like you, O Feng? My heart and my virtue are also known to you.

"All who of themselves commit crimes, robbing, stealing, practicing villainy and treachery, and who kill men or violently assault them to take their property, being reckless and fearless of death—these are abhorred by all."

The king says, "O Feng, such great criminals are greatly abhorred, and how much more detestable are the unfilial and unbrotherly—as the son who does not reverently discharge his duty to his father, but greatly wounds his father's heart, and the father who can no longer love his son, but hates him; as the younger brother who does not think of the manifest will of Heaven, and refuses to respect his elder brother, and the elder brother who does not think of the toil of their parents in bringing up their children, and is very unfriendly to his junior. If we who are charged with government do not treat parties who proceed to such wickedness as offenders, the laws of our nature given by Heaven to our people will be thrown into great disorder and destroyed. You must resolve to deal speedily with such according to the penal laws of King Wen, punishing them severely and not pardoning.

"Those who are disobedient to natural principles are to be thus subjected to the laws; much more so are the officers employed in your state as the instructors of the youth, the heads of the official departments, and the smaller officers charged with their several commissions, when they propagate other lessons seeking the praise of the people, not thinking of their duty, nor using the rules for their offices, but distressing their ruler! These lead on the people to wickedness, and are an abomination to me. Shall they be let alone? Let you quickly, according to what is recognized right, put them to death.

"And you will be yourself ruler and president. If you cannot manage your own household, with your smaller officers, and the heads of departments in the state, but use only terror and violence, you will greatly set aside the royal charge and try to regulate your state contrary to virtue. You must in everything reverence the statutes and proceed by them to the happy rule of the people. There were the reverence of King Wen and his caution; in proceeding by them to the happy rule of the people, say, 'If I can only attain to them.' So will you make me, the One Man, to rejoice."

The king says, "O Feng, when I think clearly of the people, I see that they should be led by example to happiness and tranquillity. I think of the virtue of the former wise kings of Yin, whereby they tranquilized and regulated the people, and rouse myself to realize it. Moreover, the people now are sure to follow a leader. If one does not lead them, he cannot be said to exercise a government in their state."

The king says, "O Feng, I cannot dispense with the inspection of the ancients, and I make this declaration to you about virtue in the use of punishments. Now the people are not quiet; they have not yet stilled their minds; notwithstanding my leading of them, they have not come to accord with my government. I clearly consider that severe as are the inflictions of Heaven on me, I dare not murmur. The crimes of the people, whether they are great or many, are all chargeable to me; and how much more shall this be said when the report of them goes up so manifestly to heaven!"

The king says, "Oh! Feng, be reverent! Do not do what will cause murmurings; do not use bad counsels and uncommon ways. With the determination of sincerity, give yourself to imitate the active virtue of the ancients. Hereby give repose to your mind, examine your virtue, send far forward your plans; and thus by your generous forbearance you will make the people repose in what is good and I shall not have to blame you or cast you off."

The king says, "Oh! you, Feng, you little one, Heaven's appointments are not unchanging. Think of this and do not make me deprive you of this honor. Make illustrious the charge which you have received; exalt the instructions which you have heard. And tranquilize and regulate the people accordingly."

The king speaks to this effect: "Go, Feng. Do not disregard the statutes you should reverence; ponder what I have told you; so shall you among the people of Yin enjoy honor and hand it down to your posterity."

10. THE ANNOUNCEMENT ABOUT DRUNKENNESS

This document, like the last, is a further charge to Feng at the time of his investiture.

There is a tradition that the first *chiu* (spirits) were made by Tu K'ang, who is today one of the gods of wine merchants. Another tradition places the first use of wine with Yü, who drank some and found it very pleasant, but set it aside with the prediction that states would be lost because of *chiu*.

The Karlgren translation uses the word "wine" and implies fermentation. The Legge translation uses the word "spirits" and implies distillation from rice to produce "ardent spirits." This announcement sets forth the conditions that sanction the use of spirits and goes on to stress the possible evils.

Document 10

The king speaks to the following effect: "Let you clearly make known my great commands in the country of Mei.[1]

"When your reverent father, the king Wen, laid the foundation of our kingdom in the western region, he delivered announcements and cautions to the princes of the various regions, and to all his high officers with their assistants, and the managers of affairs, saying, morning and evening, 'At sacrifices spirits should be employed.' When Heaven was sending down its favoring decree and laying the foundation of the eminence of our people, spirits were used only at the great sacrifices. When Heaven sends down its terrors and our people are thereby greatly disorganized and lose their virtue, this may be traced invariably to their

---

1. The country of Mei had been the domain of Shang north of the capital. Feng's principality must have included most of it.

indulgence in spirits. Yea, the ruin of states, small and great, has been caused invariably by their guilt in the use of spirits.

"King Wen admonished and instructed the young nobles who were charged with office, or in any employment, that they should not ordinarily use spirits; and throughout all the states he required that they should be drunk only on occasion of sacrifices, and that then virtue should preside so that there might be no drunkenness."

He said, "Let my people teach their young men that they are to love only the productions of the soil, for so will their hearts be good. Let the young also listen wisely to the constant instructions of their fathers; and let them look at all virtuous actions, whether great or small, in the same light.

"Ye people of the land of Mei, if you can employ your limbs cultivating your millet, and hastening about in the service of your fathers and elders; and if, with your carts and oxen, you traffic diligently to a distance that you may thereby filially minister to your parents; then when your parents are happy you may set forth your spirits clear and strong and use them.

"Listen constantly to my instructions, all ye my high officers and ye heads of departments, all ye, my noble chiefs: when ye have largely done your duty in ministering to your aged and serving your ruler, ye may eat and drink freely and to satiety. And to speak of greater things: when you can maintain a constant, watchful examination of yourselves and your conduct is in accord with correct virtue, then may you present the offerings of sacrifice and at the same time indulge yourselves in festivity. In such case you will indeed be ministers doing right service to your king, and Heaven likewise will approve your great virtue, so that you shall never be forgotten in the royal house."

The king says, "O Feng, in our western region, the princes of states and the young nobles, sons of the managers of affairs, who in former days assisted King Wen, were all able to obey his lessons and abstain from excess in the use of spirits; and so it is that I have now received the appointment which belonged to Yin."

The king says, "O Feng, I have heard it said that formerly the first wise king of Yin manifested a reverent awe of the bright principles of Heaven and of the lower people, acting accordingly, steadfast in his virtue, and holding fast his wisdom. From him, T'ang the Successful, down to Ti Yi,[2] all completed their royal virtue and revered their chief ministers, so that their managers of affairs respectfully discharged their helping duties and dared not to permit themselves idleness and pleasure; how much less would they dare to indulge themselves in drinking! Moreover, in the exterior domains, the princes of the Hou, Tien, Nan, and Wei states with their presiding chiefs, and in the interior domain all the various officers, directors of the several departments, inferior officers and employees, heads of great houses, and the men of distinguished name living in retirement, all eschewed indulgence in spirits. Not only did they not dare to indulge in them, but they had not leisure to do so, being occupied with helping to complete the sovereign's virtue and make it more illustrious, and helping the directors of affairs reverently to attend to his service.

"I have heard it said likewise, that the last successor of those kings was addicted to drink. No charges came from him brightly before the people, and he was as if reverently and unchangingly bent on doing and cherishing what provoked resentment. Greatly abandoned to extraordinary

2. Ti Yi was the twenty-seventh sovereign of the Shang dynasty and the father of Chou Hsin, its last ruler.

lewdness and dissipation, for pleasure's sake he sacrificed all his majesty. The people were all sorely grieved and wounded in heart; but he gave himself wildly up to drink, not thinking of restraining himself but continuing his excess until his mind was frenzied and he had no fear of death. His crimes accumulated in the capital of Shang. Though the extinction of the dynasty was imminent, this gave him no concern and he wrought not that any sacrifices of fragrant virtue might ascend to Heaven. The rank odor of the people's resentments and the drunkenness of his herd of creatures went loudly up on high, so that Heaven sent down ruin on Yin and showed no love for it—because of such excesses. There is not any cruel oppression of Heaven; people themselves accelerate their guilt and its punishment."

The king says, "O Feng, I make you this long announcement, not for the pleasure of doing so. But the ancients have said, 'Let not men look into water; let them look into the mirror of other people.' Now that Yin has lost its appointment, ought we not to look much to it as our mirror, and learn how to secure the repose of our time? I say to you: strenuously warn the worthy ministers of Yin and the princes in the Hou, the Tien, the Nan, and the Wei domains; and still more your friends, the great Recorder and the Recorder of the Interior, and all your worthy ministers, the heads of great houses; and still more those whom you serve, with whom you calmly discuss matters, and who carry out your measures; and still more those who are, as it were, your mates: your minister of War who deals with the rebellious, your minister of Instruction who is like a protector to the people, and your minister of Works who settles the boundaries; and above all: let you strictly keep yourself from drink.

"If you are informed that there are companies that drink together, do not fail to apprehend them all and send them here to Chou, where I may put them to death. As to the ministers and officers of Yin who were led to it and became addicted to drink, it is not necessary to put them to death at once; let them be taught for a time. If they follow these lessons of mine, I will give them bright distinction. If they disregard my lessons, then I, the One Man, will show them no pity. As they cannot change their way, they shall be classed with those who are to be put to death."

The king says, "O Feng, give constant heed to my admonitions. If you do not rightly manage the officers, the people will continue lost in drunkenness."

11. THE TIMBER OF THE TZU TREE

Legge found this document lacking in unity and said of it that it was the translator's greatest comfort that it was short. There are two breaks in the text marked by ellipses.

The first part may be taken as a further charge to Feng, prince of K'ang, and marks the last appearance of Feng in the *Shu*. The second part is of a different character, possibly the counsels of a minister.

The tzu tree, mentioned in the document, is the *Rottlera japonica,* prized by wood carvers. The character, according to Wieger, also means plank, wood, fellow citizen. In the Karlgren translation it becomes the catalpa tree.

Document 11

The king says, "O Feng, to secure a good understanding between the multitudes of his people and his ministers on the one hand, and the great families on the other; and again: to secure the same between all the subjects under his charge and the sovereign—is the part of the ruler of a state.

"If you regularly, in giving out your orders, say, 'My instructors whom I am to follow, my minister of Instruction, my minister of War, and my minister of Works; my heads of departments, and all ye, my officers, I will on no account put any to death oppressively. . . .' Let the ruler also set the example of respecting and encouraging the people, and these will also proceed to respect and encourage them. Then let him go on, in dealing with villainy and treachery, with murderers and harborers of criminals, to exercise clemency where it can be done, and these will likewise do the same with those who have assaulted others and injured their property. When sovereigns appointed overseers of states, they did so in order to the government of the people, and said to them, 'Do not give way to violence or oppression, but go on to show reverent regard for the friendless, and find helping connections for destitute women.' Deal with all according to this method and cherish them. And when sovereigns gave their injunctions to the rulers of states, and their managers of affairs, what was their charge? It was that they should lead the people to the enjoyment of plenty and peace. Such was the way of the kings of old. An overseer is to eschew the use of punishments."

The king says, "As in the management of a field, when the soil has been all laboriously turned up, they have to proceed by orderly arrangements to make its boundaries and water-courses; as in building a house, after all the toil on its walls, they have to plaster and thatch it; as in working with the wood of the rottlera, when the toil of the coarser and finer operations has been completed, they have to apply the paint of red and other colors. . . . So do you finish for me the work which I have begun in the state of Wei."

Now let your majesty say, "The former kings diligently employed their illustrious virtue, and produced such attachment by their cherishing of the princes, that from all the states they brought offerings, and came with brotherly affection from all quarters, and likewise showed their virtue illustrious. Let you, O sovereign, use their methods to attach the princes, and all the states will largely come with offerings. Great Heaven having given this Middle Kingdom with its people and territories to the former kings, let you, our present sovereign, display your virtue, effecting a gentle harmony among the deluded people, leading and urging them on; so also will you comfort the former kings, who received the appointment from Heaven.

"Yes, make these things your study. I say so simply from my wish that your dynasty may continue for myriads of years, and your descendants always be the protectors of the people."

12. THE ANNOUNCEMENT OF THE DUKE OF SHAO

Shih, assumed to be one of King Wen's ten sons, was duke of Shao. Shao was a region within the royal domain and Shih's appanage. He was one of the ablest among the Chou to aid in establishing the new dynasty. He was appointed Grand Guardian of the young King Ch'eng and has appeared in "The Hounds of Lü" and "The Metal-bound Coffer."

We assume the announcement that forms the subject of this document to have been composed by Shih, duke of Shao, and taken by his brother Tan, duke of Chou, to the young king, their nephew.

King Wu had planned an eastern capital but did not live to carry this plan out. The first part of the document is concerned with the new capital.

The second part of the document reviews the two previous dynasties and their founders Yü and T'ang; the young king is urged to seek the virtues of the meritorious sovereigns of Hsia and Shang. The subject of sovereign responsibility, which had been mentioned previously only in the tersest language or by oblique reference, is here expanded into a discourse on the decree of Heaven. The young King Ch'eng is reminded of kingly perils, the need for reverence as a resting place for the mind, and the responsibility attached to the decree of Heaven.

In the concluding part, the duke of Shao humbly states the purpose of his announcement.

Document 12

In the second month, on the day *yi-wei,* six days after full moon, the king went in the morning from Chou to Feng.[1] Thence the Grand Guardian preceded the duke of

1. King Ch'eng went from King Wu's capital of Hao to that of King Wen's at Feng.

Chou to survey the locality of the new capital. In the third month, on the day *wu-shen,* the third day after the first appearance of the moon on *ping-wu,* he came in the morning to Lo. He divined by the tortoise shell about the several localities and, having obtained favorable indications, he set about laying out the plan of the city. On *keng-hsü,* the third day after, he led the people of Yin to prepare the various sites on the north of the Lo. This work was completed on *chia-yin,* the fifth day after.

On *yi-mao,* the day following, the duke of Chou came in the morning to Lo and thoroughly inspected the plan of the new city. On *ting-ssu,* the third day after, he offered two bulls as victims in the northern and southern suburbs. On the morrow, *wu-wu,* at the altar to the spirit of the land in the new city, he sacrificed a bull, a ram, and a boar. After seven days, on *chia-tzu* in the morning, he gave their several orders to the people of Yin, and the presiding chiefs of the princes from the Hou, Tien, and Nan domains, from his written specifications. When the people of Yin had thus received their orders they arose and entered with vigor on their work.

When the work was drawing to a completion, the Grand Guardian went out with the hereditary princes of the various states to bring their offerings for the king. When he returned he gave them to the duke of Chou, saying, "With my hands to my head and my head to the ground, I present these to his Majesty and your Grace. Announcements for the information of the multitudes of Yin must come from you, with whom is the management of affairs.

"Oh! God dwelling in the great heavens has changed his decree respecting his great son and the great dynasty of Yin. Our king has received that decree. Unbounded is the happiness connected with it, and unbounded is the anxiety. Oh! how can he be other than reverent?

"When Heaven rejected and made an end of the decree in favor of the great dynasty of Yin, there were many of its former wise kings in Heaven. The king, however, who had succeeded to them, the last of his race, from the time of his entering into their appointment, proceeded in such a way as to keep the wise in obscurity and the vicious in office. The poor people in such a case, carrying their children and leading their wives, made their moan to Heaven. They even fled, but were apprehended again. Oh! Heaven had compassion on the people of the four quarters; its favoring decree lighted on our earnest founders. Let the king sedulously cultivate the virtue of reverence.

"Examining the men of antiquity, there was Yü, founder of the Hsia dynasty. Heaven guided his mind, allowed his descendants to succeed him, and protected them. He acquainted himself with Heaven, and was obedient to it. But in process of time the decree in his favor fell to the ground. So also is it now when we examine the case of Yin. There was the same guiding of its founder T'ang, who corrected the errors of Hsia, and whose descendants enjoyed the protection of Heaven. He also acquainted himself with Heaven, and was obedient to it. But now the decree in favor of him has fallen to the ground. Our king has now come to the throne in his youth. Let him not slight the aged and experienced, for it may be said of them that they have studied the virtuous conduct of the ancients and have matured their counsels in the sight of Heaven.

"Oh! although the king is young, yet he is the eldest son of Heaven. Let him effect a great harmony with the lower people and that will be the blessing of the present time.

Let not the king presume to be remiss in this but continually regard and stand in awe of the perilous uncertainty of the people's attachment.

"Let the king come here as the vice-regent of God and undertake the duties of government in this center of the land. Tan said, 'Now that this great city has been built, from henceforth he may be the mate of great Heaven, and reverently sacrifice to the spirits above and below; henceforth he may from this central spot administer successful government.' Thus shall the king enjoy the favoring regard of Heaven all complete, and the government of the people will now be prosperous.

"Let the king first bring under his influence those who were the managers of affairs under Yin, associating them with the managers of affairs for our Chou. This will regulate their perverse natures and they will make daily advancement. Let the king make reverence the resting place of his mind; he must maintain the virtue of reverence.

"We should by all means survey the dynasties of Hsia and Yin. I do not presume to know and say, 'The dynasty of Hsia was to enjoy the favoring decree of Heaven just for so many years,' nor do I presume to know and say, 'It could not continue longer.' The fact was simply that, for want of the virtue of reverence, the decree in its favor prematurely fell to the ground. Similarly, I do not presume to know and say, 'The dynasty of Yin was to enjoy the favoring decree of Heaven just for so many years,' nor do I presume to know and say, 'It could not continue longer.' The fact simply was that, for want of the virtue of reverence, the decree in its favor fell prematurely to the ground. The king has now inherited the decree—the same decree, I consider, which belonged to those two dynasties. Let him seek to inherit the virtues of their meritorious sovereigns; let him do this especially at this commencement of his duties.

"Oh! it is as on the birth of a son, when all depends on the training of his early life through which he may secure his wisdom in the future, as if it were decreed to him. Now Heaven may have decreed wisdom to the king; it may have decreed good fortune or bad; it may have decreed a long course of years; we only know that now is the commencement of his duties. Dwelling in this new city, let the king now sedulously cultivate the virtue of reverence. When he is fully devoted to this virtue, he may pray to Heaven for a long-abiding decree in his favor.

"In the position of king let him not, because of the excesses of the people in violation of the laws, presume also to rule by the violent infliction of death; when the people are regulated gently, the merit of government is seen. It is for him who is in the position of king to overtop all with his virtue. In this case the people will imitate him throughout the kingdom and he will become still more illustrious.

"Let the king and his ministers labor with a mutual sympathy, saying, 'We have received the decree of Heaven and it shall be great as the long-continued years of Hsia; yea, it shall not fail of the long-continued years of Yin.' I wish the king, through the attachment of the lower people, to receive the long-abiding decree of Heaven."

The duke of Shao then did obeisance with his hands to his head and his head to the ground, and said, "I, a small minister, presume with the king's heretofore hostile people and all their officers, and with his loyal friendly people, to maintain and receive his majesty's dread command and brilliant virtue. That the king should finally obtain the decree all complete, and that he should become illustrious—this I do not presume to labor for. I only bring respectfully these offerings[2] to present to his majesty, to be used in his prayers to Heaven for its long-abiding decree."

2. These offerings were the presents that princes brought to court when they sought audience with the king. We read early in the document that in this case Prince Shih, Grand Guardian and duke of Shao, had gone out with hereditary princes to the various states and returned with the offerings. Possibly this was done to test the loyalties of the various states.

13. THE ANNOUNCEMENT
CONCERNING LO

The document opens with the repetition of the misplaced section that preceded Document 9, "The Announcement to the Prince of K'ang."

The substance of this document is presented as a dialogue between the duke of Chou and King Ch'eng concerning the eastern capital. Probably it was an exchange of communications written down by Yi, Recorder to King Ch'eng. The writings begin with the characters denoting the kowtow (". . . with his hands to his head and his head to the ground . . . ") as salutations. The duke of Chou addresses his nephew King Ch'eng as his son.

In the exchanges in this document there is a sense of urgency about attending to the details of inaugurating the administration of the Chou dynasty from the city of Lo. But there is also a serene sense of confidence, or the duke of Chou would not have stated, "Henceforth I will study husbandry."

This indicates his retirement as regent and the turning over of the government to King Ch'eng, who would have been not yet twenty years old (assuming that he came to the throne at thirteen and that the duke of Chou was regent for seven years).

The sense of urgency could well stem from the conspiracy that arose among some of King Wen's ten sons upon the death of King Wu; all of which inspired Legge to a masterly summing up of a highly complex situation:

Wu died 1115 B.C. and was succeeded by his son Sung, whose reign dates from 1115 B.C. and who is known in history as Ch'eng the Completer. Ch'eng was only thirteen years old and the duke of Chou acted as his regent. It was natural he should do so, for he was the ablest of all the sons of Wen and had been devotedly

167

attached to his brother Wu, whose chief advisor he had been, and was without the shadow of any disloyal feeling.

The accession of dignity and influence which he now received, however, moved his elder brother Hsien and some of his other brothers to envy, and they had come to be engaged in a treasonable conspiracy against the throne.

We have seen how Wu, after the death of the tyrant Shou, pardoned Shou's son, generally known by the name of Wu Keng, and continued him in Yin to maintain the sacrifices to the kings of his line. To guard against the very probable contingency of rebellion, however, he placed three of his own brothers in the state with him with the title of Overseers, who should overawe both Wu Keng and old ministers of Shou. Those overseers were Hsien, known as Kuan Shu, older than the duke of Chou; Tu, known as Ts'ai Shu, immediately younger than the duke; and Ch'u, known as Ho Shu, the eighth of Wen's sons.

Perhaps Hsien thought that on the death of Wu the regency, if not the throne, should have devolved upon him. Mencius ascribed his appointment as Overseer as made upon the advice of the duke of Chou. This may have exasperated Hsien the more against his brother who had thus shelved him, he would think, away from the court. However it was induced, soon after the death of Wu, those three brothers entered into a conspiracy with Wu Keng to throw off the yoke of the new dynasty.

The serene sense of confidence rose from the fact that the conspiracy had been crushed and that other problems in the new dynasty were being solved.

The document does not make entirely clear whether King Ch'eng journeyed twice to the new city or only once. It is clear, however, that he did not remain in Lo (sometimes referred to as Ch'eng Chou), but returned to the capital at Hao. It is also clear that the duke of Chou's retirement to husbandry did not take place immediately.

Rivers that were mentioned in "The Tribute to Yü" appear again, this time with the character denoting water (*shui*).

Document 13

In the third month, when the moon began to wane, the duke of Chou commenced the foundations and proceeded to build the new great city of Lo of the eastern states. The people from every quarter assembled in great harmony. From the Hou, Tien, Nan, Ts'ai, and Wei domains, the various officers stimulated this harmony of the people and introduced them to the business that was to be done for Chou. The duke encouraged all to diligence and made a great announcement about the performance of the works.

The duke of Chou did obeisance with his hands to his head and his head to the ground, saying, "Herewith I report the execution of my commission to my son, my intelligent sovereign. The king appeared as if he would not presume to be present at Heaven's founding here the appointment of our dynasty, and fixing it, whereupon I followed the Grand Guardian and made a great survey of this eastern region, hoping to found the place where he should become the intelligent sovereign of the people. On the day *yi-mao,* I came in the morning to this capital of Lo. I first divined by the shell concerning the ground about the Li water on the north of the Ho. I then divined concerning the east of the Chien water, and the west of the Ch'an, when the ground near the Lo was indicated. Again I divined concerning the east of the Ch'an water, when the ground near the Lo was also indicated. I now send a messenger with a map, and to present the result of the divinations."

The king did obeisance with his hands to his head and his head to the ground, saying, "The duke acknowledged reverently the favor of Heaven, and has surveyed the locality where our Chou may respond to that favor. Having settled the locality, he has sent his messenger to show me the divinations, favorable and always auspicious. We two must together sustain the responsibility. He has made provision for me and my successors for myriads and tens of myriads of years, there reverently to acknowledge the favor of Heaven. With my hands to my head and my head to the ground, I receive his instructive words."

The duke of Chou said, "Let the king at first employ the ceremonies of Yin and sacrifice in the new city, doing everything in an orderly way but without display. I will marshall all the officers to attend you from Chou, merely saying that probably there will be business to be done in sacrificing. Let the king instantly issue an order to the effect that the most meritorious ministers shall have the first place in the sacrifices; and let him also say in an order, 'You, in whose behalf the above order is issued, must give me your assistance with sincere earnestness.' Truly display the record of merits, for it is you who must in everything teach the officers. My young son, can you indulge partiality? Eschew it, my young son. If you do not, the consequence hereafter will be like a fire which, a spark at first, blazes up and cannot be extinguished. Let your observance of the constant rules of right and your soothing measures be like mine. Take only the officers that are in Chou with you to the new city and make them there join their old associates, with intelligent vigor establishing their merit and with a generous largeness of soul completing the public manners; so shall you obtain an endless fame."

The duke said, "Yes, young as you are, be it yours to complete the work of your predecessors. Cultivate the spirit of reverence and you will know who among the princes sincerely present their offerings to you, and who do not. In connection with those offerings there are many observances. If the observances are not equal to the articles, it must be held that there is no offering. When there is no service of the will in the offerings of the princes, all the people will then say, 'We need not be troubled about our offerings,' and affairs will be disturbed by errors and usurpations.

"Let you, my young son, manifest everywhere my un-wearied diligence, listen to my instructions to you how to help the people observe the constant rules of right. If you do not bestir yourself in these things, you will not be of long continuance. If you sincerely and fully carry out the course of your directing father, and follow exactly my ex-ample, there will be no venturing to disregard your orders. Go, and be reverent. Henceforth I will study husbandry. There do you generously rule our people and there is no distance from which they will not come to you."

The king spoke to this effect, "O duke, you are the en-lightener and sustainer of my youth. You have set forth the great and illustrious virtues that I, notwithstanding my youth, may display a brilliant merit like that of Wen and Wu, reverently responding to the favoring decree of Heaven, to harmonize and long preserve the people of all the regions, settling the multitudes in Lo; and that I may give due honor to the great ceremony of recording the most distinguished for their merits, regulating the order for the first places at the sacrifices, and doing everything in an orderly manner without display.

"But your virtue, O duke, shines brightly above and be-low and is displayed actively throughout the four quarters. On every hand appears the deep reverence of your virtue in securing the establishment of order, so that you fail in none of the earnest lessons of Wen and Wu. It is for me, the youth, only to attend reverently, early and late, to the sacrifices."

The king said, "Great, O duke, has been your merit in helping and guiding me. Let it ever continue so."

The king said, "O duke, let me, the Little Child, return to my sovereignty in Chou and I charge you, O duke, to remain behind here. Order has been initiated throughout the four quarters of the kingdom, but the ceremonies to be honored by general observance have not yet been settled; I cannot look on your service as completed. Commence on a great scale what is to be done by your remaining here, setting an example to my officers and greatly preserving the people whom Wen and Wu received. By your good government you will be a help to the whole kingdom."

The king said, "Remain, O duke. I will certainly go. Your services are devoutly acknowledged and reverently rejoiced in. Do not, O duke, occasion me this difficulty. I on my part will not be weary in seeking the tranquillity of the people. Do not let the example which you have afforded me cease. So shall the kingdom enjoy for generations the benefit of your virtue."

The duke of Chou did obeisance with his hands to his head and his head to the ground, saying, "You have charged me, O king, to come here. I undertake the charge and will protect the people whom your accomplished grandfather, and your glorious and meritorious father King Wu, received by the decree of Heaven. I will enlarge the reverence which I cherish for you. But my son, come frequently and inspect this settlement. Pay great honor to old statutes and to the good and wise men of Yin. Good government here will make you indeed the new sovereign of the kingdom, and an example of royal respectfulness to all your successors of Chou."

The duke proceeded to say, "From this time, by the government administered in this central spot, all the states will be conducted to repose. And this will be the completion of your merit, O king.

"I, Tan, with the numerous officers and managers of affairs, will consolidate the achievements of our predecessors in response to the hopes of the people. I will afford an example of sincerity to future ministers of Chou, seeking to render complete the pattern intended for the enlightenment of you, my son, and thus to carry fully out the virtue of your accomplished grandfather."

Afterwards, on the arrival of a message and gifts from the king, the duke said, "The king has sent messengers to admonish the people of Yin, and with a soothing charge to me, along with two flagons of the black-millet herb-flavored spirits, saying, 'Here is a pure sacrificial gift, which with my hands to my head and my head to the ground I offer for you to enjoy its excellence!' I dare not keep this by me, but offer it in sacrifice to King Wen and King Wu." In doing so, he prayed, "May he be obedient to, and observant of your course! Let him not bring on himself any evil or illness! Let him satisfy his descendants for myriads of years with your virtue! Let the people of Yin enjoy prolonged prosperity!" He also said to the messengers, "The king has sent you to Yin and we have received his well-ordered charges, sufficient to direct us for myriads of years. But let the people ever be able to observe the virtue cherished by my son."

On the day *wu-ch'en,* the king, being in the new city, performed the annual winter sacrifice, offering moreover one red bull to King Wen and another to King Wu. He then ordered a declaration to be prepared, which was done by Yi in the form of a prayer, and it simply announced the remaining behind of the duke of Chou. The king's guests, on occasion of the killing of the victims and offering the sacrifice, were all present. The king entered the grand apartment and poured out the libation. He gave a charge to the duke of Chou to remain and Yi, the preparer of the document, made the announcement in the twelfth month. Thus through the space of seven years the duke of Chou grandly sustained the decree which Wen and Wu had received.

14. THE NUMEROUS OFFICERS

This document is classed among the announcements and is addressed to the numerous officers of the previous dynasty who had been resettled in the new city of Lo. Here are the usual justifications of the attack on the Shang dynasty with persuasions to its survivors to cooperate in the establishment of the new government.

Document 14

In the third month, at the commencement of the government in the new city of Lo, the duke of Chou announced the royal will to the officers of the Shang dynasty, saying, "The king speaks to this effect: 'Ye numerous officers who remain from the dynasty of Yin, great ruin came down on Yin from the cessation of forbearance in compassionate Heaven and we, the lords of Chou, received its favoring decree. We felt charged with its bright terrors, carried out the punishments which kings inflict, rightly disposed of the appointment of Yin, and finished the work of God. Now, ye numerous officers, it was not our small state that dared to aim at the appointment belonging to Yin. But Heaven was not with Yin, for indeed it would not strengthen its misrule. It therefore helped us. Did we dare to seek the throne of ourselves? God was not for Yin, as appeared from the mind and conduct of our inferior people, in which there is the brilliant dreadfulness of Heaven.'

"I have heard the saying, 'God leads men to tranquil security,' but the sovereign of Hsia would not move to such security, whereupon God sent down corrections indicating his mind to him. Chieh, however, would not be warned by God but proceeded to greater dissoluteness and sloth and excuses for himself. Then Heaven no longer regarded nor heard him but took away his great appointment and inflicted extreme punishment. Then Heaven charged your founder, T'ang the Successful, to set Hsia aside and by means of able men to rule the kingdom. From T'ang the Successful down to Ti Yi, every sovereign sought to make his virtue illustrious and duly attended to the sacrifices. And thus it was that, while Heaven exerted a great establishing influence, preserving and regulating the house of Yin, its sovereigns on their part were humbly careful not to lose the favor of God and strove to manifest conduct corresponding to that of Heaven. But in these times, their successor showed himself greatly ignorant of the ways of Heaven; much less could it be expected of him that he would be regardful of the earnest labors of his fathers for the country. Greatly abandoned to dissolute idleness, he gave no thought to the bright principles of Heaven and the awfulness of the people. On this account God no longer protected him but sent down the great ruin which we have witnessed. Heaven was not with him because he did not make his virtue illustrious. Indeed, with regard to the overthrow of all states, great and small, throughout the four quarters of the kingdom, in every case reasons can be given for their punishment.

"The king speaks to this effect: 'Ye numerous officers of Yin, the case now is this, that the kings of our Chou, from their great goodness, were charged with the work of God. There was the charge to them: "Cut off Yin." They proceeded to perform it, and announced the execution of their service to God. In our affairs we have followed no double aims. Ye of the royal house of Yin must now simply follow us.

" 'May I not say that you have been very lawless? I did not want to remove you. The thing came from your own city. When I consider also how Heaven has drawn near to Yin with so great tribulations, it must be that what was there was not right.'

"The king says, 'Ho! I declare to you, ye numerous officers, it is simply on account of these things that I have removed you and settled you here in the west;[1] it was not that I, the One Man, considered it a part of my virtue to interfere with your tranquillity. The thing was from Heaven; do not offer resistance; I shall not presume to have any subsequent charge concerning you; do not murmur against me. Ye know that your fathers of the Yin dynasty had their archives and statutes, showing how Yin superseded the appointment of Hsia. Now, indeed, ye say further, "The officers of Hsia were chosen and employed in the royal court of Shang and had their duties among the mass of its officers." But I, the One Man, listen only to the virtuous and employ them; and it was with this view that I ventured to seek you in your capital of Shang once sanctioned by Heaven, and removed you here to Lo. I thereby follow the ancient example and have pity on you. Your present nonemployment is no fault of mine; it is the decree of Heaven.'

"The king says, 'Ye numerous officers, formerly, when I came from Yen, I greatly mitigated the penalty and spared the lives of the people of your four states.[2] At the same time I made evident the punishment appointed by Heaven, and removed you to this distant abode, that you might be near the ministers who had served in our honored capital, and learn their much obedience.'

---

1. Lo was the eastern capital of Chou, but the officers of the previous dynasty who resettled in Lo were west of their capital of Chao-ko.
2. Yen was the region to which the duke of Chou had gone to put down the revolt that resulted from the conspiracy of Wu Keng, son of Chou Hsin (Shou), and the duke's brothers Kuan Shu, Ts'ai Shu, and Ho Shu. The four states were the principalities of the four traitors.

"The king says, 'I declare to you, ye numerous officers of Yin, I have not put you to death and therefore I reiterate the declaration of my charge. I have now built this great city here in Lo, considering that there was no central place in which to receive my guests from the four quarters and also that you, ye numerous officers, might here with zealous activity perform the part of ministers to us, with the obedience ye would learn. Ye have still here, I may say, your grounds and may still rest in your duties and dwellings. If you can reverently obey, Heaven will favor and compassionate you. If you do not reverently obey, you shall not only lose your lands, but I will also carry to the utmost Heaven's inflictions on your persons. Now you may here dwell in your villages and perpetuate your families; you may pursue your occupations and enjoy your years in this Lo; your children also will prosper; all from your being removed here.'

"The king says, 'Whatsoever I may now have spoken is on account of my anxiety about your residence here.' "

15. AGAINST LUXURIOUS EASE

As the duke of Chou looks toward the time that he will turn over the government to King Ch'eng, he comments on some of the previous rulers and their reigns. From earliest time, diligence was singled out as a primary virtue, and a life of ease was considered the open door to vices. This document is classed among the instructions.

Document 15

The duke of Chou said, "Oh! the superior man rests in this: that he will indulge in no luxurious ease. He first understands how the painful toil of sowing and reaping conducts to ease, and thus he understands how the lower people depend on this toil for their support. I have observed among the lower people that where the parents have diligently labored in sowing and reaping, their sons often do not understand this painful toil but abandon themselves to ease, and to village slang, and become quite disorderly. Or where they do not do so, they still throw contempt on their parents, saying, 'Those old people have heard nothing and know nothing.'"

The duke of Chou said, "Oh! I have heard that aforetime T'ai Wu, one of the kings of Yin, was grave, humble, reverent, and timorously cautious. He measured himself with reference to the decree of Heaven and cherished a reverent apprehension in governing the people, not daring to indulge in useless ease. It was thus that he enjoyed the throne seventy and five years.

"If we come to the time of Wu Ting, he toiled at first away from the court and among the lower people. When he came to the throne and occupied the mourning shed, it may be said that he did not speak for three years. Afterwards he was still inclined not to speak; but when he did speak, his words were full of harmonious wisdom. He did not dare to indulge in useless ease but admirably and tranquilly presided over the regions of Yin until throughout them all, small and great, there was not a single murmur. It was thus that he enjoyed the throne fifty and nine years. In the case of Tsu Chia, he refused to be king unrighteously, and was at first one of the lower people.[1] When he came to the throne, he knew on what they must depend for their support and was able to exercise a protecting kindness toward their masses. He did not dare to treat with contempt the wifeless men and widows. Thus it was that he enjoyed the throne thirty and three years.

"The kings that arose after these from their birth enjoyed ease. Enjoying ease from their birth, they did not know the painful toil of sowing and reaping, and had not heard of the hard labors of the lower people. They sought for nothing but excessive pleasure; and so not one of them had long life. They reigned for ten years, for seven or eight, for five or six, or perhaps only for three or four."

The duke of Chou said, "Oh! there likewise were King T'ai and King Chi of our own Chou, who were humble and reverently cautious. King Wen dressed meanly, gave himself to the work of tranquilization and to husbandry. Admirably mild and beautifully humble, he cherished and protected the inferior people and showed a fostering kindness to the wifeless men and widows. From morning to midday, and from midday to sundown, he did not allow himself leisure to eat; thus seeking to secure the happy harmony of the myriads of the people. King Wen did not

1. The Karlgren translation states that Tsu Chia was preceded to the throne by two brothers; he had not expected to reign.

dare to go to excess in his excursions or his hunting, and from the various states he would receive only the correct amount of contribution. The appointment of Heaven came to him in the middle of his life, and he enjoyed the throne for fifty years." [2]

The duke of Chou said, "Oh! from this time forward, let you who have succeeded to the throne imitate Wen's avoiding of excess in sightseeing, indulgence in ease, excursions, hunting; and from the myriads of the people receive only the correct amount of contribution. Do not allow yourself the leisure to say, 'Today I will indulge in pleasure.' This would not be holding out a lesson to the people, nor the way to secure the favor of Heaven. Men will on the contrary be prompt to imitate you and practice evil. Become not like Shou the king of Yin, who went quite astray and became abandoned to drunkenness."

The duke of Chou said, "Oh! I have heard it said that, in the case of the ancients, their ministers warned and admonished them, protected and loved them, taught and instructed them; and among the people there was hardly one who would impose on them by extravagant language or deceiving tricks. If you will not listen to this and profit by it, your ministers will imitate you and the correct laws of the former kings, both small and great, will be changed and disordered. The people, blaming you, will disobey and rebel in their hearts; yea, they will curse you with their mouths."

The duke of Chou said, "Oh! those kings of Yin, T'ai Wu, Wu Ting, and Tsu Chia, with King Wen of our Chou —these four men carried their knowledge into practice. If it was told them, 'The lower people murmur against you and revile you,' then they paid great and reverent attention to their conduct. With reference to the faults imputed to

2. A reference to Wen's becoming Chief of the West in 1185 B.C.

them they said, 'Our faults are really so,' thus not simply shrinking from the cherishing of anger. If you will not listen to this and profit by it, when men with extravagant language and deceptive tricks say to you, 'The lower people are murmuring against you and reviling you,' you will believe them. Doing this, you will not be always thinking of your princely duties and will not cultivate a large and generous heart. You will confusedly punish the guiltless and put the innocent to death. There will be a general murmuring, concentrated upon your person."

The duke of Chou said, "Oh! let the king, who has succeeded to the throne, make a study of these things."

16. THE PRINCE SHIH

King Ch'eng, the young son of Wu the tranquilizing king, was sustained by two uncles: Shih, duke of Shao and the Grand Guardian, and Tan, duke of Chou, the regent. The duke of Chou had already expressed his wish for retirement; now his brother, the duke of Shao, has apparently expressed a similar desire.

It is natural that the duke of Chou, in setting forth these declarations to persuade his brother to remain active in the affairs of the new government, should refer to past ministers. We assume that the two brothers had long been harmoniously associated for the common good and had experienced together the good auspices of "the voices of phoenixes."

The document is classified as an announcement. Two possible breaks in the text are indicated by ellipses.

Document 16

The duke of Chou spoke to the following effect: "Prince Shih, unpitying Heaven sent down ruin on Yin. Yin has lost its appointment to the throne, which our house of Chou has received. I do not dare, however, to say as if I knew, 'The foundation will ever truly abide in prosperity. If Heaven aid sincerity . . .' Nor do I dare to say, as if I knew, 'The end will issue in our misfortunes.' Oh! you have said, O prince, 'It depends on ourselves.' I also do not dare to rest in the favor of God, not forecasting at a distance the terrors of Heaven in the present time, when there is no murmuring or disobedience among the people . . . the issue is with men. Should our present successor to his fathers prove greatly unable to reverence Heaven above and the people below, and so bring to an end the glory of his predecessors, could we in the retirement of our families be ignorant of it? The favor of Heaven is not easily preserved;

183

Heaven is difficult to count on. Men lose its favoring appointment because they cannot pursue and carry out the reverence and brilliant virtue of their forefathers. Now I, Tan, the Little Child, am not able to make the king correct. I can only conduct him to the glory of his fathers and make him who is my young charge partaker of that." He also said, "Heaven is not to be depended on. Our course is only to seek the prolongation of the virtue of the tranquilizing King Wu, that Heaven may not find occasion to remove its favoring decree which King Wen received."

The duke said, "Prince Shih, I have heard that aforetime, when T'ang the Successful had received the appointment to the throne, he had with him I Yin, making his virtue like that of great Heaven; that T'ai Chia had the same I Yin; that T'ai Wu had I Chih and Ch'en Hu through whom his virtue was made to affect God, and Wu Hsien who regulated the royal house; that Tsu Yi had Wu Hsien's son; and that Wu Ting had Kan P'an. These ministers carried out their principles, and displayed their merit, preserving and regulating the dynasty of Yin. While its ceremonies lasted, those sovereigns became counterparts to Heaven when deceased; and Yin's duration extended over many years. Heaven thus determinately maintained its favoring appointment and Shang was replenished with men. The various heads of great surnames and members of the royal house, holding employments, all held fast their virtue and showed an anxious solicitude for the kingdom. The smaller ministers, and the guardian princes in the Hou and Tien domains, hurried about on their services. Thus did they all exert their virtue and aid their sovereign so that whatever affairs he, the One Man, had in hand throughout the land, an entire faith was reposed in their justice as in the indications of the shell or the divining stalks."

The duke said, "Prince Shih, Heaven gives length of days to the just and the intelligent. It was thus that those ministers maintained and regulated the dynasty of Yin. Chou Hsin, who came last to the throne granted by Heaven, was extinguished by its terrors. If you but think of the distant future, we shall have the decree in favor of Chou made sure; and its good government will be brilliantly exhibited in our newly-founded state."

The duke said, "Prince Shih, aforetime when God was inflicting calamity on Yin, he encouraged anew the virtue of the tranquilizing king, till at last the great favoring decree was concentrated in his person. But that King Wen was able to conciliate and unite the portion of the great kingdom which we came to possess, was owing to his having such ministers as his brother of Ko, Hung Yao, San Isheng, T'ai Tien, and Nan-kung Kuo."

He said further, "But for the ability of those men to go and come in his affairs, developing his constant lessons, there would have been no benefits descending from King Wen on the people. And it also was from the determinate favor of Heaven that there were these men of firm virtue, acting according to their knowledge of the dread majesty of Heaven, to give themselves to enlighten King Wen and lead him forward to his high distinction and universal rule, until his fame reached the ears of God and he received the appointment that had been Yin's. There were still four of those men who guided King Wu to the possession of the revenues of the kingdom and afterward, along with him, in great reverence of the majesty of Heaven, slew all his enemies. These four men, moreover, made King Wu so illustrious that his glory overspread the kingdom and the people universally and greatly proclaimed his virtue. Now with me Tan, the Little Child, it is as if I were floating on a great stream. With you, O Shih, let me from this time endeavor to cross it. Our young sovereign is powerless, as if he had not yet ascended the throne. You must by no means lay the whole burden on me. If you draw yourself up without an effort to supply my deficiencies, no good will flow to the people from our age and experience. We shall not hear the voices of the phoenixes, and how much less can it be thought that we shall be able to make the king's virtue equal to Heaven!"

The duke said, "Oh! consider well these things, O prince. We have received the appointment to which belongs an unlimited amount of blessing, but it has great difficulties attached to it. What I announce to you are counsels of a generous largeness. I cannot allow the successor of our kings to go astray."

The duke said, "The former king laid bare his heart and gave full charge to you, constituting you one of the guides and patterns for the people, saying, 'Let you with intelligence and energy second and help the king; let you with sincerity support and convey forward the great decree. Think of the virtue of King Wen and enter greatly into his boundless anxieties.' "

The duke said, "What I tell you, O prince, are my sincere thoughts. O Shih, Grand Guardian, if you can but reverently survey with me the decay and great disorders of Yin and thence consider the dread majesty of Heaven which warns us! Am I not to be believed, that I must reiterate my words? I simply say, 'The establishment of our dynasty rests with us two.' Do you agree with me? Then you also will say, 'It rests with us two.' And the favor of Heaven has come to us so generously—it should be ours to feel as if we could not sufficiently respond to it. If you can but reverently cultivate your virtue now, and bring to light our men of eminent ability, then when you resign your position to some successor in a time of established security, I will interpose no objection.

"Oh! it is by the earnest service of us two that we have come to the prosperity of the present day. We must both go on, abjuring all idleness, to complete the work of King Wen until it has grandly overspread the kingdom, until from the corners of the sea and the sunrising, there shall not be one who is disobedient to the rule of Chou."

The duke said, "O prince, have I not spoken in accord with reason in these many declarations? I am only influenced by anxiety about the appointment of Heaven, and about the people."

The duke said, "Oh! you know, O prince, the ways of the people, how at the beginning they can be all we could desire. But it is the end that is to be thought of. Act in careful accord with this fact. Go and reverently exercise the duties of your office."

17. THE CHARGE TO CHUNG OF TS'AI

After the death of Ts'ai Shu (one of the conspirators against the new dynasty mentioned in Document 13, "The Announcement Concerning Lo"), his son Hu, Chung of Ts'ai, was enfeoffed with his father's territory of Ts'ai.

The first part of the document serves as an introduction to the charge, which is given by the duke of Chou speaking for the king. Hu and King Ch'eng were both grandsons of King Wen; the duke of Chou was a mutual uncle.

The charge itself conforms to two ideals of ancient China: that no line should ever be entirely extinguished (this would terminate its sacrifices) and that sons should not be punished for their fathers' crimes. The genuineness of this document has been challenged.

Document 17

When the duke of Chou was in the place of prime minister and directed all the officers, the king's uncles spread abroad an evil report, in consequence of which the duke put to death the prince of Kuan in Shang; confined the prince of Ts'ai in Koh-lin with an attendance of seven chariots; and reduced the prince of Huo to be a private man, causing his name to be erased from the registers for three years. The son of the prince of Ts'ai having displayed a reverent virtue, the duke of Chou made him a high minister and, when his father died, requested a decree from the king investing him with the country of Ts'ai.

"The king speaks to this effect: 'My little child, Hu, you follow the virtue of our ancestors and have changed from the conduct of your father. You are able to heed your ways. I therefore appoint you to be a marquis in the east. Go to your fief, and be reverent!

" 'In order that you may cover the faults of your father, be loyal, be filial. Urge your steps in your own way, diligent and never idle, and so shall you hand down an example to your descendants. Follow the constant lessons of your grandfather King Wen, and be not, like your father, disobedient to the royal orders.

" 'Great Heaven has no partial affections; it helps only the virtuous. The people's hearts have no unchanging attachment; they cherish only the kind. Acts of goodness are different, but they contribute in common to good order. Acts of evil are different, but they contribute in common to disorder. Be cautious!

" 'In giving heed to the beginning think of the end. The end will then be without distress. If you do not think of the end, it will be full of distress—even of the greatest.

" 'Exert yourself to achieve your proper merit. Seek to be in harmony with all your neighbors. Be a bulwark to the royal house. Live in amity with your brothers. Tranquilize and help the lower people.

" 'Follow the course of the Mean and do not by aiming to be intelligent throw old statutes into confusion. Watch over what you see and hear. Do not, for one-sided words, deviate from the right rule. Then I, the One Man, will praise you.'

"The king says, 'Oh! my little child, Hu, go—and do not idly throw away my charge.' "

18. THE NUMEROUS REGIONS

From the documents in the *Shu,* we infer that submission to the new dynasty was gained by enfeoffing loyal nobles, by making punitive expeditions against rebellious factions, and by alternately persuading and threatening the general populace. This announcement was addressed to a large assembly of princes and nobles who were thought to be at least secretly sympathetic to the rebellion that had recently been put down. The occasion is King Ch'eng's triumphant return from Yen to his capital at Hao (Ch'eng never moved his residence from Hao to the city of Lo, also called Ch'eng Chou). The duke, as regent, speaks for the king.

Document 18

In the fifth month, on the day *ting-hai,* the king came from Yen to Hao, the honored capital of Chou. The duke of Chou said,

"The king speaks to the following effect: 'Ho! I make an announcement to you of the four states and the numerous other regions. Ye who were the officers and people of the prince of Yin, I have dealt very leniently·as regards your lives, as ye all know. You depended on the decree of Heaven and did not keep with perpetual awe before your thoughts the preservation of your sacrifices.

" 'God sent down correction on Hsia, but the sovereign only increased his luxury and sloth, and would not speak kindly to the people. He showed himself dissolute and dark, and would not yield for a single day to the guidance of God: this is what you have heard. He depended on the decree of God in his favor, and did not cultivate the means for the people's support. Also, by great inflictions of punishment he increased the disorder of the states of Hsia. The

190

first cause of his evil course was inner misrule, which made him unfit to deal well with the multitudes. Nor did he endeavor to find and employ men whom he could respect and who might display a generous kindness to the people; but where any of the people of Hsia were covetous and fierce, he daily honored them and they practiced cruel tortures in the cities. Heaven on this sought a true lord for the people, and made its distinguished and favoring decree light on T'ang the Successful, who punished and destroyed the sovereign of Hsia. Heaven's refusal of its favor to Hsia was decided. The righteous men of your numerous regions were not permitted to continue long in their posts of enjoyment. The many officers whom Hsia's last sovereign honored were unable intelligently to maintain the people in the enjoyment of their lives but, on the contrary, aided one another in oppressing them until of the hundred ways of securing prosperity they could not promote one.

" 'In the case indeed of T'ang the Successful, it was because he was the choice of your numerous regions that he superseded Hsia and became the lord of the people. He paid careful attention to the essential virtue of a sovereign in order to stimulate the people, and they on their part imitated him and were stimulated. From him down to Ti Yi, the sovereigns all made their virtue illustrious and were cautious in the use of punishments; thus also exercising a stimulating influence over the people. When they, having examined the evidence in criminal cases, put to death those chargeable with many crimes, they exercised the same influence; and they did so also when they liberated those who were not purposely guilty. But when the throne came to your last sovereign, he could not with the good will of your numerous regions continue in the enjoyment of the favoring decree of Heaven.'

"Oh! the king speaks to the following effect: 'I announce and declare to you of the numerous regions, that Heaven had no set purpose to do away with the sovereign of Hsia or with the sovereign of Yin. But it was the case that your last ruler, being in possession of your numerous regions, abandoned himself to great excess, and depended on the favoring decree of Heaven, making trifling excuses for his conduct. And so in the case of the last sovereign of Hsia; his plans of government were not of a tendency to secure his enjoyment of the kingdom. Heaven sent down ruin on him, and the chief of the territory of Shang put an end to the line of Hsia. In truth, the last sovereign of your Shang was luxurious to the extreme of luxury, while his plans of government showed neither purity nor progress. Thus Heaven sent down such ruin on him.

" 'The wise, through not thinking, become foolish; and the foolish, by thinking, become wise. Heaven for five years waited kindly and forbore with the descendant of T'ang, to see if he would indeed prove himself the ruler of the people; but there was nothing in him deserving to be regarded. Heaven then sought among your numerous regions, making a great impression by its terrors to stir up someone who would look reverently to it, but in all your regions there was not one deserving of its favoring regard. But there were the kings of our Chou, who treated well the multitudes of the people and were able to sustain the burden of virtuous government. They could preside over all services to spirits and to Heaven. Heaven thereupon instructed us, increased our excellence, made choice of us, and gave us the decree of Yin, to rule over your numerous regions.

" 'Why do I now presume to make these many declarations? I have dealt very leniently as regards the lives of you, the people of these four states. Why do you not show a sincere and generous obedience in your numerous regions? Why do you not aid and cooperate with the kings of our Chou, to secure the enjoyment of Heaven's favoring decree? You now still dwell in your dwellings and cultivate your fields; why do you not obey our kings and consolidate the decree of Heaven? The paths which you tread are continually those of unrest; have you in your hearts no love for yourselves? Do you refuse so greatly to acquiesce in the ordinance of Heaven? Do you triflingly reject that decree? Do you of yourselves pursue unlawful courses, scheming by your alleged reasons for the approval of upright men? I simply instructed you and published my announcement; with trembling awe I secured and confined the chief criminals. I have done so twice and for three times. But if you do not take advantage of the leniency with which I have spared your lives, I will proceed to severe punishments and put you to death. It is not that we, the sovereigns of Chou, hold it virtuous to make you untranquil; but it is you yourselves who accelerate your crimes and sufferings.'

"The king says, 'Oh! ho! I tell you, ye many officers of the various regions, and you, ye many officers of Yin, now have ye been hurrying about doing service to my overseers for five years. There are among you the junior assistants, the chiefs, and the numerous directors, small and great; see that ye all attain to the discharge of your duties. Want of harmony in the life rises from the want of it in one's inner self; strive to be harmonious. Want of concord in your families arises from the want of it in your conduct; strive to be harmonious. When intelligence rules in your cities, then will you be proved attentive to your duties. Do not be afraid, I pray you, of the evil ways of the people; and moreover, by occupying your offices with a reverent harmony, you will find it possible to select from your cities individuals on whose assistance you can count. You may thus long continue in this city of Lo cultivating your fields. Heaven will favor and compassionate you and we, the sovereigns of Chou, will greatly help you and confer rewards, selecting you to stand in our royal court. Only be attentive to your duties, and you may rank among our great officers.'

"The king says, 'Oh! ye numerous officers, if you cannot exhort one another to pay sincere regard to my charges, it will further show that you are unable to honor your sovereign; and all the people will also say, "We will not honor him." Thus will ye be proved slothful and perverse, greatly disobedient to the royal charges. Throughout your numerous regions you will bring on yourselves the terrors of Heaven and I will then inflict on you its punishments, removing you from your country.'

"The king says, 'I do not wish to make these many declarations, but it is in a spirit of awe that I lay my commands before you.' He further says, 'You may now make a new beginning. If you cannot reverently realize the harmony which I enjoin, do not hereafter murmur against me.'"

19. THE ESTABLISHMENT
OF GOVERNMENT

Some Chinese commentators find this document confused,
"head and tail in disorder, and without connection." We assume
that it was written after the duke of Chou had retired from the
regency. In the last paragraph, the duke of Chou addresses the
historiographer as if commenting upon the document he had
just composed. It is classified among the instructions.

Document 19

The duke of Chou spoke to the following effect: "With
our hands to our heads and our heads to the ground, we
make our declarations to the Son of Heaven, the king who
has inherited the throne."

In such manner accordingly all the other ministers cautioned the king, saying, "In close attendance on your majesty there are the regular presidents, the regular ministers,
and the officers of justice; the keepers of the robes also, and
the guards."

The duke of Chou said, "Oh! admirable are these officers. Few, however, know to be sufficiently anxious about
them.

"Among the ancients who exemplified this anxiety there
was Yü, founder of the Hsia dynasty. When his house was
in its greatest strength, he sought for able men who should
honor God in the discharge of their duties. His advisers,
when they knew of men thoroughly proved and trustworthy
in the practice of the nine virtues, would then presume to
inform and instruct their sovereign, saying, 'With our hands
to our heads and our heads to the ground, O sovereign, we
would say, Let such an one occupy one of your high offices:

Let such an one be one of your pastors: Let such an one be one of your officers of justice. By such appointments you will fulfill your duty as sovereign. If you judge by the face only, and therefrom deem men well schooled in virtue and appoint them, then those three positions will all be occupied by unrighteous individuals.' The way of Chieh, however, was not to observe this precedent. Those whom he employed were cruel men. And he left no successor.

"After this there was T'ang the Successful who, rising to the throne, grandly administered the bright ordinances of God. To fill the three high positions he employed those who were equal to them; and those who were called possessors of the three kinds of ability would display that ability. He then studied them strictly and greatly imitated them, making the utmost of them in their three positions and with their three kinds of ability. The people in the cities of Shang were thereby all brought to harmony, and those in the four quarters of the kingdom were brought greatly under the influence of the virtue thus displayed. Oh! when the throne came to Shou, his character was all violence. He preferred men of severity who deemed cruelty a virtue to share in the government of his states; and at the same time men who counted idleness a virtue shared the offices of his court. God then sovereignly punished him and caused us to possess the great land and enjoy the favoring decree, which Shou had received, and govern all the people in their myriad realms.

"Then subsequently there were King Wen and King Wu, who knew well the minds of those whom they put in the three positions and saw clearly the minds of those who had the three grades of ability. Thus they could employ them to serve God with reverence, and appointed them as presidents and chiefs of the people. In establishing their government, the three things which principally concerned them were to find the men for high offices, the officers of justice, and the pastors. They had also the guards; the keepers of the robes; their equerries; their heads of small departments; their personal attendants; their various overseers; and their treasurers. They had their governors of the larger and smaller cities assigned in the royal domain to the nobles; their men of arts,[1] their overseers whose offices were beyond the court; their grand historiographers; their heads of departments—all good men of constant virtue.

"In the external states there were the minister of Instruction, the minister of War, and the minister of Works, with the many officers subordinate to them. Among the wild tribes, such as the Wei, the Lu, and the Ch'eng, in the three Po[2] and at the dangerous passes, they had wardens.

"King Wen was able to make the minds of those in the three high positions his own. So it was that he established regular officers and superintending pastors who were men of ability and virtue. He would not appear himself in the various notifications, in litigations, and in precautionary measures. There were the officers and pastors to attend to them, whom he simply taught to be obedient to his wishes and not disobedient. Yea, as to litigations and precautionary measures, he would seem as if he did not presume to know about them. He was followed by King Wu, who carried out his work of settlement and did not presume to

1. In addition to the mechanical arts, those artists recognized in the service of government were officers of prayer, clerks, archers, charioteers, doctors, and diviners.
2. The three Po had been capitals of the Shang kings. The dangerous passes were routes of easy ingress into the kingdom by the wild tribes. Such passes were attended by wardens.

supersede his righteous and virtuous men; who entered into his plans and employed, as before, those men. Thus it was that they unitedly received this vast inheritance.

"Oh! young son, the king, from this time forth be it ours to establish the government, appointing the high officers, the officers of the laws, and the pastors; be it ours clearly to know what courses are natural to these men and then fully to employ them in the government, that they may aid us in the management of the people whom we have received and harmoniously conduct all litigations and precautionary measures. And let us never allow others to come between us and them. Yea, in our every word and speech, let us be thinking of these officers of complete virtue to regulate the people that we have received.

"Oh! I, Tan, have received these excellent words of others and tell them all to you, young son, the king. From this time forth, O accomplished son of Wu, accomplished grandson of Wen, do not err in regard to the litigations and precautionary measures; let the proper officers manage them. From of old to the founder of Shang, and downward to King Wen of our Chou, in establishing government, when they appointed high officers, pastors, and officers of the laws, they settled them in their positions, and allowed them to unfold their talents; thus giving the regulation of affairs into their hands. In the kingdom, never has there been the establishment of government by the employment of artful-tongued men; with such men, unlessoned in virtue, never can a government be distinguished in the world. From this time forth, in establishing government, make no use of artful-tongued men but seek for good officers and get them to use all their powers in aiding the government of our country. Now, O accomplished son of Wu, accomplished grandson of Wen, young son, the king, do not err in the matter of litigations; there are the officers and pastors to attend to them.

"Have well arranged also your military accouterments and weapons so that you may go beyond the steps of Yü and traverse all under the sky, even to beyond the seas, everywhere meeting with submission: so shall you display the bright glory of King Wen, and render more illustrious the great achievements of King Wu.

"Oh! from this time forth, may our future kings in establishing the government be able to employ men of constant virtue!"

The duke of Chou spoke to the following effect: "O Grand Historiographer, the duke of Su, the minister of Crime, dealt reverently with all the criminal matters that came before him and thereby perpetuated the fortunes of our kingdom. Here was an example of anxious solicitude for future ministers, whereby they may rank with him in the ordering of the appropriate punishments."

With this document, the duke of Chou passes from the pages of the *Shu ching*. Legge states, in one of his unstinting footnotes: "The duke of Chou was undoubtedly one of the greatest men whom China has produced; and I do not know the statesmen of any nation with whom his countrymen need shrink from comparing him." Legge also relates a legend that connects Tan, the duke of Chou, to the invention of the compass. This legend is included in selections from Legge's long quotation from P. De-Mailla, in his *Histoire Générale de la Chine*:

This same sixth year of his reign, King Ch'eng, after having established his different officers, received the news that the ambassadors of a foreign kingdom were come to bring him presents and do him homage. This kingdom, situated to the south of Cochin-China, had never sent anybody to China. The king gave orders that the ambassadors should be conducted to the court and that great honors everywhere should be paid to them.

The duke of Chou received them very well, treated them with distinction, and accepted their presents, among which was a white pheasant—a species heretofore unknown; after which he made the inquiry be put to them on what business they had come.

They replied by interpreters that the elders of their country said loudly that for three years they had had neither winds nor tempest, no unseasonable rains nor great waves of the sea, and that there must be some special cause for such favor of Heaven; that apparently the throne of China was occupied by a sage who had procured for them these benefits.

After that, the duke conducted them to the ancestral temple of the reigning family, where he caused to be displayed on the one side the presents which they had brought and on the other those which King Ch'eng was sending to their prince. Among these were five chariots of a new invention. They accommodated the travelers and at the same time indicated the route which they kept by means of a small box, made in the form of a pavilion or dome suspended from the roof, in which was a hand that always pointed to the south, whatever side the chariots might turn. It was on this account that they were called "chariot of the south."

This machine was very useful to the envoys for when they arrived on the borders of the sea they took to some barques and, by means of this compass, they needed only one year to return to their own kingdom.

This legend of the south-pointing chariots is one of several concerning the origin of the compass. The *Shu ching* makes no mention of these ambassadors from the south.

20. THE OFFICERS OF CHOU

This document outlines the official system of the Chou dynasty. Its genuineness, however, has been challenged.

It is classed among the instructions. The time is estimated to be in the ninth or tenth year of the reign of King Ch'eng, who would then be in his early twenties. The duke of Chou is in retirement, and King Ch'eng has assumed his kingly duties.

Document 20

The king of Chou brought the myriad regions of the kingdom to tranquillity; he made a tour of inspection through the Hou and Tien tenures; he punished on all sides the chiefs who had refused to appear at court; thus securing the repose of the millions of the people. All the princes in the six tenures acknowledged his virtue. He then returned to the honored capital of Chou and strictly regulated the officers of the administration.

The king said, "It was the grand method of former times to regulate the government while there was no confusion and to secure the country while there was no danger." He said, "Yao and Shun, having studied antiquity, established a hundred officers. At court, there were the General Regulator and the Chief of the Four Mountains; abroad, there were the pastors of the provinces and the princes of states. Thus the various departments of government went on harmoniously and the myriad states all enjoyed repose. Under the dynasties of Hsia and Shang, the number of officers was doubled and they were able still to secure good government. Those early intelligent kings, in establishing their government, cared not so much about the number of the offices as about the men to occupy them. Now I, the Little Child, cultivate with reverence my virtue, concerned day and night about my deficiencies. I look up to those former dynasties, and seek to conform to them while I instruct and direct you, my officers.

"I appoint the Grand Master, the Grand Assistant, and the Grand Guardian. These are the three *kung*.[1] They discourse about the principles of reason and adjust the states, harmonizing also and regulating the operations in nature of heaven and earth. These offices need not always be filled; there must first be the men for them.

"I appoint the Junior Master, the Junior Assistant, and the Junior Guardian. These are called the three *ku*. They assist the *kung* to diffuse widely the transforming influences, and display brightly with reverence the powers of heaven and earth—assisting me, the One Man.

"I appoint the prime minister, who presides over the ruling of the various regions, has the general management of all the other officers, and secures uniformity within the four seas; the minister of Instruction, who presides over the education in the states, diffuses a knowledge of the duties belonging to the five relations of society, and trains the millions of the people to obedience; the minister of Religion, who presides over the sacred ceremonies of the country, regulates the services rendered to the spirits and manes,[2] and makes a harmony between high and low; the minister of War, who presides over the military administration of the country, commands the six hosts, and secures the tranquillity of all the regions; the minister of Crime, who pre-

1. Literally, three dukes. The inference is that the work appointed by the sovereign to be done by three dukes had now been constituted as three offices of government.
2. Spirits and manes: spirits of heaven, earth, and the deceased.

sides over the prohibitions of the country, searches out the villainous and secretly wicked, and punishes oppressors and disturbers of the peace; and the minister of Works, who presides over the land of the country, settles the four classes of the people,[3] and secures at the proper seasons the produce of the ground.

"These six ministers with their different duties guide their several subordinates and set an example to the nine pastors of the provinces, enriching and perfecting the condition of the millions of the people. In six years the lords of the five tenures appear once at the royal court; after a second six years, the king makes a tour of inspection in the four seasons and examines the various regulations and measures at the four mountains. The princes appear before him each at the mountain of his quarter; advancements and demotions are awarded with great intelligence."

The king said, "Oh! all ye men of virtue, my occupiers of office, pay reverent attention to your charges. Be careful in the commands you issue for, once issued, they must be carried into effect and cannot be retracted. Extinguish all selfish aims by your public feeling and the people will have confidence in you and be gladly obedient. Study antiquity as a preparation for entering on your offices. In deliberating on affairs, form your determinations by help of such study and your measures will be free from error. Make the regular statutes of our own dynasty your rule; do not with artful speeches introduce disorder into your offices. To accumulate doubts is the way to ruin your plans; to be idle and indifferent is the way to ruin your government. Without study, you stand facing a wall and your management of affairs will be full of trouble.

3. The four classes of the people were the officers (scholars), farmers, laborers, and merchants.

"I warn you, my high ministers and officers, that exalted merit depends on the high aim; a patrimony is enlarged only by diligence; it is by means of bold decision that future difficulties are avoided. Pride comes along with rank, unperceived; and extravagance in the same way with emolument. Let reverence and economy be real virtues with you, unaccompanied with hypocritical display. Practice them as virtues and your minds will be at ease; you will daily become more admirable. Practice them in hypocrisy and your minds will be toiled; you will daily become more stupid. In the enjoyment of favor think of peril and never be without a cautious apprehension; he who is without such apprehension finds himself amidst what is really to be feared. Push forward the worthy and show deference to the able; and harmony will prevail among all your officers. When they are not harmonious the government becomes a mass of confusion. If those whom you advance be able for their offices, the ability is yours; if you advance improper men, you are not equal to your position."

The king said, "Oh! ye charged with the threefold business of government, and ye great officers, reverently attend to your departments and conduct well the affairs under your government, so as to assist your sovereign and secure the lasting happiness of the millions of the people; so shall there be no dissatisfaction throughout the myriad states."

21. THE CHÜN CH'EN

Between "The Officers of Chou" (Document 20 of Part V) and "The Chün Ch'en," two documents have been lost. The second contained the account of the death of Tan, duke of Chou, with the announcement made by King Ch'eng at his bier.

Now the duke's successor, Chün Ch'en, is appointed. This document is the charge to him delivered by King Ch'eng in the eastern capital of Ch'eng Chou, which had been built at Lo (Part V, Documents 13 and 14). We assume that Chün Ch'en, like the duke of Chou, will govern the conquered people of Yin from this capital. King Ch'eng always lived in his western capital at Hao, so we assume that following this charge the king returns to Hao. The time is about 1105–1100 B.C.

Nothing conclusive is known about the identity of Chün Ch'en except, by the evidence of his being called Chün, that he was a prince. No information about his principality is given. The genuineness of the document has been challenged.

Document 21

The king spoke to the following effect: "Chün Ch'en, it is you who are possessed of excellent virtue, filial and respectful. Being filial, and friendly with your brethren, you can display these qualities in the exercise of government. I appoint you to rule this eastern border. Be reverent.

"Formerly, the duke of Chou acted as teacher and guardian of the myriads of the people, who cherish the remembrance of his virtue. Go and with sedulous care enter upon his charge; act in accord with his regular ways; exert yourself to illustrate his lessons; so shall the people be regulated. I have heard that he said, 'Perfect government has a piercing fragrance and influences the spiritual intelligences. It is not the millet which has the piercing fragrance; it is

205

bright virtue.[1] Let you make this lesson of the duke of Chou your rule, being diligent from day to day and not presuming to indulge in luxurious ease. Ordinary men, when they have not yet seen a sage, are full of desire, as if they should never get a sight of him; and after they have seen him they are still unable to follow him. Be cautioned by this! You are the wind; the inferior people are the grass. In revolving the plans of your government, never hesitate to acknowledge the difficulty of the subject. Some things have to be abolished and some new things to be enacted; going out and coming in, seek the judgment of your people about them and, when there is a general agreement, exert your own powers of reflection. When you have any good plans or counsels, enter and lay them before your sovereign in the palace. Thereafter, when you are acting abroad in accord with them, say, 'This plan or this view is all due to our sovereign.' Oh! if all ministers were to act thus, how excellent would they be, how distinguished!"

The king said, "Chün Ch'en, give their full development to the great lessons of the duke of Chou. Do not make use of your power to exercise oppression; do not make use of the laws to practice extortion. Be gentle, but with strictness of rule. Promote harmony by the display of an easy forbearance.

"When any of the people of Yin are amenable to punishment, if I say 'Punish,' do not therefore punish; and if I say 'Spare,' do not therefore spare. Seek the due Mean. Those who are disobedient to your government and uninfluenced by your instructions, you will punish—remembering that the end of punishment is to make an end of punish-

1. There was a grass called *ch'ang* that was very fragrant and used to flavor spirits—in this case, spirits distilled from the black millet. According to Wieger, there was a sacrificial wine designated *ch'ang*.

ing. Those who are inured to villainy and treachery, those who violate the regular duties of society, and those who introduce disorder into the public manners: those three classes you will not spare, though their particular offenses be but small.

"Be not passionate with the obstinate and dislike them. Seek not every quality in one individual. You must have patience and you will be successful; have forbearance and your virtue will be great. Mark those who discharge their duties well and also mark those who do not. Advance the good to induce those who are not to follow their example.

"The people are born good and are changed by external things, so that they resist what their superiors command and follow what they themselves love. Let you but reverently observe all the statutes and they will become virtuous, they will thus all be changed and truly advance to a great degree of excellence. Then shall I, the One Man, enjoy much happiness and your excellent services will be famous through long ages!"

22. THE TESTAMENTARY CHARGE

King Ch'eng reigned for thirty-seven years. From "The Charge to Chün Ch'en" to this document, his reign is almost a blank. Ssu-ma Ch'ien chronicles only a coinage of round money with a square hole in the center and regulations concerning the making of cloth, which was to be in lengths of forty-four cubits, two cubits two inches wide.

"The Testamentary Charge" records the death and funeral of King Ch'eng. It is one of the most interesting, and difficult, sections in the entire *Shu*. But Legge found it possible, from diligent reading of the Chinese commentators—especially Chu Hsi—and close observation of Chinese architecture, to reconstruct for us the setting and events of this occasion, as whole animals are reconstructed from a few bones in the workrooms of museums. The following projection is culled from his voluminous notes.

The king lies ill in his private apartments at the palace. The palace is almost a city in itself. It is a series of buildings following one after another in a straight line through courtyards and gates. These gates were gates in name only, being large areas covered by roofs supported on pillars.

Each space in the palace has its special use. At ceremonies and sacrifices, the worthies were stationed according to prearranged plans. The Chou dynasty became increasingly ritualistic, with all activities becoming more and more formalized.

Outside the fifth gateway it was usual for the king to meet with his ministers on the business of government. Between this gate and the private apartments beyond was the hall where private audiences were granted and the sovereign feasted those whom he wished to honor. It is here that the dying king rallies himself to make his testamentary charge, which he delivers leaning forward against a stool. In general, people sat on mats, but stools were provided for the old or the ill to lean forward against.

208

His attendants have arrayed Ch'eng in his kingly garments and crown (ceremonial cap) to address his ministers. Among them is the Grand Guardian Shih, duke of Shao, brother of the deceased duke of Chou. The charge is given within a ceremonial tent of canopy and curtains set up outside the sovereign's private chamber. After the king has expressed his last wishes, this tent will be carried out into the courtyard to be used in the funeral.

When the king has died, it is time for his son Chao, who will be known as King K'ang, to participate in the rites and then, when the services are over, to retire to the mourning shed to remain for the period of mourning ("twenty-five months, nominally three years"). Shih, duke of Shao, makes these arrangements; the marquis of Ch'i ceremoniously conducts Chao to a side apartment, there to be chief mourner.

The testamentary charge will now be inscribed on tablets. But the sacrificial funeral rites will not be performed for seven days, when the deceased king will be shrouded and coffined. Many things are being done during this period before the actual funeral. Precious relics are brought out and arranged in special order; the meanings attached to many of these are now lost to us. There is mention made of "the great lessons," which may be the instructions written by the duke of Chou that King Ch'eng urged Chün Ch'en to illustrate by his actions. Four of the five royal chariots are brought in; possibly the one not admitted was the war chariot—to demonstrate that King Ch'eng will no longer go on punitive expeditions. Everything that is done, is done as if the king were still living.

In the revolving sphere that characterizes Chinese conceptual thought, the king, while giving his testamentary charge, was to be considered already dead; now dead, his presence is experienced as a living entity. We assume that these solemn preparations proceeded to the sound of musical stones, lutes, bamboo tubes, and rattle drums.

When the time for the sacrifices arrives, the Grand Guardian and the minister of Religion ascend to the hall by the east, or king's own, steps because the authority of King Ch'eng reposes in them, not as yet conveyed to his son. And the king's son Chao ascends to the hall using the guests' steps, being not yet sovereign.

There are two symbols of importance for the ceremonies. One is the cup that will hold the sacrificial wine, which, we suppose, will have been strained through the three-ribbed rush described in "The Tribute to Yü" as being brought in by tribute bearers. The other is the mace-cover, which has incised in it the counterfoils for the tokens of rank, perhaps the "five jade symbols of rank" we read of in "The Canon of Shun." The cup and the mace-cover will be passed to the new king by the minister of Religion.

Seven days have passed between the death of King Ch'eng and the raising of the sacrifice to him. Princes from the fiefs have come in, bringing gifts of horses for the new king, and offerings. The last of the funeral ceremonies is about to begin. All the worthies taking part understand the ritual, know where to stand, which way to face, what to do, when to begin, and the moment of stopping. Chao is standing at the top of the western steps with his face to the north. The historiographer stands by King Ch'eng's coffin with his face to the east to read the testamentary charge as delivered by King Ch'eng to his ministers.

In response to the historiographer, the new king bows twice. The minister of Religion, with his face to the north, now presents the cup and mace-cover to Chou's new sovereign; the favoring appointment of heaven is descending upon Chao, who will reign tranquilly for twenty-six years and will be known posthumously as King K'ang. Now he accepts the mace-cover, passes it to an attendant, and takes the cup. Three times he advances to the place between the pillars where the sacrificial spirits are waiting. Three times he fills the cup, goes to the east of the coffin, and stands with his face to the west. Three times he approaches a spot where the spirit of his father is thought to be, and there, three times, he sacrifices, pouring out the wine on the ground and three times placing the cup on a bench placed there for that purpose.

The Grand Guardian informs the spirit of the dead king that the testamentary charge has been communicated. The young king, by his sacrifice, has acknowledged the charge to the spirit of his father.

The services are over. The private apartments had, for this time, through the presence of the coffin and by means of the sacrifices, been converted into a sort of ancestral temple. The princes leave the hall and go out into a courtyard where they await audience of the new sovereign.

Document 22

In the fourth month, when the moon began to wane, the king was indisposed. On the day *chia-tzu* he washed his hands and face; his attendants put on him his cap and robes; and he sat up, leaning on a gem-adorned bench. He then called together the Grand Guardian Shih, the earls of Jui and T'ung, the duke of Pi, the marquis of Wei, the duke of Mao, the master of the warders, the master of the guards, the heads of the various departments, and the superintendents of affairs.

The king said, "Oh! my illness has greatly increased and it will soon be over with me. The malady daily comes on with more violence and maintains its hold. I am afraid I may not find another opportunity to declare my wishes about my successor; and therefore I now lay my charge upon you with special instructions. The former rulers, our kings Wen and Wu, displayed in succession their equal glory, making sure provision for the support of the people and setting forth their instructions. The people accorded a practical submission without any opposition and the influence of their example and instructions extended to Yin;

and the great appointment of Heaven was secured. After them, I, the stupid one, received with reverence the dread decree of Heaven, and continued to keep the great instructions of Wen and Wu, not daring blindly to transgress them.

"Now Heaven has laid affliction on me and it seems as if I should not again rise or be myself. Let you take clear note of these my words, and in accord with them watch reverently over my eldest son Chao, and greatly assist him in the difficulties of his position. Be kind to those who are far off and help those who are near. Promote the tranquillity of the states, small and great, and encourage them to well-doing. I think how a man has to govern himself in dignity and with decorum; do not allow Chao to proceed heedlessly on the impulse of improper motives."

Immediately on receiving this charge, the ministers and others withdrew. The tent was then carried out into the court; and on the next day, *yi-ch'ou,* the king died.

The Grand Guardian then ordered Chung Huan and Nan Kung Mao to instruct Lü Chi, the marquis of Ch'i, with two shield-and-spearmen and a hundred guards, to meet the prince Chao outside the south gate and conduct him to one of the side apartments near to that where the king lay, there to be as chief mourner.

On the day *ting-mao,* two days after the king's death, he ordered the charge to be recorded on tablets and the forms to be observed in publishing it. Seven days after, on *kuei-yu,* as Chief of the West and premier, he ordered the proper officers to prepare the wood for all the requirements of the funeral.

The serving men set out the screens, ornamented with figures of axes, and the tents. Between the window and the door, facing the south, they placed the threefold mat of fine bamboo splints with its striped border of white and black silk, and the usual bench adorned with different-colored gems. In the side-space on the west, which faced the east, they placed the threefold mat of fine grass with its border of painted silk and the usual bench carved and adorned with gems. Before the western side-chamber, and facing the south, they placed the threefold mat of fine bamboo with its dark mixed border and the usual lacquered bench.

They set forth also the five pairs of jade and the precious things of display. There were the red knife, the great lessons, the large round-and-convex symbol of jade, and the rounded and pointed maces—all in the side-space on the west; the large piece of jade, the pieces contributed by the wild tribes of the east, the heavenly musical stone, and the river plan[1]—all in the side-space on the east; the dancing habits of Yin, the large tortoise shell, and the large drum—all in the western apartment; the spear of Tui, the bow of Ho, and the bamboo arrows of Ch'ui—all in the eastern apartment.

The grand carriage was by the guests' steps facing the south; the next was the eastern or host's steps, facing the south. The front carriage was placed before the left lobby and the one that followed it before the right lobby.

Two men in brownish leather caps, holding three-cornered halberds, stood inside the gate leading to the private apartments. Four men in caps of spotted deerskin, holding spears with blades upturned from the base of the point, stood one on each side of the steps east and west and near to the platform of the hall. One man in a great officer's cap, and holding an axe, stood in the hall near the steps at the

1. The river plan, named here with the relics set out for this occasion, is sometimes called the Ho map. This is a reference to the dragon-horse that rose from the waters of the Ho and gave Fu Hsi the idea for the eight trigrams on which the *I ching, Book of Changes* is based.

east end. One man in a great officer's cap, and holding an axe of a different pattern, stood in the hall near the steps at the west end. One man in a great officer's cap, and holding a lance, stood at the front and east of the hall close by the steps. One man in a great officer's cap, and holding a lance of a different pattern, stood in the corresponding place on the west. One man in a great officer's cap, and holding a pointed weapon, stood by the steps on the north side of the hall.

The king, in a linen cap and the variously figured skirt, ascended by the guests' steps followed by the high ministers, great officers, and princes of states, in linen caps and dark-colored skirts. Arrived in the hall, they all took their proper places. The Grand Guardian, the Grand Historiographer, and the minister of Religion were all in linen caps and red skirts. The Grand Guardian bore the great mace. The minister of Religion bore the cup and the mace-cover. These two ascended by the steps on the east.

The Grand Historiographer bore the testamentary charge. He ascended by the guests' steps on the west and advanced to the king with the tablets containing the charge, and said, "Our royal sovereign, leaning on the gem-adorned bench, declared his last charge and commanded you to continue the observance of the lessons and to take the rule of the kingdom of Chou, complying with the great laws and securing the harmony of all under the sky, so as to respond to and display the bright instructions of Wen and Wu."

The king twice bowed low and then arose, and replied, "I am utterly insignificant and but a child, how should I be able to govern the four quarters of the kingdom with a corresponding reverent awe of the dread majesty of Heaven!" He then received the cup and the mace-cover. Thrice he slowly and reverently advanced with a cup of spirits to the east of the coffin; thrice he sacrificed to the spirit of his father; and thrice he put the cup down. The minister of Religion said, "It is accepted."

The Grand Guardian received the cup, descended the steps, and washed his hands. He then took another cup, placed it on a half-mace which he carried, and repeated the sacrifice. He then gave the cup to one of the attendants of the minister of Religion and did obeisance. The king returned the obeisance. The Grand Guardian took a cup again and poured out the spirits in sacrifice. He then just tasted the spirits, returned to his place, gave the cup to the attendant, and did obeisance. The king returned the obeisance. The Grand Guardian descended from the hall, after which the various sacrificial articles were removed and the princes all went out at the temple gate and waited.

23. THE ANNOUNCEMENT
OF KING K'ANG

King K'ang was the posthumous title conferred upon Chao; it has the meaning of "he who caused the people to be tranquil and happy." Chao reigned from 1078–53 B.C., the third sovereign of the Chou dynasty. He is not to be confused with Chao, the fourth sovereign of the Chou dynasty, whose reign is passed over in the documents of the *Shu*.

The time of this document is immediately after the solemn sacrificial services for King Ch'eng. The princes are waiting to greet the new king and offer their presents. Chao comes from the hall to make this announcement. The princes are ceremoniously ushered into the courtyard. The king addresses them as uncles, meaning particularly those who carry the same surname. But the term uncle often carries a further meaning of affectionate respect.

Following this announcement, the new king will enter his period of mourning, living outside the palace in a rough shed and afflicting himself with various austerities. The genuineness of this document has been challenged.

Document 23

The king came forth and stood in the space within the fourth gate of the palace. The Grand Guardian led in the princes of the western regions by the left half of the gate, and the duke of Pi those of the eastern regions by the right half. All the princes then caused their teams of light bay horses, with their manes and tails dyed red, to be exhibited and, as the king's guests, lifted up their rank-symbols and the other presents they had brought, saying, "We your servants, defenders of the throne, venture to bring the productions of our territories and lay them here." With

216

these words they all did obeisance twice, laying their heads on the ground. The king, as the righteous successor to the virtue of those who had gone before him, returned their obeisance.

The Grand Guardian and the earl of Jui, with all the rest, then advanced and bowed to each other; after which they did obeisance twice with their heads to the ground, and said, "O Son of Heaven, we venture respectfully to declare our sentiments. Great Heaven altered its decree which the great house of Yin had received, and Wen and Wu of our Chou grandly received the same and carried it out, manifesting their kindly government in the western regions. His recently ascended majesty King Ch'eng, rewarding and punishing exactly in accord with what was right, fully established their achievements and transmitted this happy state to his successors. Let you, O king, now be reverent. Maintain your armies in great order; and do not allow the rarely equalled appointment of our high ancestors to come to harm."

The king spoke to the following effect: "Ye princes of the various states, chiefs of the Hou, Tien, Nan, and Wei domains, I, Chao, the One Man, make an announcement in return for your advice. The former rulers Wen and Wu were greatly just and enriched the people. They did not occupy themselves to find out people's crimes. Pushing to the utmost and maintaining an entire impartiality and sincerity, they became gloriously illustrious all under heaven. Then they had officers brave as bears and grizzly bears, and ministers of no double heart, who helped them maintain and regulate the royal house. Thus did they receive the true favoring decree from God, and thus did great Heaven approve of their ways and give them the four quarters of the land. Then they appointed and set up principalities and established bulwarks to the throne for the sake of us, their successors.

"Now do you, my uncles, I pray you, consider with one another and carry out the service which the dukes, your predecessors, rendered to my predecessors. Though your persons be distant, let your hearts be in the royal house. Enter thus into my anxieties and act in accord with them so that I, the Little Child, may not be put to shame."

The dukes and all the others, having heard this charge, bowed to one another and hastily withdrew. The king put off his cap and assumed again his mourning dress.

24. THE CHARGE TO THE DUKE OF PI

Kao, the duke of Pi, was a scion of the house of Chou. He has appeared briefly in "The Testamentary Charge" and "The Announcement of King K'ang." At the time of this document he would have reached a venerable age. It is said that he served four kings: Wen, Wu, Ch'eng, and K'ang (Chao).

This charge is given by King K'ang to the duke upon his succession to the office of Grand Master. This office is not to be confused with that of Grand Guardian, which was filled by Shih, the duke of Shao. The duke of Chou had been Grand Master as well as regent; Chün Ch'en succeeded him; now the duke of Pi succeeds Chün Ch'en.

It is 1067 B.C. King K'ang (Chao, son of King Ch'eng) has occupied the throne for twelve years. The genuineness of this document has been challenged.

Document 24

In the sixth month of his twelfth year, the day of the new moon's appearance was *keng-wu,* and on *jen-shen,* the third day after, the king walked in the morning from Hao, the honored capital of Chou to Feng and there, with reference to the multitudes of Ch'eng Chou, gave charge to the duke of Pi to protect and regulate the eastern border.

The king spoke to the following effect: "Oh! Grand Master, it was when Wen and Wu had diffused their great virtue all under heaven, that they therefore received the appointment which Yin had enjoyed. The duke of Chou acted as assistant to my royal predecessors, tranquilized and established their kingdom. Cautiously did he deal with the refractory people of Yin, and removed them to the city of Lo,[1] that they might be quietly near the royal house and be

1. Ch'eng Chou.

transformed by its lessons. Six and thirty years have elapsed; the generation has been changed; manners have altered. Through the four quarters of the land there is no occasion for anxiety and I, the One Man, enjoy repose.

"The prevailing ways now tend to advancement and now to degeneracy, and measures of government must be varied according to the manners of the time. If you now do not manifest your approval of what is good, the people will not be led to stimulate themselves in it. But your virtue, O duke, is strenuous and you are cautiously attentive to the smallest things. You have been helpful to and brightened four reigns; with deportment all correct guiding the inferior officers so there is not one who does not reverently take your words as a law. Your admirable merits were many and great in the times of my predecessors; I, the Little Child, have but to let my robes hang down and fold my hands, while I look up for the complete effect of your measures."

The king said, "Oh! Grand Master, I now reverently charge you with the duties of the duke of Chou. Go! Signalize the good, separating the bad from them; give tokens of your approbation in their neighborhoods,[2] reducing the evil by distinguishing the good, thus establishing the influence and reputation of virtue. When the people will not obey your lessons and statutes, mark off the boundaries of their hamlets—making them fear to do evil, and desire to do good. Define anew the borders and frontiers and be careful to strengthen the guardposts through the territory, in order to secure tranquillity within the four seas.

"In measures of government to be consistent and constant, and in proclamations a combination of completeness

2. Tokens of approbation were inscribed monuments set up in conspicuous places. Setting up such testimonials continued into modern times.

and brevity, are valuable. There should not be the love of what is extraordinary. Among the customs of Shang was the flattery of superiors; sharp-tonguedness was the sign of worth. The remains of these manners are not yet obliterated. Let you, O duke, bear this in mind. I have heard the saying, 'Families which have for generations enjoyed places of emolument seldom observe the rules of propriety. They become dissolute and do violence to virtue, setting themselves in opposition to the way of Heaven. They ruin the formative principles of good; encourage extravagance and display; and tend to carry all future ages on the same stream with them.' Now the officers of Yin had long relied on the favor which they enjoyed. In the confidence of their prideful extravagance they extinguished their sense of righteousness. They displayed before men the beauty of their robes— proud, licentious, arrogant, and boastful. The natural result was that they should end in being thoroughly bad. Although their lost minds have in a measure been recovered, it is difficult to keep them under proper restraint. If with their property and wealth they can be brought under the influence of instruction, they may enjoy lengthened years, virtue, and righteousness—these are the great lessons. If you do not follow in dealing with them these lessons of antiquity, wherein will you instruct them?"

The king said, "Oh! Grand Master, the security or the danger of the kingdom depends on those officers of Yin. If you are not too stern with them nor too mild, their virtue will be truly cultivated. The duke of Chou exercised the necessary caution at the beginning of the undertaking; Chün Ch'en displayed the harmony proper to the middle of it; and you, O duke, can bring it at last to a successful issue. You three princes will have been one in aim and will have equally pursued the proper way. The penetrating power of your principles and the good character of your measures of government will exert an enriching influence on the character of the people, so that the wild tribes, with their coats buttoning on the left,[3] will all find their proper support in them and I, the Little Child, will long enjoy much happiness. Thus, O duke, there in Ch'eng Chou will you establish forever the power of Chou and you will have an inexhaustible fame. Your descendants will follow your perfect pattern, governing accordingly.

"Oh! do not say, 'I am unequal to this'; but exert your mind to the utmost. Do not say, 'The people are few'; but attend carefully to your business. Reverently follow the accomplished achievements of the former kings and complete the excellence of the government of your predecessors."

After this charge, King K'ang reigned for fourteen more quiet and uneventful years. According to Ssu-ma Ch'ien, the reigns of both King K'ang and his father, King Ch'eng, marked a long period of profound tranquillity during which, for more than forty years, punishments were set aside.

This period was marked by the deaths of many who had been helpful in the founding of the Chou dynasty: most notable was the death of Shih, the duke of Shao. Other decedents were the count of Wei, who was active both in the Shang and Chou dynasties; Hu, a young nephew of the duke of Chou, called Chung of Ts'ai, who is the subject of Document 17 of Part V; and Feng, another younger brother of the duke of Chou, called the prince of K'ang or K'ang Shu, and the subject of Document 9 of Part V.

3. Confucius once praised Kuan Chung, a minister of Ch'i in the seventh century B.C., for his services against the wild tribes of his time, saying that but for him they would all be wearing their hair unbound and buttoning the lappets of their jackets on the left side (Analects, XIV.18).

In 1052 B.C., King K'ang was succeeded by his son King Chao, who reigned for fifty-one years. There are no documents in the *Shu* concerning this long reign. The notices in Ssu-ma Ch'ien and other sources, Legge tells us, were unfavorable. Many see the first evidence of the Chou decline beginning at this time. About 1039 B.C., the duke of Lü was murdered by a younger brother; King Chao was unable to punish the murderer. The king himself, it is said, drowned in the Han while on a hunting trip.

The next document will take us into the reign of King Mu in the first millennium B.C.

25. THE CHÜN YA

This short document is a charge to Chün Ya, whose surname is not known. He is here appointed minister of Instruction, and it is intimated that both his father and grandfather had held the same office. The second paragraph describes the duties of the minister of Instruction.

The charge is made by King Mu who reigned 1001–947 B.C. The genuineness of this document has been challenged.

The grand banner mentioned by the king was carried aloft whenever he went to sacrifice. On it were figures of the sun and moon, with dragons lying along its breadth, one above the other, head above tail. Meritorious ministers had their names inscribed on it during their lifetimes and, after their deaths, were believed to share in the sacrifices of the ancestral temple.

Document 25

The king spoke to the following effect: "Oh! Chün Ya, your grandfather and your father, one after the other, with true loyalty and honesty labored in the service of the royal house, accomplishing a merit that was recorded on the grand banner. I, the Little Child, have become charged by inheritance with the line of government transmitted from Wen and Wu, from Ch'eng and K'ang. I also keep thinking of their ministers who aided them in the good government of the kingdom. The trembling anxiety of my mind makes me feel as if I were treading on a tiger's tail, or walking upon spring ice. I now give you charge to assist me; be as my limbs to me, as my heart and backbone. Continue their old service and do not disgrace your grandfather and father.

"Diffuse widely the knowledge of the five invariable relations of society and reverently seek to produce a harmonious observance of the duties belonging to them among the people. If you are correct in your own person, none will dare to be but correct. The minds of the people cannot attain to the right mean of duty; they must be guided by your attaining to it. In the heat and rains of summer, the inferior people may be described as murmuring and sighing. And so it is with them in the great cold of winter. How great are their hardships! Think of their hardships in order to seek to promote their ease; and the people will be tranquil. Oh! how great and splendid were the plans of King Wen! How greatly were they carried out by the energy of King Wu! All in principle correct, deficient in nothing, they are for the help and guidance of us their descendants. Let you with reverence and wisdom carry out your instructions, enabling me to honor and follow the example of my immediate predecessors and to respond to and display the bright decree conferred on Wen and Wu; so shall you be the mate of your bygone fathers."

The king spoke to the following effect: "Chün Ya, let you take for your rule the lessons afforded by the courses of your excellent fathers. The good or the bad order of the people depends on this. You will thus follow the practice of your grandfather and father and make the good government of your sovereign illustrious."

26. THE CHARGE TO CH'IUNG

This section is another short charge by King Mu, on the appointment of Ch'iung to be High Chamberlain. He is addressed as *Po,* indicating his place in his family as the eldest.

The genuineness of this document has been challenged. The second paragraph describes the duties of the High Chamberlain.

Document 26

The king spoke to the following effect: "Po Ch'iung, I come short in virtue to succeed the former kings on the great throne. I am fearful; and conscious of the peril of my position. I rise at midnight and think how I can avoid falling into errors. Formerly Wen and Wu were endowed with all intelligence, august and sage, while their ministers, small and great, all cherished loyalty and goodness. Their servants, charioteers, chamberlains, and followers were all men of correctness, morning and evening waiting on their sovereign's wishes or supplying his deficiencies. Those kings, going out and coming in, rising up and sitting down, were thus made reverent. Their every warning or command was good. The people yielded a reverent obedience and the myriad regions were all happy. But I, the One Man, am destitute of goodness and really depend on the officers about me to help my deficiencies, applying the line to my faults and exhibiting my errors, thus correcting my bad heart and enabling me to be the successor of my meritorious predecessors.

"Now I appoint you to be High Chamberlain, to see that all the officers in your department and my personal attendants are upright and correct, that they strive to promote the virtue of their sovereign and together supply my deficiencies. Be careful in selecting your officers. Do not employ men of artful speech and insinuating looks, men whose likes and dislikes are ruled by mine, one-sided men and flatterers; but employ good men. When these household officers are correct, the sovereign will be correct; when they are flatterers, the sovereign will consider himself a sage. His virtue or his want of it equally depends on them. Cultivate no intimacy with flatterers, nor get them to do duty for me as my ears and eyes; they will lead their sovereign to disregard the statutes of the former kings. If you choose the men not for their personal goodness but for the sake of their bribes, their offices will be made of no effect, your great want of reverence for your sovereign will be apparent, and I will hold you guilty."

The king said, "Oh! be reverent! Ever help your sovereign to follow the regular laws of duty he should exemplify."

27. THE MARQUIS OF LÜ
ON PUNISHMENT

This document is the only one of the three documents from the reign of King Mu to appear in the Karlgren translation. Although this is a charge by King Mu, it is assumed that it was the marquis himself who prepared the code for the king to deliver to his princes and judges. The king is recorded as having been in his hundredth year at the time of this charge, 952 B.C., and as living to be at least 105.

During King Mu's reign, the house of Chou declined. According to Ssu-ma Ch'ien, Mu warred with the wild tribes against the advice of his ministers, losing their respect and also the loyalty of the princes.

The first part of the document is the historiographer's account of the circumstance in which King Mu gave this address. This is followed by the king's résumé of the lessons on punishment from antiquity.

The second part is concerned with general matters addressed to the princes and judges.

Then the subject of redemptions is gone into thoroughly. This portion has been the subject of much controversy in China, where the document is simply called "Lü's Punishments." Some critics condemn it and imply that Confucius should not have given this document a place in the *Shu ching, Book of History.* Others say that no such large scale redemption of punishments existed in China before Mu's time. Official corruption would seem to be the natural result of such a system. But Legge states that redemption of punishments entered into the penal code of every subsequent dynasty.

The last part of the document is again general, with the usual exhortations for reverence.

In this document appears the name of Ch'ih Yu, said to have lived in the twenty-sixth century B.C. His is the oldest name to be mentioned in the *Shu*. His name follows the phrase, "According to the teachings of ancient times . . . ," which intimates some kind of a continuous record of events, whether by means of an oral tradition, knotted strings, or primitive ideographs inscribed on material now vanished.

Document 27

In reference to the charge to the marquis of Lü: when the king had occupied the throne until he reached the age of a hundred years, he gave great consideration to the appointment of punishments in order to deal with the people of the four quarters.

The king said, "According to the teachings of ancient times, Ch'ih Yu was the first to produce disorder—which spread among the quiet, orderly people until all became robbers and murderers, owl-like and yet self-complacent in their conduct, traitors and villains snatching and filching, dissemblers and oppressors.

"Among the people of Miao, they did not use the power of goodness but the restraint of punishments. They made the five punishments engines of oppression, calling them the laws. They slaughtered the innocent and were the first also to go to excess in cutting off the nose, cutting off the ears, castration, and branding. All who became liable to those punishments were dealt with without distinction, no difference being made in favor of those who could offer some excuse. The people were gradually affected by this state of things and became dark and disorderly. Their hearts were no more set on good faith; they violated their oaths and covenants. The multitudes who suffered from the oppressive terrors and were in danger of being murdered declared their innocence to Heaven. God surveyed the people, and there was no fragrance of virtue arising from them, but the rank smell of their cruel punishments.

"The great Shun[1] compassionated the innocent multitudes that were in danger of being murdered and made the oppressors feel the terrors of his majesty. He restrained and finally extinguished the people of Miao, so that they should not continue to future generations. Then he commissioned Ch'ung and Li[2] to make an end of the communications between earth and heaven; and the descents of spirits ceased. From the princes down to the inferior officers, all helped with clear intelligence the spread of the regular principles

1. That this sovereign was Shun is a deduction; the text refers to a great but unnamed *ti,* meaning supreme sovereign.

2. Ch'ung and Li are not met elsewhere in the *Shu;* the Chinese commentaries offer no reliable or, for the purpose of this edition, relevant opinion as to their origin. What is quoted below from Legge's footnotes sheds light on a religious attitude as expressed by Kuan Yi Fu, a minister to a king of Ch'u at the cusp of the fourth and fifth centuries B.C.

The minister speaks in reply to a question asking what is meant by the statement that Ch'ung and Li "brought it about that there was no intercourse between heaven and earth." Kuan Yi Fu "gave his own view of it to the following effect":

> Anciently, the people attended to the discharge of their duties to one another and left the worship of spiritual beings—the seeking intercouse with them, invoking and effecting their descent on earth—to the officers who were appointed for that purpose. In this way things proceeded with great regularity. The people minded their own affairs and the spirits minded theirs. Tranquillity and prosperity were the consequence.
>
> But in the time of Shao Hao (twenty-sixth century B.C.) a change took place through the lawlessness of Chiu Li. The people intruded into the functions of the regulators of the spirits and their worship. They abandoned their duties to their fellowmen and tried to bring down spirits from above. The spirits themselves, no longer kept in check and subject to rule, made their appearance irregularly and disastrously. All was confusion and calamity when Chuan Hsü (2510–2433 B.C.) took the case in hand. He appointed Ch'ung, the minister of the South, to the superintendency of heavenly things—to prescribe the rules for the spirits; and Li, the minister of Fire (or of the North), to the superintendency of earthly things—to prescribe the rules for the people. In this way both spirits and people were brought back to their former regular courses and there was no unhallowed interference of the one with the other.
>
> This was the work described in the text: ". . . to make an end of the communications between earth and heaven; and the descents of spirits ceased."

of duty; the solitary and widows were no longer overlooked. The great Shun with an unprejudiced mind carried his enquiries down among the people, and the solitary and widows laid before him their complaints against the Miao. He awed the people by the majesty of his virtue and enlightened them by its brightness. He thereupon charged the three princely ministers to labor with compassionate anxiety in the people's behalf. Po-i delivered his statutes to prevent the people from rendering themselves obnoxious to punishment; Yü reduced to order the water and the land, and presided over the naming of the hills and rivers; Ch'i spread abroad a knowledge of agriculture and the people extensively cultivated the admirable grains. When the three princes had accomplished their work, it was abundantly well with the people. The minister of Crime, Kao Yao, exercised among them the restraint of punishment in exact adaptation to each offense and taught them to reverence virtue. The greatest gravity and harmony in the sovereign and the greatest intelligence in those below him, thus shining forth to all quarters of the land, all were rendered diligent in cultivating their virtue. Hence, if anything more were wanted, the clear adjudication of punishments effected the regulation of the people and helped them to observe the regular duties of life. The officers who presided over criminal cases executed the law fearlessly against the powerful and faithfully against the wealthy. They were reverent and cautious. They had no occasion to make choice of words to vindicate their conduct. The virtue of Heaven was attained to by them; from them was the determination of so great a matter as the lives of men. In their low sphere they yet corresponded to Heaven and enjoyed its favor."

The king said, "Ah! you who direct the government and

preside over criminal cases through all the land, are you not constituted the shepherds of Heaven? To whom ought you now to look as your pattern? Is it not to Po-i, spreading among the people his lessons to avert punishments? And from whom ought you now to take warning? Is it not from the people of Miao? They would not examine into the circumstances of criminal cases and did not make choice of good officers who saw to the right apportioning of the five punishments. They chose the violent and bribe-snatchers to determine and administer them so as to hold them guiltless and sent down calamity on Miao. The people had no plea to allege in mitigation of their punishment and their name was cut off from the world."

The king said, "Oh! lay it to heart. My uncles, and all ye, my brethren and cousins, my sons and my grandsons,[3] listen all of you to my words in which, it may be, you will receive a most important charge. You will only tread the path of satisfaction by being daily diligent; do not have occasion to beware of the want of diligence. Heaven, in its wish to regulate the people, allows us for a day to make use of punishments. Whether crimes have been premeditated, or are unpremeditated, depends on the parties concerned. Let you deal with them to accord with the mind of Heaven and thus serve me, the One Man. Though I would put them to death, do not you therefore put them to death; though I would spare them, do not you therefore spare them. Reverently apportion the five punishments so as fully to exhibit the three virtues.[4] Then shall I, the One Man, enjoy

3. While King Mu means those princes bearing the same surname as he does, actual sons and grandsons were probably present, as he was then (so it is said) in his hundredth year.

4. The three virtues are those of "The Great Plan": correctness and straightforwardness, strong government, and mild government; the sixth of the nine divisions (Part V, Document 4).

felicity; the people will look to you as their sure dependence; the repose of such a state will be perpetual."

The king said, "Ho! come, ye rulers of states and territories, I will tell you how to make punishments a blessing. It is yours now to give repose to the people. What should you be most concerned about the choosing of—should it not be the proper men? What should you deal with most reverently—should it not be punishments? What should you calculate the most carefully—should it not be to whom these will reach?

"When both parties are present with their documents and witnesses complete, let the judges listen to the fivefold statements that may be made. When they have examined and fully made up their minds on those, let them adjust the case to one of the five punishments. If the five punishments do not meet it, let them adjust it to one of the five redemption fines; and if these, again, are not sufficient for it, let them reckon it among the five cases of error.[5]

"In settling the five cases of error there are evils to be guarded against: being warped by the influence of power, or by private grudge, or by female solicitation, or by bribes, or by applications. Any one of these things should be held equal to the crime before the judges. Let you carefully examine, and prove yourselves equal to every difficulty.

"When there are doubts as to the infliction of any of the five punishments, that infliction should be forborne. When there are doubts as to the infliction of any of the five fines, it should be forborne. Let you carefully examine and prove yourselves equal to overcome every difficulty. When you

5. The five cases of error are those cases that arose from inadvertence. Previously in this paragraph, mention was made of the "fivefold statements"—apparently an emphasis, perhaps unwarranted, to fit a numerical category of five.

have examined and many things are clear, in addition form a judgment from studying the appearance of the parties. If you find nothing out on examination, do not listen to the case any more. In everything stand in awe of the dread majesty of Heaven.

"When, in a doubtful case, the punishment of branding is forborne, the fine to be laid on instead is 600 ounces of copper; but you must first have satisfied yourselves as to the crime. When the case would require the cutting off the nose, the fine must be double this; with the same careful determination of the crime. When the punishment would be the cutting off the feet, the fine must be 3000 ounces; with the same careful determination of the crime. When the punishment would be castration,[6] the fine must be 3600 ounces; with the same determination. When the punishment would be death, the fine must be 6000 ounces; with the same determination. Of crimes that may be redeemed by the fine in lieu of branding there are 1000; and the same number of those that would otherwise incur cutting off the nose. The fine in lieu of cutting off the feet extends to 500 cases; that in lieu of castration, to 300; and that in lieu of death, to 200. Altogether, set against the five punishments, there are 3000 crimes. In the case of others not exactly defined, you must class them with the next higher or next lower offenses, not admitting assumptive and disorderly pleadings and not using obsolete laws. Examine and act lawfully, judging carefully, proving yourselves equal to every difficulty.

"Where the crime should incur one of the higher punishments, but there are mitigating circumstances, apply to it the next lower. Where it should incur one of the lower punishments, but there are aggravating circumstances, apply to it the next higher. The light and heavy fines are to

6. In the case of females, the punishment was solitary confinement.

be apportioned in the same way by the balance of circumstances. Punishments and fines should also be light in one age, and heavy in another. To secure uniformity in this seeming irregularity, there are certain relations of things to be considered and the essential principle to be observed.

"The chastisement of fines is short of death, yet it will produce extreme distress. Therefore persons of artful tongues should not determine criminal cases, but really good persons whose awards will hit the right Mean. Examine carefully where there are any discrepancies in the statements: the view which you were resolved not to follow, you may see occasion to follow; with compassion and reverence settle the cases; examine carefully the penal code and deliberate with all about it that your decisions may be likely to hit the Mean and be correct; whether it be the infliction of a punishment or a fine, examine carefully, mastering every difficulty. When the case is thus concluded, all parties will acknowledge the justice of the sentence; and when it is reported, the sovereign will do the same. In sending up reports of cases, they must be full and complete. If a man have been tried on two counts, his two punishments must be recorded."

The king said, "Oh! let there be a feeling of reverence. Ye judges and princes of the same surname with me, and of other surnames, know all that I speak in much fear. I think with reverence of the subject of punishment, for the end of it is to promote virtue. Now Heaven, wishing to help the people, has made us its representatives here below. Be intelligent and pure in hearing each side of a case. The right ordering of the people depends on the impartial hearing of the pleas on both sides; do not seek for your own private advantage by means of those pleas. Gain so got by the decision of cases is no precious acquisition; it is an accumulation of guilt and will be recompensed with many judgments: you should ever stand in awe of the punishment of Heaven. It is not Heaven that does not deal impartially with men; men ruin themselves. If the punishment of Heaven were not so extreme, nowhere under the sky would the people have good government."

The king said, "Oh! ye who shall hereafter inherit the dignities and offices of the present time, to whom are ye to look for your models? Must it not be to those who promoted the virtue belonging to the unbiased nature of the people? I pray you give attention to my words. The wise men of antiquity by their use of punishments obtained boundless fame. Everything relating to the five punishments exactly hit with them the due Mean. Hence came their excellence. Receiving from your sovereigns the good multitudes, behold in the case of those men punishments made felicitous!"

28. THE CHARGE TO THE MARQUIS WEN

Between "The Marquis of Lü on Punishments" and this document, seven reigns and two centuries have passed, a period for which no documents appear in the *Shu*. It is known from other sources that the dynasty declined steadily to culminate in the disorders of King Yu's reign (781–770 B.C.).

King Yu, as Chieh of the Hsia dynasty and Shou of the Shang, became the thrall of a notorious woman, Pao Ssu. As she gained ascendancy, King Yu degraded his rightful queen, a daughter of the prince of Shen, and set aside her son I Ch'iu; Pao Ssu was made queen and her son declared heir to the throne. In addition to the usual debaucheries and depravities, King Yu treated the enfeoffed nobles in a trifling manner, losing their loyalty.

The prince of Shen called in the Dog Jung, a barbarian tribe, to assist him in attacking the capital. He did not intend the death of King Yu, only those of Pao Ssu and her son. But the Dog Jung, once on the attack, could not be controlled. They sacked and overran the capital. King Yu fled, but the Dog Jung followed and killed him. They took Pao Ssu captive and, according to Couling, forced her to commit suicide.

When several of the feudal princes decided to come to the aid of the house of Chou despite their humiliations at the hand of King Yu, the capital lay in ruins. The Dog Jung remained hostile, forcing the dynasty to give up its capital at Hao. The influence and power of the dynasty was over.

The princes rallied to bring I Ch'iu back from Shen and hailed him as king. He is known as King P'ing and is the author of this charge to the marquis Wen. The first act of his reign was to transfer the capital from the ruins of Hao to Loyang, thus fulfilling (more than two centuries later and under disastrous circumstance) the wishes of the duke of Chou. The date was 770 B.C., after which the dynasty became known as Eastern Chou.

The marquis Wen, to whom this charge is addressed upon his appointment to be chief of several other princes, was one of the feudal princes who came to aid the royal house when it was attacked and overrun by the Dog Jung. He was a lord of Chin, not to be confused with the state of Ch'in, a principality that was to become one of the largest and most powerful in the kingdom. Wen was the sacrificial name of I Ho, the name by which King P'ing addresses him in the document. I Ho was his style, a designation assumed at the time of his marriage. His personal name was Ch'iu. He was a descendant of King Wu's son Yü, who is mentioned here for the first time. Yü had been made marquis of T'ang; the name T'ang was later changed to Chin.

Document 28

The king spoke to the following effect: "Uncle I Ho, how illustrious were Wen and Wu! Carefully did they make their virtue brilliant, until it rose brightly on high and the fame of it was widely diffused here below. Therefore God caused his favoring decree to light upon King Wen. There were ministers thereafter who aided and illustriously served their sovereigns, following and carrying out their plans, great and small, so that my fathers sat tranquilly on the throne.

"Oh! an object of pity am I, who am but as a Little Child. Just as I have succeeded to the throne, Heaven has severely chastised me. Through the interruption of the royal bounties that ceased to descend to the inferior people, the invading barbarous tribes of the west have greatly injured our kingdom. Moreover, among the managers of my affairs there are none of age and experience and distinguished ability in their offices. I am thus unequal to the difficulties of my position and say to myself, 'My granduncles and uncles, you ought to compassionate my case.' Oh! if there were those who could establish their merit in behalf of me, the One Man, I might long enjoy repose upon the throne.

"Uncle I Ho, you render still more glorious your illustrious ancestor. You were the first to imitate the example of Wen and Wu, collecting the scattered powers and continuing the all but broken line of your sovereign. Your filial piety goes back to your accomplished ancestor and is equal to his. You have done much to repair my losses and defend me in my difficulties and of you, being such, I am full of admiration."

The king said, "Uncle I Ho, return home, survey your multitudes, and tranquilize your state. I reward you with a jar of spirits distilled from the black millet and flavored with aromatic herbs, with a red bow and a hundred red arrows;[1] with a black bow and a hundred black arrows; and with four horses. Go, my uncle. Show kindness to those who are far off and help those who are near at hand; cherish and secure the repose of the inferior people; do not idly seek your ease; exercise an inspection and benign compassion in your capital and all your borders; thus completing your illustrious virtue."

1. When a prince received a gift of a bow and arrows, it invested him with the power officially to punish any who were disobedient to the royal commands. In addition, the gift was a tribute of the prince's merit.

29. THE SPEECH AT PI

This document is out of chronologic order; it belongs to the reign of King Ch'eng. In the Karlgren translation, it appears in the same position among the documents as here.

There is a tradition that attributes this speech to Po Ch'in, son of the duke of Chou, who was duke of Lu for over fifty years and died in 1063 B.C.

During the reign of King Ch'eng, the wild tribes, as we know from many of the documents of the early Chou, were frequently in rebellion. This speech has reference to hostilities in subduing the wild tribes along the Huai.

We do not know the exact year. The place is Pi in the province of Hsü. Po Ch'in appears at the head of his host and commands silence. He briefs his army on the plan and logistics of this punitive expedition and issues his commands.

Document 29

The duke said, "Ah! ye men, make no noise, but listen to my commands. We are going to punish those wild tribes of the Huai and of Hsü, which have risen up together.

"Have in good repair your buff coats and helmets; have the laces of your shields well secured; presume not to have any of them but in perfect order. Prepare your bows and arrows; temper your lances and spears; sharpen your pointed and edged weapons; presume not to have any of them but in good condition.

"We must now largely let the oxen and horses loose and not keep them in enclosures; ye people, do you close your traps and fill up your pitfalls and do not presume to injure any of the animals so let loose. If any of them be injured, you shall be dealt with according to the regular punishments.

240

"When the horses or cattle are seeking one another, or when your followers, male or female, abscond, presume not to leave the ranks to pursue them. But let them be carefully returned. I will reward you among the people who return them according to their value. But if you leave your places to pursue them, or if you who find them do not restore them, you shall be dealt with according to the regular punishments.

"And let none of you presume to commit any robbery or detain any creature that comes in your way, to jump over enclosures and walls to steal people's horses or oxen, or to decoy away their servants or female attendants. If you do so, you shall be dealt with according to the regular punishments.

"On the day *chia-hsü* I will take action against the hordes of Hsü. Prepare the roasted grain and other provisions; and presume not to have any deficiency. If you have, you shall suffer the severest punishment. Ye men of Lu, from the three environing territories and the three tracts beyond,[1] be ready with your posts and planks. On *chia-hsü* I will commence my intrenchments: dare not but be provided with a supply of these. If you be not so provided, you shall be subjected to various punishments short only of death. Ye men of Lu, from the three environing territories and the three tracts beyond, be ready with the forage and do not dare to let it be other than abundant. If you do, you shall suffer the severest punishment."

1. Outside the capital city was an environing territory called the *chiao;* beyond, was the *sui*. The *chiao* of the royal domain was divided again into six *hsiang,* which furnished the six royal hosts. The *sui* furnished subsidiary hosts.

30. THE SPEECH BY THE MARQUIS OF CH'IN

The state of Ch'in (not to be confused with the state of Chin) at the time of this speech was one of the most powerful in the kingdom. Ultimately, about 200 B.C., one of its princes would unify all of China, found the modern empire, and assume the title of Ch'in Shih Huang Ti, Ch'in designating the imperial dynasty—the first of more than twenty until the founding of the republic in 1912.

The time is 631 B.C., more than two centuries away from the Warring States period. But already the feudal princes are intriguing and warring. The royal house of Chou is only nominally the head of the kingdom, relegated to performing the sacrifices. The states of Ch'in and Chin have been besieging the capital of the principality of Cheng and threaten to obliterate that state. The background to this document offers rare insight into the almost infinite complexities of the disorders to culminate in the Warring States period.

Suddenly the marquis of Ch'in is induced to withdraw from the siege, leaving three officers on friendly terms at the court of Cheng with the understanding that they would defend the state from aggression.

However, these officers acted as spies. In 629 B.C. one of the spies sent word that he was in charge of one of the gates and, if the marquis would mount a surprise attack, the state of Cheng could be added to the territories of Ch'in.

The marquis of Ch'in is known to history as Duke Mu. It was the custom of the historiographers to elevate their lord one degree. This indicates that this document had been among the chronicles of Ch'in, which was only a marquisate.

A year later the marquis, now listening to the promptings of ambition, sent a large force under three of his ablest commanders to attack Cheng; but Cheng was warned in advance and the attack failed.

While returning to Ch'in, the unsuccessful army was attacked by the forces of their late co-besieger, Chin. The men of Ch'in were nearly annihilated, and the three commanders were taken prisoner.

The marquis of Chin intended to put his three prisoners to death, but he was persuaded by his mother to send them to the marquis of Ch'in (Duke Mu). The marquis was confident that Duke Mu would sacrifice the prisoners to his anger for their failure to take Cheng.

Instead, the marquis of Ch'in left his capital to meet the returning prisoners and took upon himself the blame for their lack of success. This is probably the supreme instance of sovereign responsibility within the documents of the *Shu*. Following this, according to one tradition, he made this speech to the commanders, which was preserved for the benefit of his ministers.

Document 30

The duke said, "Ah! my officers, listen to me without noise. I solemnly announce to you the most important of all sayings. It is this which the ancients have said, 'Thus it is with all people: they mostly love their ease. In reproving others there is no difficulty; but to receive reproof and allow it to have free course—this is difficult.' The sorrow of my heart is that the days and months have passed away. It is not likely they will come again so that I might pursue a different course.

"There were my old counsellors: I said, 'They will not accommodate themselves to me,' and I hated them. There were my new counsellors: I would for the time give my confidence to them. So indeed it was with me. But hereafter I will take advice from the men of yellow hair[1] and then I

---

1. Yellow hair means fading, indicative of age.

shall be free from error. That good old officer! His strength is exhausted, but I would rather have him as my counsellor. That dashing brave officer! His shooting and charioteering are faultless but I would not wish to have him. As to men of quibbles, skillful at cunning words, and able to make the good man change his purposes, what have I to do to make much use of them?

"I have deeply thought and thus concluded: Let me have but one resolute minister, plain and sincere, without other ability but a straightforward mind; and possessed of generosity regarding the talents of others, as if he himself possessed them. When he finds accomplished and sage men, loving them in his heart more than his mouth expresses, really showing himself able to forbear with them—such a minister would be able to preserve my descendants and people and would indeed be a giver of benefits.

"But if the minister, when he finds men of ability, be jealous and hates them; if, when he finds accomplished and sage men, he oppose them and does not allow their advancement, showing himself really not able to forbear with them—such a man will not be able to protect my descendants and people; and will he not be a dangerous man?

"The decline and fall of a state may arise from One Man. The glory and tranquillity of a state may also arise from the goodness of One Man."

This closes the collection of sparse and cryptic documents known as the *Shu ching, Book of History*.

Down through the literature of China we can trace the heritage of the *Shu* ricocheting from school to school, writer to writer—spiraling through the ages from the earliest historiographers among the black-haired people into the homogeneity of our global village.

Twenty-two kings were to follow King P'ing before the Chou was finally superseded by the Ch'in dynasty. Mencius, a philosopher who lived in the last years of the Chou dynasty, had this to say as he reflected on the many centuries of the existence of the longest dynasty in the history of China:

Chieh and Shou losing the throne arose from their losing the people; to lose the people means to lose their hearts. There is a way to get the kingdom: get the people—and the kingdom is got. There is a way to get the people: get their hearts—and the people are got. There is a way to get their hearts: it is simply to collect for them what they like and not to lay on them what they dislike.

The people turn to a benevolent ruler as water flows downward and as wild beasts fly to the wilderness.

As the otter aids the deep waters, driving the fish into them, and the hawk aids the thickets, driving the little birds to them, so accordingly Chieh and Shou aided T'ang and Wu—driving the people to them.

If among the present rulers of the kingdom there were one who loved benevolence, all the other princes would aid him by driving the people to him. Although he might not wish to become sovereign, he could not avoid becoming so.

The case of one of the present princes wishing to become sovereign is like having to seek mugwort three years old to cure a seven years' sickness. If it have not been stored, the patient may not get it. If the princes do not set their wills on benevolence, all their days will be in sorrow and disgrace and they will be involved in death and ruin.

This is illustrated in the passage from "The T'ai Chia" (Document 5 of Part IV)—"When heaven sends down calamities it is still possible to escape them. When we occasion the calamities ourselves, it is not possible any longer to live."

From the Prolegomena of James Legge

Introduction to the
Chinese Classics Generally

The books now recognized as of highest authority in China are comprehended under the denominations of *Five ching* and *Four shu*.[1] The term *ching* is of textile origin, and signifies the warp threads of a web and their adjustment. An easy application of it is to denote what is regular and insures regularity. As used with reference to books, it indicates their authority on the subjects of which they treat. The *Five ching* are the five canonical works, containing the truth upon the highest subjects from the sages of China, which should be received as law by all generations. The term *shu* simply means writings or books: *the pencil speaking.* It may be used of a single character or of books containing thousands of characters.

The *Five ching* are: *I ching, Book of Changes; Shu ching, Book of History; Shih ching, Book of Odes; Li chi, Book of Rites;* and *Ch'un ch'iu, Spring and Autumn Annals,* a chronicle of events from 722 to 481 B.C. The authorship, or compilation rather, of all these works is loosely attributed to Confucius. But much of the *Li chi* is from later hands. Of the *I,* the *Shu,* and the *Shih,* it is only in the *I ching* that we find additions attributed to Confucius himself, in the shape of appendixes. The *Ch'un ch'iu* is the only one of the *Five ching* that can be described as his own "making."

The Four Books is an abbreviation for "The Books of the Four Philosophers." The first is *Lun yü* or *Confucian Analects,* occupied chiefly with the sayings of Confucius. He is the philosopher to whom it belongs. The second is the *Ta hsüeh, Great Learning,* now commonly attributed to Tseng Shen, disciple of Confucius. He is the philosopher of it. The third is *Chung yung, Doctrine of the Mean.* Its composition is ascribed to K'ung Chi,

1. Commonly called *Five Classics* and *Four Books.*

249

grandson of Confucius. He is the philosopher of it. The fourth contains the works of Mencius.

This arrangement of the classical books, commonly supposed to have originated with the scholars of the Sung dynasty, is defective. The *Great Learning* and the *Doctrine of the Mean* are both found in the *Li chi, Book of Rites.*

The oldest enumerations of the classical books specify only the *Five ching.* The *Yo chi, Book of Music,* the remains of which now form part of the *Li chi, Book of Rites,* was sometimes added, making the *Six ching.* A division was also made into *Nine ching* consisting of *I ching, Book of Changes; Shih ching, Book of Odes; Shu ching, Book of History; Chou li, Rites of Chou; I li, Ceremonial Usage; Li chi, Book of Rites;* and the three annotated editions of the *Ch'un ch'iu, Spring and Autumn Annals* by Tso Ch'iu Ming, Kung Yang Kao, and Ku Liang Ch'ih.

In the famous compilation of classical books undertaken by order of T'ang T'ai Tsung, second emperor of the T'ang dynasty (reigned A.D. 627–649), and which appeared in the reign of his successor, there are *Thirteen ching:* the *Lun yü* or *Confucian Analects,* the *Erh ya, Literary Expositer* (the precursor of the dictionaries which Chinese literature possesses in abundance), the *Hsiao ching, Classic of Filial Piety,* and the works of Mencius, in addition to the *Six ching.*

A distinction, however, was made among the works thus comprehended under the same common name. *Mencius,* the *Lun yü* or *Analects,* the *Ta hsüeh, Great Learning,* the *Chung yung, Doctrine of the Mean,* and the *Hsiao ching, Classic of Filial Piety* were spoken of as the *Smaller Classics.* It thus appears, contrary to the ordinary opinion on the subject, that the *Ta hsüeh* and *Chung yung* had been published as separate treatises before the Sung dynasty and that the *Four Books,* as distinguished from the *Greater Classics,* had also previously found a place in the literature of China.

In the memoirs of the Former Han dynasty (202 B.C.-A.D.

9) we have one chapter which we may call the "History of Literature." It commences thus:

After the death of Confucius there was an end of his exquisite words; and when his seventy disciples had passed away, violence began to be done to their meaning. It came about that there were five different editions of the *Ch'un ch'iu,* four of the *Shih,* and several of the *I ching.* Amid the disorder and collisions of the Warring States (482–221 B.C.), truth and falsehood were in a greater state of warfare, and a sad confusion marked the words of the various scholars. Then came the calamity inflicted under the Ch'in dynasty (221–206 B.C.) when the literary monuments were destroyed by fire in order to keep the people in ignorance. But by-and-by there arose the Han dynasty, which set itself to remedy the evil wrought by the Ch'in. Great efforts were made to collect slips and tablets,[2] and the way was thrown wide open for the bringing in of books.

In the time of Han Wu Ti (141–86 B.C.), portions of books being lacking and tablets lost, so that ceremonies and music were suffering great damage, the emperor was moved to sorrow and said, "I am very sad for this." He therefore formed the plan of repositories in which books might be stored, and appointed officers to transcribe books on an extensive scale, embracing the works of the various scholars, that they might all be placed in the repositories.

Han Ch'eng Ti (reigned 32–6 B.C.), finding that a portion of the books still continued dispersed or missing, commissioned Ch'en Neng, the superintendent of guests, to search for undiscovered books throughout the empire. By special edict he ordered the chief of the Banqueting House, Liu Hsiang, to examine the classical works, along with the commentaries on them, the writings of the scholars, and all poetical productions; the master-controller of infantry, Jen Huang, to examine books on the art of war; the grand historiographer, Yin Hsien, to examine books treating the art of divination; and the imperial physician, Li Chu Kuo, to examine the books on medicine. Whenever any book

2. Slips and tablets of bamboo, on which the "literary monuments" were written.

was done with, Liu Hsiang forthwith arranged it, indexed it, and made a digest of it that was presented to the emperor. Hsiang died while this work was in progress. Han Ai Ti (reigned 6 B.C.–A.D. 2) appointed his son, Liu Hsin, master of the imperial carriages, to complete his father's work. On this, Hsin collected all the books and presented a report of them under seven divisions.

The first of these divisions seems to have been a general catalogue containing, perhaps, only the titles of the works included in the other six. The second embraced the classical works. From the abstract of it, which is preserved in the chapter referred to, we find that there were 294 collections of the *I ching, Book of Changes* from thirteen different individuals or editors; 412 collections of the *Shu ching, Book of History* from nine different individuals; 416 volumes of the *Shih ching, Book of Odes* from six different individuals; of the books of rites, 555 collections from thirteen different individuals; of the books on music, 165 collections from six different editors; 948 collections of history, under the heading of the *Ch'un ch'iu,* from twenty-three different individuals; 229 collections of the *Lun yü,* including the *Confucian Analects* and kindred fragments, from twelve different individuals; of the *Hsiao ching,* embracing also the *Erh ya* and some other portions of the ancient literature, 59 collections from eleven different individuals; and finally, of the lesser learning, being works on the form of the characters, 45 collections from eleven different individuals. The works of Mencius were included in the second division among the writings of what were deemed orthodox scholars, of which there were 836 collections from fifty-three different individuals.

The above important document is sufficient to show how the emperors of the Han dynasty, as soon as they had made good their possession of the empire, turned their attention to recover the ancient literature of the nation, the classical books engaging their first care, and how earnestly and effectively the scholars of the time responded to the wishes of their rulers. The ordinance of the Ch'in dynasty against possessing classical books (with the exception of the *I ching*) was repealed by the second sovereign of the Han, Hui Ti, in the fourth year of his reign. A large portion of the *Shu ching* was recovered in the time of the third emperor, 180–158 B.C., while in the year 137 B.C. a special board of literati was constituted and put in charge of the *Five ching*.

The collections reported on by Liu Hsin suffered damage in the troubles which began A.D. 8 and continued till the rise of the Later or Eastern Han dynasty in the year 25. The founder of it zealously promoted the undertaking of his predecessors and additional repositories were required for the books which were collected. His successors, Han Ming Ti, Han Chang Ti, and Han Ho Ti, took part themselves in the studies and discussions of the literary tribunal and the emperor Han Ling Ti, between A.D. 172–178, had the text of the *Five ching* cut in slabs of stone and set up in the capital outside the gate of the Grand College.

Since the Han, successive dynasties have considered the literary monuments of the country to be an object of their special care. Many of them have issued editions of the classics embodying the commentaries of preceding generations. The evidence is complete that the classical books of China have come down from at least a century before our Christian era substantially the same as we have them at present.

But it still remains to inquire in what condition we may suppose the books were when the scholars of the Han dynasty commenced their labors upon them. They acknowledge that the tablets—we cannot here speak of manuscripts—were mutilated and in disorder. Was the injury they had received of such an extent that all the care and study put forth on the remains would be of little use? This question can be answered satisfactorily only by an examination of the evidence which is adduced for the text of each particular classic. But it can be made apparent that there is nothing in the nature of the case to interfere with our believing that the materials were sufficient to enable the scholars to execute the work intrusted to them.

The burning of the ancient books by order of the founder of the Ch'in dynasty is always referred to as the greatest disaster the classical books sustained, and with this is coupled the slaughter of many of the literati by the same monarch. The account which we have in the *Historical Records* is the following:

In his 34th year,[3] the emperor, returning from a visit to the south which had extended as far as Yüeh, gave a feast in his palace at Hsien-yang. The great scholars, amounting to seventy men, appeared and wished him long life. One of the principal ministers, Chou Ch'ing Ch'eh, came forward and said, "Formerly, the State of Ch'in was only 1,000 li in extent, but Your Majesty, by your spirit-like efficacy and intelligent wisdom, has tranquilized and settled the whole empire and driven away all barbarous tribes. Wherever the sun and moon shine, all rulers appear before you as guests acknowledging subjection. You have formed the states of the various princes into provinces and districts where the people enjoy a happy tranquillity, suffering no more from the calamities of war and contention. This condition of things will be transmitted for 10,000 generations. From the highest antiquity there has been no one in awful virtue like Your Majesty."

The emperor was pleased with this flattery. Shun Yü Yüeh, one of the great scholars, a native of Ch'i, advanced and said, "The sovereigns of Yin and Chou, for more than a thousand years, invested their sons and younger brothers, and meritorious ministers, with domains and rule and could thus depend upon them for support and aid; that I have heard. But now Your Majesty is in possession of all within the seas, and your sons and younger brothers are nothing but private individuals. The issue will be that someone will arise to play the part of T'ien Ch'ang,[4] or of the six nobles of Chin. Without the support of your own family, where will you find aid? That a state of things not modeled from the lessons of antiquity can long continue; that I have not heard. Ch'ing is now showing himself to be a flatterer who increases the errors of Your Majesty, and not a loyal minister."

3. Meaning, Legge tells us, the thirty-fourth year after Ch'in Shih Huang Ti had ascended the throne.

4. T'ien Ch'ang murdered his sovereign, duke Chien of Ch'i, in 481 B.C.

The emperor requested the opinions of others on this representation and the premier, Li Ssu said, "The five emperors were not one the double of the other, nor did the three dynasties accept one another's ways.[5] Each had a peculiar system of government, not for the sake of contrariety, but as required by changed times. Now Your Majesty has laid the foundations of imperial sway that it will last for 10,000 generations. This is indeed beyond what a stupid scholar can understand. And moreover, Yüeh only talks of things belonging to the three dynasties, which are not fit to be models to you. At other times, when the princes were all striving together, they endeavored to gather the wandering scholars about them. But now the empire is in a stable condition; laws and ordinances issue from one supreme authority. Those of the people who abide in their homes should give their strength to the toils of husbandry, while those who become scholars should study the various laws and prohibitions. Instead of doing this, however, the scholars do not learn what belongs to the present day but study antiquity. They go on to condemn the present time, leading the masses of the people astray and to disorder.

At the risk of my life, I, the prime minister, say: Formerly, when the nation was disunited and disturbed, there was no one who could give unity to it. The princes therefore stood together; constant references were made to antiquity to the injury of the present state; baseless statements were dressed up to confound actuality, and men made a boast of their own peculiar learning to condemn what their rulers appointed. And now, when Your Majesty has consolidated the empire and, distinguishing black from white, has constituted a stable unity, they still honor their peculiar learning and stand together; they teach men what is contrary to your laws. When an ordinance has been issued, every one sets to discussing it with his learning. In the court, they are dissatisfied in heart; out of it, they keep talking in the streets. While they make a pretence of supporting their master, they consider it fine to have extraordinary views of their own. And

5. The five emperors cited by Li Ssu are generally acknowledged to be the legendary sage rulers Fu Hsi, Shen Nung, Huang Ti (also called the Yellow Emperor), and the sovereigns Yao, and Shun. The three dynasties were the Hsia, Shang (or Yin), and Chou.

so they lead the people to be guilty of murmuring and evil speaking. If these things are not prohibited, Your Majesty's authority will decline and parties will be formed. The best way is to prohibit them. I pray that all the records in charge of the historiographers be burned, excepting those of the state of Ch'in; that, with the exception of those officers belonging to the Board of Great Scholars, all who presume to keep copies of the *Shih ching, Book of Odes,* or of the *Shu ching, Book of History,* or of the books of the Hundred Schools, be required to go with them to the officers in charge of the several districts, and burn them; that all who may dare to speak together about the *Shih* and the *Shu* be put to death and their bodies exposed in the market-place; that those who make mention of the past, so as to blame the present, be put to death along with their relatives; that officers who know of the violation of those rules and not inform against the offenders shall be held equally guilty with them; and that whoever shall not have burned their books within thirty days after the issuing of the ordinance, be branded and sent to labor on the wall for four years. The only books which should be spared are those on medicine, divination, and husbandry. Whoever wants to learn the laws may go to the magistrates and learn of them."

The imperial decision was "Approved."

The destruction of the scholars is related more briefly. In the year after the burning of the books, the resentment of the emperor was excited by the remarks and flight of two scholars who had been favorites with him. He determined to institute a strict inquiry about all of their class in Hsien-yang to find out whether they had been making ominous speeches about him and disturbing the minds of the people. The investigation was committed to the Censors[6] and, it being discovered that upwards of 460 scholars had violated the prohibitions, they were all buried alive in pits as a warning to the empire, while degradation and banishment were employed more strictly than before against all

6. The duty of Censors was to report to the throne on all subjects connected with the welfare of the people.

who fell under suspicion. The emperor's eldest son, Fu Su, remonstrated with him saying that such measures against those who repeated the words of Confucius and sought to imitate him would alienate all the people from their infant dynasty. His interference offended his father so much that he was sent from court to be with the general who was superintending the building of the great wall.

No attempts have been made by Chinese critics and historians to discredit the record of these events, though some have questioned the extent of the injury inflicted on the monuments of their ancient literature. It is important to observe that the edict against the books did not extend to the *I ching, Book of Changes,* exempted as being a work on divination. Nor did it extend to the other classics which were in the charge of the Board of Great Scholars. There ought to have been no difficulty in finding copies when the Han dynasty superseded that of Ch'in, and probably there would have been none but for the sack of the capital in 206 B.C. by Hsiang Yü, the formidable opponent of the founder of the House of Han. Then, we are told, the fires blazed for three months among the palaces and public buildings, and must have proved as destructive to the copies of the Great Scholars as the edict of the tyrant had been to the copies among the people.

It is to be noted also that the life of Ch'in Shih Huang Ti lasted only three years after the promulgation of his edict. We may believe that vigorous efforts to carry the emperor's edict into effect would not be continued longer than the life of its author. The calamity inflicted on the ancient books of China could not have approached anything like a complete destruction of them. There would be no occasion for the scholars of the Han dynasty, in regard to the bulk of their ancient literature, to undertake more than the work of recension and editing. The idea of forgery on a large scale by the Han scholars is out of the question.

CHRONOLOGIC TABLE

Ruler	First Year of Reign, B.C.	Years of Reign
Yao	2357	100
Shun	2255	50

Hsia Dynasty, with Title of *Hou*, or Sovereign

Yü	2205	8
Ch'i	2197	9
T'ai K'ang	2188	29
Chung K'ang	2159	13
Hsiang	2146	27
Usurpation	2119	40
Shao K'ang	2079	22
Ch'u	2057	17
Huai	2040	26
Mang	2014	18
Hsieh	1996	16
Pu Chiang	1980	59
Chiung (Pien)	1921	21
Chin	1900	21
K'ung Chia	1879	31
Kao	1848	11
Fa	1837	19
Chieh Kuei (Cheo)	1818	52

Shang (Yin) Dynasty, with Title of *Wang*, or King

T'ang (Ch'eng T'ang)	1766	13
T'ai Chia	1753	33
Wu Ting	1720	29
T'ai Keng	1691	25
Hsiao Chia	1666	17
Yung Chi	1649	12
T'ai Wu (T'ai Mou)	1637	75
Chung Ting	1562	13
Wai Jen	1549	15
Ho Tan Chia	1534	9
Tsu Yi	1525	19
Tsu Hsin	1506	16
Wu Chia	1490	25
Tsu Ting	1465	32

Ruler	First Year of Reign, B.C.	Years of Reign
Nan Keng	1433	25
Yang Chia	1408	7
P'an Keng	1401	28
Hsiao Hsin	1373	21
Hsiao Yi	1352	28
Wu Ting	1324	59
Tsu Keng	1265	7
Tsu Chia	1258	33
Lin Hsin	1225	6
Keng Ting	1219	21
Wu Yi	1198	4
T'ai Ting	1194	3
Ti Yi	1191	37
Chou Hsin	1154	32

Chou Dynasty, with Title of *Wang,* or King

Wu	1122	7
Ch'eng	1115	37
K'ang	1078	26
Chao	1052	51
Mu	1001	55
Kung	946	12
I	934	25
Hsiao	909	15
I	894	16
Li	878	51
Hsüan	827	46
Yu	781	11
P'ing	770	51
Huan	719	23
Chuang	696	15
Hsi	681	5
Hui	676	25
Hsiang	651	33
Ch'ing	618	6
K'uang	612	6
Ting	606	21
Chien	585	14
Ling	571	27
Ching	544	25
Ching	519	44
Yüan	475	7

Ruler	First Year of Reign, B.C.	Years of Reign
Ching Ting	468	28
K'ao	440	15
Wei Lieh	425	24
An	401	26
Lieh	375	7
Hsien	378	48
Shin Tsing	320	6
Nan	314	29
Tung Chou Chün	255	
Formal end of dynasty	249	

The western feudal state of Ch'in was in the ascendant. King Nan attacked it, but was defeated. After his death in 255 B.C., Ch'in was the *de facto* dynasty. A scion of the house of Chou designated himself Tung Chou Chün (Eastern Chou Prince) and attempted to restore the Chou dynasty to power. He was unsuccessful. One by one, Ch'in extinguished the remaining feudal states: Han, Chao, Wei, Ch'u, and Chi.

In 221 B.C. King Cheng of Ch'in designated himself Shih Huang Ti (First Emperor) and founded the Ch'in dynasty and the empire that was to last until A.D. 1912.

SELECTED BIBLIOGRAPHY

Carr, Edward Hallett. *What is History? The George Macaulay Treveleyan Lectures delivered at the University of Cambridge January–March 1961.* Alfred A. Knopf, New York, 1964.

Chang Chi-yun. *Chinese History of Fifty Centuries: Ancient Times.* Vol. 1. Translated by Chu Li-hen. Yangmingshan Publishing Co., Taipei, Taiwan, 1962.

Couling, Samuel. *Encyclopaedia Sinica.* Ch'eng Wen Publishing Co., Taipei, Taiwan, 1967.

Creel, Herrlee Glessner. *The Birth of China: a Survey of the Formative Period of Chinese Civilization.* Reynal & Hitchcock, New York, 1937.

————. *Sinism. A Study of the Evolution of the Chinese World-View.* Open Court Publishing Co., Chicago and LaSalle, Ill., 1929.

Dawson, Raymond, ed. *The Legacy of China.* Oxford, 1964.

Feng, Han-chi. *The Chinese Kinship System.* Harvard-Yenching Institute Series No. 22, Cambridge, n.d.

Gernet, Jacques. *Ancient China from the Beginnings to the Empire.* Translated from the French by Raymond Rudorff. University of California Press, Berkeley and Los Angeles, 1968.

Hegel, Georg Wilhelm Friedrich. *Lectures on the Philosophy of History.* Translated by J. Sibree. Dover Publishing Co., New York, 1956.

Karlgren, Bernhard: *see* Museum of Far Eastern Antiquities.

Kolb, Albert. *Ostasien: China–Japan–Korea.* Quelle & Mayer, Heidelberg, 1963. Scheduled for publication in English by Methuen & Co., Ltd. as *East Asia: China, Japan, Korea.* U.S. agents, Barnes and Noble, N.Y.

Latourette, Kenneth Scott. *The Chinese, Their History and Culture.* Second Edition Revised; Two volumes in one. The Macmillan Co., New York, 1942. Bibliographies will be found at the end of chapters; the general reader who wishes to pursue a specialized interest will find them of great value.

Legge, James. *The Chinese Classics.* 1861–72. Eight volumes in five.

————. Reprint: five volumes in four. Ch'eng Wen Publishing Co., Taipei, Taiwan, n.d.

————. *The Shoo King*. The Author's Hongkong; Trubner & Co., London, 1865.

————. *The Shû King*. (So titled in the original publications.) *The Sacred Books of the East*. Vol. 3. Edited by F. Max Müller; Clarendon Press, Oxford, 1879. Reprinted by Motilal Banarsidass Co., Delhi 7, 1966.

Li, Dun J. *The Ageless Chinese: A History*. Charles Scribner's Sons, New York, 1965.

Museum of Far Eastern Antiquities, Stockholm. Bulletins 20 and 21, 1948 and 1949: Glosses on *The Book of Documents*. Bulletin 22, 1950: *The Book of Documents*. All the bulletins of the Museum of Far Eastern Antiquities are of note. Many contain illustrations of unusual interest. Bulletins 20–22 are concerned entirely with the *Shu ching, Book of History* (*Book of Documents*).

Random House Dictionary of the English Language. The Unabridged Edition. Random House, New York, 1966. This dictionary lists far more Chinese words and terms than usually found in dictionaries.

Smith, D. Howard. *Chinese Religions*. Holt, Rinehart and Winston. New York, Chicago, San Francisco, 1968.

Tuchman, Barbara W. *Can History Be Served Up Hot?* New York Times Book Review, March 8, 1964. An essay that explores possible answers to *What is History?* by Edward Hallet Carr.

Watson, William. *Early Civilization in China*. Thames and Hudson, London, 1966. Profusely and brilliantly illustrated.

Weber, Max. *The Religion of China, Confucianism and Taoism*. Translated and edited by Hans H. Gerth with an introduction by C. K. Yang. The Free Press, New York, 1968. This is a translation of the first volume of Weber's Collected *Essays in the Sociology of Religion*.

Wieger, Dr. L., S. J. *Chinese Characters, Their Origin, Etymology, History, Classification and Signification. A thorough study from Chinese documents*. Translated into English by L. Davrout, S. J.; second edition, enlarged and revised according to the fourth French edition. Paragon Book Reprint Corp., Dover Publications, Inc., New York, 1965.

Yutang, Lin. *My Country and My People*. Reynal & Hitchcock, New York, 1935.

INDEX-GLOSSARY

As yet, there is no wholly satisfactory system of romanization—the transliteration of Chinese characters into the Roman alphabet. There are also national differences as well as different systems. Therefore the reader may wish to keep in mind that certain words in this index sometimes appear in other indexes with alternative initial letters. For example: An as Nan; Ch as Ts or K; G as K; Hs as S or H; I as Yi or E; K as Ch; Nan as An; Ts as Ch; Yi as I. For the purposes of this edition, names have been kept as uniform and simple as possible.

Ancestorism. The practice of ceremonial sacrifice to decedents in the belief that mutual assistance is thus maintained. 84, 114, 121, 135–136, 144, 208–211. *See also* Guests of the king; Music; Personators; Sacrifices.

Announcements. Documents addressed to the general populace; one of six classifications found in the *Shu ching*. *See also* Canons; Charges; Counsels; Instructions; Speeches.

Aheng. *See* I Yin

An-yi. Hsia capital. 77*n*

Archery. 33

Arranger of the Ancestral Temple. Government officer. 17

Astronomy. *See* Hsi, the brothers and the minister, and Ho, the brothers and the minister.

Black-haired people. *See* China, the Chinese.

Black River. 48, 49, 51

Book-burning during Ch'in dynasty. 253–256

Book of History. See *Shu ching, Book of History*.

Book of Changes. See *I ching, Book of Changes*.

Book of Music. See *Yo chi, Book of Music*.

Book of Odes. See *Shih ching, Book of Odes*.

Book of Rites. See *Li chi, Book of Rites*.

Bright Valley. 4

Brilliant Capital. 4

Canons. Documents of an exalted nature; one of six classifications found in the *Shu ching. See also* Announcements; Charges; Counsels; Instructions; Speeches.

Censors. 256

Ceremonial Usage. See I li, Ceremonial Usage.

Ch'an (river). 47, 52, 169

Ch'ang. *See* Wen, King.

Chang (river). 42

Ch'ao (place). 63

Chao, King. Third sovereign of Chou dynasty, posthumously named King K'ang. 209–222

Chao, King. Fourth sovereign of Chou dynasty. 223

265

Chao-ko. Shang (Yin) capital. 177*n*

Charges. Documents addressed to princes or high officers when invested with authority; one of six classifications found in the *Shu ching. See also* Announcements; Canons; Counsels; Instructions; Speeches.

Chen (marsh). 45

Cheng (state). 242–243

Ch'eng. A wild tribe. 197

Ch'eng Chou. Lo, Eastern Chou capital.

Ch'eng, King, named Sung. Second sovereign of Chou dynasty. 135–178, 188–215, 222, 240

Ch'en Hu. Minister to T'ai Wu. 184

Ch'en Neng (person). 251

Chi (river). 43, 44, 52

Ch'i (river). 49, 52

Ch'i (mountain). 42, 49, 50

Ch'i (place). 94

ch'i. The yarrow plant. 129*n*

Ch'i. Second sovereign of Hsia dynasty. 55–56

Ch'i, count of Wei. *See* Wei, Count Ch'i of.

Chi, King. Father of King Wen. 135–136, 180

Ch'i, marquis of. *See* Lü Chi.

Ch'i (Chi). Minister of Agriculture under Shun. 15, 30, 31, 41, 111, 122, 231

Ch'iang (person). 16

Chiang (principal river). 40, 46, 47, 51

Ch'iang. Western tribe. 119

chiao, "territory."

Chi Chou. Province, location of capital. 40, 42, 59, 62

Chief of the Four Mountains. Government officer. 3, 6, 13, 15, 16, 201

Chieh (rocks). 40, 43, 50

Chieh. Last sovereign of Hsia dynasty. 62–63, 67–70, 72–74, 245

Ch'ien (hill). 50

Ch'ien (river). 46, 47, 48

Chien (river). 47, 52, 169

Chien, duke of Ch'i. 254*n*

Chih. *See* I Yin.

Ch'ih Jen. An ancient historiographer. 88

Ch'ih Yu (person). 228, 229

Chin (state). 242

Ch'in (state). 242, 243

Ch'in dynasty. 242, 251, 252, 253

Ch'in, marquis of (Duke Mu). 242–244

Chin, marquis of. 243

China, the Chinese. Designations of foreign origin for the country and inhabitants referred to in the *Shu ching,* variously, as "Middle Kingdom," "myriad regions," flowery and great land," "all under Heaven," "all within the four seas," and "black-haired people."

Chinese calendar. Chinese chronology has no fixed point such as the birth of Christ. In the *Shu ching* documents, chronology of years is within the reigns of sovereigns. The names of days result from a cyclical system of stems and branches attributed to Huang Ti (ca. 2637 B.C.). The Ten Heavenly Stems are *chia, yi, ping, ting, wu, chi, keng, hsin, jen, kuei.* The Twelve Earthly Branches are *tzu, ch'ou, yin, mao, ch'en, ssu, wu, wei, shen, yu, hsü, hai.* During the Han dynasty these stems and branches also began to indicate years sequentially, within the Chinese cycle of sixty, which is equivalent to the West's use of a cycle of one hundred years. 5, 55

Chinese names. In addition to his surname and personal name received at birth, the Chinese acquired a *tzu,* or style. Sometimes he was given an official name, *kuan ming,* and a geographical designation might be added. Also, a posthumous name was often bestowed, his honorific designation. Sovereigns received *miao hao,* or temple names, which were their dynastic titles. No rule accounts for the name under which individuals are best known.

ching, "book" or "canon"; in general, "classic."

Ching (river). 49, 52

ch'ing. See Musical stones.

Ching Chou. Province. 46, 104

Ch'ing Chou. Province. 43

Ching, Mount. 46, 47, 49, 50

Ch'in Shih Huang Ti. 242, 254, 257

Chi-shih (mountain). 49, 51

Ch'iu. *See* Wen, marquis.

Chiu Li (person). 230*n*

Ch'iung (Po Ch'iung). High Chamberlain under King Mu. 226–227

chou, "province."

Chou. The dynasty and state: beginnings of, 94, 102, 111–112, 121; decline of, 223, 228, 237, 242, 245; official system of, 201–204

Chou, duke of (Chou kung), named Tan. Fourth son of King Wen and regent during minority of King Ch'eng. 111, 135–200, 205

Chou Ch'ing Ch'eh. Minister under Ch'in Shih Huang Ti. 254

Chou Hsin, named Shou. Last sovereign of Shang (Yin) dynasty. 102–108, 113–123, 245

Chou li, Rites of Chou. 250

Chu (person). 16

Ch'ü (river). 49, 52

Ch'u, named Ho Shu. Eighth son of King Wen. 168

Ch'u, prince of. Minister under Chou Hsin. 103

Chu of Tan. Son of Yao. 5, 34

Chuan Hsü (person). 230*n*

Chu-ch'iao (place). 123

Ch'uei. Minister of Works under Shun. 16

Chu Hsi. A commentator. 94, 208

Ch'ui, arrows of. 213

Chün Ch'en. Successor to duke of Chou. 205–207

Ch'un ch'iu, Spring and Autumn Annals. 249, 250, 251, 252

Ch'ung. Minister of the South under Chuan Hsü. 230

Ch'ung Hua. *See* Shun.

Chung Huan (person). 212

Chung Hui. A chief minister to T'ang. 69–71

Chung K'ang. Fourth sovereign of Hsia dynasty. 60, 62

Ch'ung, Mount. 14

Chung-nan (mountain). 49

Chung-yen. Brother of Chou Hsin. 102

Ch' un-wu (mountain). 49

Chün Ya. Minister of Instruction under King Mu. 224–225

Chung yung, Doctrine of the Mean. 249, 250.

Ch'u-sou (mountain). 49

Chu-ye (marsh). 49

Chu-yü (mountain). 50

Classic of Filial Piety. See *Hsiao ching, Classic of Filial Piety.*

Coinage. 208

Communication, minister of Government officer. 17

Compass. 199–200

Confucian Analects. See *Lun yü, Confucian Analects.*

Confucius. 22, 50*n*, 116*n*, 222*n*, 228, 249, 251, 257

Counsels. Documents on the subject of government; one of six classifications found in the *Shu ching. See also* Announcements; Canons; Charges; Instructions; Speeches.

Cowrie shells. 91

Crime, minister of. Government officer. 202–203

Dark Valley. 5

DeMailla, P. Author of *Histoire Generale de la Chine.* 199–200

Divination. 23–24, 129–131, 135–136, 140–143

Doctrine of the Mean. See *Chung yung*

Dog Jung. Tribe. 237

Domains, Five. 34, 41, 53–54, 146, 155, 169

Eastern Chou dynasty. 112, 238

Ehr ya, Literary Expositor. 250, 252

Eight musical instruments (of metal, stone, silk, bamboo, gourds, earth, leather, wood). 14, 32

Eight trigrams. 39, 40. *See also* Divination.

Equalizing quarter. Measure of weight. 59

Fa. *See* Wu, King.

Fang Ch'i. Minister under Yao. 5

Fang Hsün. *See* Yao.

Feng (river). 49, 52

Feng. *See* K'ang, prince of.

Feng. King Wen's capital. 121, 161

Filial piety, duty, or virtue. 25*n*, 80, 149–150, 154, 205, 239

Five cardinal duties (or virtues). *See* Five orders of relationships.

Five ching. Five Classics. 249, 253

Five colors (usually considered to have been black, red, green, white, and yellow). 32, 44

Five degrees of nobility. *kung,* duke; *hou,* marquis (not to be confused with *hou,* the title of the sovereign during Hsia dynasty); *pai,* earl; *tz'u,* viscount; *nan,* baron.

Five elements. 126

Five orders of relationship (or society). 11, 124, 202, 224

Five punishments. Branding on

the forehead, *mo;* cutting off the nose, *pi;* cutting off the legs, *yüeh;* castration, *kung;* death inflicted in various ways, *ta p'i. See also* Punishments.

Forester. Government officer. 16

Four Mountains Ministry. 40

Four shu. Four books.

Fu Ch'ien (plain). 50

Fu Hsi. Inventor of trigrams. 39, 40

Fu Su. Son of Ch'in Shih Huang Ti. 257

Fu Yen (place). 94, 96

Fu Yüeh. *See* Yüeh.

General Regulator. Government officer. 12, 15, 201

Gernet, Jacques. 46*n*

Go, prince of. Minister under Chou Hsin. 103

God. As the term is used in the *Shu ching,* "God" designates a force, the Prime Mover, *Shang Ti,* not to be confused with the Christian concept, an anthropomorphic deity, or related to Yahweh and Jehovah.

Government. 96–97, 127, 195–199, 201–204

Government officers. 15–17, 195–199, 201–203. *See also* individual entries.

Grand Assistant. Government officer. 202

Grand Guardian. *See* Shih, duke of Shao.

Grand Guardian. Government officer. 202

Grand Master. Government officer. 202

Greater Classics. 250

Great Learning. See *Ta hsüeh, Great Learning.*

Great Plan. 125

Great Scholars, Board of. 256, 257

Guests of the king. Persons entrusted with maintaining the ceremonial sacrifices of ancestorism, including those of a conquered house. 144, 173, 216. *See also* Ancestorism.

Han (principal river). 40, 46, 47, 51, 52

Han Ai Ti. 252

Han Chang Ti. 253

Han Ch'eng Ti. 251

Han dynasty. 250, 251, 252, 253, 257

Han Hui Ti. 253

Han Huo Ti. 253

Han Ling Ti. 253

Han Ming Ti. 253

Han Wu Ti. 251

Hao. Western capital of Chou. 168, 190, 205, 237

Heaven: appointment of, 35, 147, 148, 160; decree of, 139, 161–166; as deity, 70, 97; mind of, 83, 115

Heaven, Son of. A designation of the sovereign. 28 and throughout documents *passim.*

Heng (river). 42

Heng, Mount. 3, 40, 46, 50

High Chamberlain. Government officer. 226–227

Historical Records (Shih chi), by Ssu-ma Ch'ien. 31*n,* 46*n,* 254

Historiographer, or Grand His-

Historiographer (*continued*) toriographer. Court officer. 136, 137, 195, 214

Ho, bow of. 213

Ho, the brothers. Astronomers under Yao. 3–5

Ho. Minister of Board of Astronomy under Chung K'ang. 60–62

Ho (principal river). 40–52 *passim,* 122*n*, 169

Ho. A tributary of the Chiang. 48

Ho-li Mountains. 50

Ho map. *See* River plan.

Ho Shu. *See* Ch'u.

Host. Usually 3,000 soldiers. 241*n*

Hou. One of Five Domains. 121, 146, 155, 156, 162, 169, 184, 201, 217

Hsi, the brothers. Astronomers under Yao. 3–5

Hsi. Minister of Board of Astronomy under Chung K'ang. 60–62

Hsia. First hereditary dynasty. 39, 62, 63

Hsiang. Fifth sovereign of Hsia dynasty. 62

Hsiang. Half-brother to Shun. 7

Hsiang Yü (person). 257

Hsiao ching, Classic of Filial Piety. 250, 252

Hsiao Hsin. 18th sovereign of Shang (Yin) dynasty. 94

Hsiao Yi. 19th sovereign of Shang (Yin) dynasty. 94

Hsi-ch'eng (mountain). 50

Hsi-chih (mountain). 49

Hsi Ch'ing (hill). 48, 50

Hsieh. Minister of Instruction under Shun. 15, 67

Hsien, named Kuan Shu. Son of King Wen. 135, 137, 168, 188

Hsien-yang (place). 256

Hsiung (person). 16

Hsiung-ehr (mountain). 50, 52

Hsü Chou. Province. 44, 240–241

Hu, lord of. 55–56

Hu (person). 16

Hua, Mount. 3, 40, 48, 51, 121, 122*n*

Huai (river). 40, 44, 45, 46, 52

Huai. Tribe. 240–241

Huan (river). 48

Huang (Hwang) Ho. *See* Ho.

Huan Tou. Minister under Yao. 6, 14, 26, 27

Hu, Chung of Ts'ai. 188–189, 222

Hu-k'ou (hill). 42, 50

Hung Yao. Minister under King Wen. 185

Huo, prince of. 188

Hu Wei. Commentator. 52*n*

I (river in Hsü Chou). 44

I (river in Yü Chou). 47, 52

I, prince of Ch'iung. 57

I, tribes of. 54

I. Usurper in Hsia dynasty. 62, 63

I Chih. Minister under T'ai Wu. 184

I ching, Book of Changes. 39, 94, 104, 111, 249–257 *passim*

I Ch'iu. *See* P'ing, King.

I Ho. *See* Wen, marquis.

I li, Ceremonial Usage. 250

Instruction, minister of. Government officer. 156, 202

Instructions. Documents regarded as lessons, either from

antiquity or by ministers of the sovereign; one of six classifications found in the *Shu ching*. *See also* Announcements; Canons; Charges; Counsels; Speeches.

I Yin, named Aheng or Chih. A chief minister under T'ang and under T'ai Chia. 72, 74–84, 94, 99

Jen Huang. An officer under Han Ch'eng Ti. 251

Jo River. 49, 50

Jui, earl of. 211, 217

Junior Assistant. Government officer. 202

Junior Guardian. Government officer. 202

Junior Master. Government officer. 202

Kan (place). 55

K'ang, King. *See* Chao, King

K'ang, prince of (K'ang Shu), marquis of Wei, named Feng. Ninth son of King Wen. 146–160, 211, 222

Kan P'an. Minister under Wu Ting. 98, 184

Kao, duke of Pi. *See* Pi, duke of.

Kao Tsung. *See* Wu Ting, King.

Kao Yao. Minister of Crime under Shun. 15, 16, 21–22, 26–32, 35, 231

Keng. A capital of Shang (Yin) dynasty. 85

Ko (marsh). 47, 52

Ko (principality). 69

Ko. Minister under King Wen. 185

Ko, earl of. 69, 70

Koh-lin (place). 188

Kowtow. 167

Kuan Chung. Minister. 222*n*

Kuan Shu. *See* Hsien

Kuan Yi Fu. Minister to a king of Ch'u. 230*n*

kuei. Jade scepter, symbol of rank. 135, 136

Kuei (river). 7

K'uei. Director of Music under Shun. 17, 30, 34, 35

Ku Liang Ch'ih. Commentator. 250

Kun. Father of Yü. 3, 6, 11, 14, 42*n*, 126

K'ung Chi. Grandson of Confucius. 249

Kung Liu (person). 122

Kung Yang Kao. Commentator. 250

Kunlun Mountains. 40, 49, 61*n*

Ku Sou. Father of Shun. 25

Lai. Tribe. 44

Lei-hsia (marsh). 43

Lei Shou (hill). 50

Li. Measure of length approximately one-third of a mile.

Li (river). 51, 169

Li (state). 104

Li. Minister of Fire (or of the North) under Chuan Hsü. 230

Li, Mount. Home of Shun. 25

Liang (mountain). 42

Liang Chou. A province. 48, 104

Li chi, Book of Rites. 249, 250

Li Chu Kuo. Imperial physician under Han Ch'eng Ti. 251

Li Ssu. Minister under Ch'in Shih Huang Ti. 255

Literary Expositor. See *Ehr ya, Literary Expositor*.

Little Child. A designation of the sovereign used by himself to communicate his humility. *See also* One Man.

Liu Hsiang. Officer under Han Ch'eng Ti. 251, 252

Liu Hsin. Son of Liu Hsiang. 252, 253

Lo (river). 40, 41, 47, 48, 51, 52, 162, 169

Lo (Loyang, Ch'eng Chou). Eastern Chou capital. 146, 162, 167–169, 177–178, 190, 194, 205, 219, 222, 237

Loyang. See Lo

Lu (fief). 240, 241

Lu. Western tribe. 119, 197

Lü. Wild tribe. 133

Lü, duke of. 223

Lü, marquis of. 228, 229

Lü Chi, marquis of Ch'i. 209, 212

Lung. Minister of Communication under Shun. 17

Lung-men (mountain). 49, 51

Lun yü, or *Confucian Analects.* 249, 250, 252

Man, tribes of. 54

Mandate of Heaven. *See* Heaven, decree of.

Mao, duke of. 211

Mao. Western tribe. 119

Mao Tse-tung. 30

Mean. Early references to what would later emerge as the concept of *chung yung,* or the golden mean, the practice of non-deviating mind and of harmony. 22, 23, 71, 189, 206, 235, 236

Meeting Ho (river). 51

Mei (place). 153, 154

Mei Hsi. Concubine of Chieh. 63

Mencius. 245

Mencius, works of. 250, 252

Meng (Meng-tsin) (ford). 51, 113, 123

Meng (hill). 44, 48

Meng (marsh). 46

Meng-chu (marsh). 47

Metal(s). 45, 46*n*, 47, 48, 234

Miao. Tribe. 11, 14, 18, 19, 24, 25, 34, 49, 229–232

Middle Chiang (river). 52

Middle Kingdom. *See* China, the Chinese.

Mien (river). 48

Min (hill). 48

Min, Mount. 50, 51

Ming-t'iao (place). 74

mou (or *mu*). Unit of area, approximately one-sixth of an acre.

Mourning shed. 95, 179, 209, 216

Moving Sands. 50, 51*n*

Mu (tract of land). 108, 119, 123

Mu, Duke. *See* Ch'in, marquis of.

Mu, King. Fifth sovereign of Chou dynasty. 224–236

Music. 13*n*, 14, 17, 30, 32–35, 45*n*, 209

Music, Director of. Government officer. 17

Musical stones. 17, 44, 45*n*

Myriad. 10,000; an idiom meaning any large number.

Myriad regions. A designation of the realm of the sovereign, it being proper to speak of his domain in hyperbole. *See also* China, the Chinese.

Myriad states. Those states lying beyond the royal domain.

Nan. One of Five Domains. 146, 155, 156, 162, 169, 217
Nan Ch'ao (place). 69
Nan-chiao (place). 4
Nan-kung Kuo. Minister under King Wen. 185
Nan Kung Mao (person). 212
Nei-fang (mountain). 50
Nestbuilders. 41
Niao-shu (hill). 49, 50, 52
Nine branches or classes of kindred. 4, 27
Nine Chiang (river). 46, 47, 50, 51
Nine ching. 250
Nine Ho (river). 51

Official Book of Chou, The. 33n
One Man. A designation of the sovereign used by himself to communicate his role as one ruler as opposed to the multitudes ruled.

P'ang. Western tribe. 119
P'an Keng. 17th sovereign of Shang (Yin) dynasty. 85–93
Pao Heng (I Yin). 99n
Pao Ssu. Concubine of King Yu. 237
Pastor (sometimes referred to as "shepherd"). Government officer in charge of a province. 13, 15, 198, 232
Pei-wei (mountain). 50
P'eng-li (lake). 45
P'eng-li (marsh). 51
People's Republic of China. 30
Personators of the dead. Individuals, preferably grandsons, who represented decedents during sacrificial ceremonies of ancestorism. 57, 61, 100. *See also* Ancestorism.
pi. Jade disk, symbol of Heaven and indicative of rank. 135
P'i (person). 16
Pi (place). 240
Pi, duke of (Kao). Grand Master under King K'ang. 211, 216, 219–222
Pi Kan (person). 115, 117, 123
P'ing, King (I Ch'iu). 13th sovereign of Chou dynasty. 237–239
Po (hill). 48
Po. A Shang (Yin) dynasty capital. 67, 79, 197
P'o. Western tribe. 119
Po Ch'in, duke of Lu. Son of duke of Chou. 240–241
Po Ch' iung. *See* Ch'iung
Po-ch'ung (hill). 50
Po-i. Arranger in the Ancestral Temple under Shun. 17, 50n, 231, 232
Po Yü (person). 16
Prime Minister. Government officer. 202
Provinces, nine. 31, 42–49, 82
Provinces, twelve, 14, 34
Punishments: during Chou dynasty, 148–152, 158–159, 206–207, 240–241; during Hsia dynasty, 61–62; Marquis of Lü on, 228–236; during Shang (Yin) dynasty, 88–89, 91, 103, 191; under Shun, 14–22

Rank, symbols of. 13, 32, 54, 97, 135, 145, 210
Recorder. Government officer. 156, 167

Recorder of the Interior. Government officer. 156

Religion. *See* Ancestorism; Sacrifices.

Religion, minister of. Government officer. 202

Rites of Chou. See Chou li, Rites of Chou.

River plan (Ho map). 213

Sacrifices. 12–13, 49, 88, 97, 101, 107; during Chou dynasty, 114, 121, 162–164, 170–174. *See also* Ancestorism.

San Isheng. Minister under King Wen. 185

San Miao. *See* Miao.

San-wei. Region in the west. 14, 49, 51

Sha-ch'u (place). 103

shan, "mountain"

Shang (Yin). The dynasty and state. 39, 72, 102–108, 113–124, 147–186 *passim,* 201

Shang (principality). 63, 67

Shang Yung (person). 123

Shao, duke of. *See* Shih, duke of Shao.

Shao (region). 161

Shao Hao (person). 230*n*

Shen, prince of. 237

Shi, chief of. 62

shih, "annalists," "recorders," "historiographers."

Shih, duke of Shao. Grand Guardian under King Wu and King Ch'eng. 133–134, 135*n*, 161–166, 183–187, 209–218, 222

Shih ching, Book of Odes. 111, 249–256 *passim*

Shou. The name of Chou Hsin and the designation by which he usually appears in later literature. *See* Chou Hsin.

shu, literally, "the pencil speaking"; "book(s)."

Shu. Western tribe. 119

Shu (person). 16

Shu Ch'i (person). 50*n*

Shu ching, Book of History. 249–256 *passim*

shui, "water."

Shun, named Ch'ung Hua, posthumously designated Yü. Successor to Yao. 6–7, 11–25, 30–35, 230–231

Shun Yü Yüeh. Scholar of Ch'in dynasty. 254, 255

Six ching. 250

Six tenures. 201

Six treasuries of nature. 21, 53

Smaller Classics. 250

Somber Capital. 5

"Sovereign responsibility." 26–28, 73, 82–84, 151, 243; as "royal perfection," 127–129

Speeches. Documents addressed to armed hosts; one of six classifications found in the *Shu ching. See also* Announcements; Canons; Charges; Counsels; Instructions.

Spring and Autumn Annals. See Ch'un ch'iu, Spring and Autumn Annals

Ssu (river). 44, 45, 52

Ssu-ma Ch'ien. Historian of Han dynasty. 82, 100, 208, 222, 223, 228

Stag Tower. 123

Standard stone. Standard of weight kept in the royal treasury. 59

Standard tube. Measure of both length and capacity. 13

Su, duke of. Minister of Crime under King Wu. 199

Su, prince of. 103

sui, "territory."

Sung. *See* Ch'eng, King.

Sung dynasty. 250

Surnames. 53, 184, 235

T'a (river). 43

Ta Chi. Concubine of Chou Hsin. 103, 108, 117

Ta hsüeh, Great Learning. 249, 250

T'ai (state). 122*n*

t'ai chi. Primal ether out of which all things were fashioned by interactions of yang and yin. 131*n*

T'ai, King (T'ai Wang), named Tan Fu. 94, 122, 135, 136, 180

Tai, Mount. 3, 13, 40, 43, 44

T'ai Chia. Second sovereign of Shang (Yin) dynasty. 74–84

T'ai-hang (mountain). 50

T'ai-hua (mountain). 50

T'ai K'ang. Third sovereign of Hsia dynasty. 55, 57

T'ai Tien. Minister under King Wen. 185

T'ai Wu (T'ai Mou). Seventh sovereign of Shang (Yin) dynasty. 179, 181, 184

T'ai-yo Mountain. 50

T'ai-yüan (place). 42

Ta-lü (plain). 42, 51

Tan. *See* Chou, duke of.

Tan Fu. *See* T'ai, King.

T'ang. Dynastic designation of Yao

T'ang (principality). 59

T'ang (small state). 3

Tang dynasty. 250

T'ang the Successful. Founder of Shang (Yin) dynasty. 63, 67–76, 83

Tang T'ai Tsung. 250

Tan-huai (place). 42

T'ao (principality). 59

T'ao-ch'iu (hill). 52

T'ao-lin (place). 121

Ta-pie (mountain). 50, 51

Ta-ye (lake). 44

Tenures. *See* Domains.

Thirteen ching. 250

Three Chiang (river). 45

"Three years." Idiom which may indicate a long time as well as 36 months.

Throne, ceding of. 6, 12, 21, 23–24, 39

ti, "emperor" or "supreme sovereign."

Ti-ch'u (hill). 51

Ti-chu (mountain). 50

Tien. One of Five Domains. 121, 146, 155, 156, 162, 169, 184, 201, 217

T'ien Ch'ang (person). 254

Ti Yi, King. 27th sovereign of Shang (Yin) dynasty. 102, 155, 191

T'o (river). 46, 47, 48, 51

"Treading on a tiger's tail." An idiom meaning to blunder. 224

Tribute, articles of. 42–49 *passim,* 133

Trigrams. 39, 40

Ts'ai (hill). 48

Ts'ai. Interior, or royal, domain of Five Domains. 146, 169

Ts'ai (territory). 188

Ts'ai Ch'en. Commentator. 131*n*

Ts'ai Shu. *See* Tu.

Ts'ang-lang (river). 51

Tseng Shen. Disciple of Confucius. 249

Tsi (river). 44

Tso Ch'iu Ming. Commentator. 250

Tsu. Usurper in Hsia dynasty. 63

Tsü (river). 43

Tsu Chi. Minister under Wu Ting. 100–101

Tsu Chia. 22nd sovereign of Shang (Yin) dynasty. 180, 181

Tsu I. Minister under Chou Hsin (Shou). 104–105

Tsu Keng. Son of Wu Ting. 100–101

Tsu Yi. 11th sovereign of Shang (Yin) dynasty. 85, 184

Tu, named Ts'ai Shu. Son of King Wen. 168, 188

t'uan. Summaries of hexagrams. 111

Tui, spear of. 213

Tu K'ang (person). 153

T'ung (place). 78

T'ung, earl of. 211

T'ung-po (mountain). 50, 52

Tung-yüan (tract of land). 44

T'u-shan (place). 34

Wai-fang (mountain). 50

"Walking on spring ice." Idiom meaning proceeding in peril. 224

wang, "king"

Wang Ts'ia. Commentator. 52*n*

Wang-wu (mountain). 50

War, minister of. Government officer. 156, 202

Warring States period. 112, 251

Wei. One of Five Domains. 121, 146, 155, 156, 169

Wei (marquisate). 146, 159

Wei (river). 44, 48, 49, 52

Wei. Western tribe. 119, 197

Wei, Count Ch'i of. Brother of Chou Hsin (Shou). 102, 106–107, 117, 123, 125–132, 144–145, 222

Wei, marquis of. *See* K'ang, prince of.

Wen (river). 44, 52

Wen, King (Wen Wang), named Ch'ang. Apotheosized as founder of Chou dynasty. 94, 104, 111, 118, 122, 147, 153–154, 180–181, 196–197, 198–239 *passim*

Wen, marquis, named I Ho or Ch'iu. 238–239

Wen Ming. *See* Yü.

Western Chou dynasty. 112

Western Ho (river). 49

Works, minister of. Government officer. 156, 202

Writing as form of communication. 33*n*, 77, 79, 95

Wu, King (Wu Wang), named Fa. First sovereign of Chou dynasty, called "the tranquilizer." 111–143, 161, 167–245 *passim*

Wu Hsien. Minister under T'ai Wu. 184

wu hsing. *See* Five punishments.

Wu Keng. Son of Chou Hsin (Shou). 144, 168

Wu Ting, King. Third sovereign of Shang (Yin) dynasty. 84

Wu Ting, King. 20th sovereign of Shang (Yin) dynasty, posthumously designated Kao Tsung. 84, 94–100, 179–180

Yang (river). 51
Yang Chou. Province. 45
yao. Interpretations of lines of hexagrams. 111
Yao, named Fang Hsün. Sovereign, posthumously designated T'ang. 3–7, 12, 14, 59n
Yarrow stalks (*ch'i*). 129n
Yellow River. *See* Ho.
Yen (river). 52
Yen (state). 177, 190
Yen Chou. Province. 43
Yi. Forester under Shun. 16, 19–21, 24–25, 30–31, 41
Yi, Mount. 44
Yi. Recorder under King Ch'eng. 167, 174
Yin dynasty. *See* Shang. The dynasty and state.
Yin, marquis of. 60–62
Ying-ta. Commentator. 44n
Yin Hsien. Grand historiographer under Han Ch'eng Ti. 251
Yo, Mount. 42
Yo chi, Book of Music. 30, 250
Yü. Dynastic designation of Shun.

Yü (hill). 44
Yu (island). 14
Yü (principality). 6
Yü, marquis of T'ang, later changed to Chin. Son of King Wu. 238
Yü, the Great (Ta Yü), named Wen Ming. Founder of Hsia dynasty. 15, 19–33, 39–55, 58–59, 125, 153, 163, 195
Yu, King. 12th sovereign of Chou dynasty. 237
Yü, Mount. 14, 44
Yü Chou. Province. 47
Yüeh (Fu Yüeh). Chief minister to second King Wu Ting. 94–99
Yü-i (place). 4, 44
Yü kung. Canon "Tribute to Yü"
Yu Li. Place of imprisonment. 104, 111
Yün (marsh). 46
Yung (marsh). 52
Yung (river). 43
Yung. Western tribe. 119
Yung Chou. Province. 49, 104
Yung-po (marsh). 47